BLESSED
—— BY ——
DISTRESS

How to Use Suffering to Evolve Your
Brain and Transform Your Life

Introducing the
SatoriWest Method

BLESSED —BY— DISTRESS

How to Use Suffering to Evolve Your Brain and Transform Your Life

Introducing the
SatoriWest Method

Jeff Skolnick, MD PhD

BLESSED BY DISTRESS

How to Use Suffering to Evolve
Your Brain and Transform Your Life

Introducing the **SatoriWest Method**

Copyright © 2022 by Jeff Skolnick

Published by SatoriWest Publishing, Seattle, WA 98126
All rights reserved. No part of this book may be reproduced or transmitted in
any form or by any means without written permission from the publisher.

For information contact

SatoriWest Publishing, Seattle, WA 98126
www.SatoriWest.com

Production Management:
Robyn M Fritz MA MBA Cht, Alchemy West

Copyediting:
Laurel Robinson, Laurel Robinson Editorial Services

Design and Layout:
Robert Lanphear, Lanphear Design

Email: info@SatoriWest.com
Library of Congress Control Number: 2021921004
Print ISBN: 978-1-7360816-2-4
E-Book ISBN: 978-1-7360816-3-1

Dedication

To my spiritual teachers in Zen and secular nonduality and to the hundreds of patients with whom I have interacted personally or were touched by the SatoriWest Method's curriculum. Thank you for teaching and inspiring me.

Contents

Preface / xiii
    The Story of SatoriWest and Me \ xiii

Introduction \ 1

PART I: The Human Condition \ 5

1: Life Is Hard \ 7
    You Are Not Alone \ 7
    Fueling Up for the Journey \ 10
    Your First Shift \ 11
    A Note About Suffering \ 12
    Conclusion \ 14

2: Surface Reasons for Suffering \ 17
    Birth \ 17
    Childhood \ 18
    Adolescence and Late Teens \ 19
    Adulthood \ 21
    Aging \ 23
    Insecurity \ 24
    Illness \ 25
    Loss \ 26
    Old Age \ 27

PART II: Tunnel Vision \ 31

3: The Human Brain–Tunnel Vision: Parts One, Two, and Three \ 33
    The Brain's Survival Wiring and Tunnel Vision \ 34
    Tunnel Vision, Facet One: Attention \ 36
    Tunnel Vision, Facet Two: Control \ 38
    Tunnel Vision, Facet Three: Awareness \ 41
    Point of Clarification \ 45

4: The Human Mind–Tunnel Vision: Parts Four Through Eight \ 47
  Human Intelligence, Imagination and Ego
    as Objects of Attention \ 48
      Human Intelligence \ 48
      Human Imagination \ 49
      Sense of Self \ 51
  Quick Recap \ 52
  Tunnel Vision, Facet Four: Suggestibility \ 53
  Tunnel Vision, Facet Five: Imagination \ 56
  Tunnel Vision, Facet Six: Ego \ 59
  Tunnel Vision, Facet Seven: Thinking \ 64
  Tunnel Vision, Facet Eight: Time \ 72
  The Eight Facets of Tunnel Vision \ 74

5: The Downward Spiral of Tunnel Vision \ 77

6: The Immediate Rewards of Tunnel Vision \ 83
  The Rewards of Tunnel Vision \ 83
  The "Cultural" Rewards of Tunnel Vision \ 91
  The Familiarity of Tunnel Vision \ 93
  Conclusion \ 95

7: Traversing Levels of Tunnel Vision \ 97
  Degrees of Tunnel Vision \ 99
      Cultural Tunnel Vision (Attention Is Not as Constricted) \ 100
      Toxic Tunnel Vision (Attention Is More Tightly Focused) \ 101
      Crisis Tunnel Vision (Attention Is Very Constricted) \ 102
  The Name of the Game: See Cultural Tunnel Vision in Yourself \ 102
  The Downward Spiral from Cultural to Toxic to Crisis \ 108

PART III: Perspective \ 111

8: The Core of Human Potential \ 113
  Defining Perspective \ 115
      Facet One: Attention \ 115
      Facet Two: Control \ 117

Facet Three: Awareness \ 118
Facet Four: Suggestibility \ 119
Facet Five: Imagination \ 120
Facet Six: Ego \ 121
Facet Seven: Thinking \ 122
Facet Eight: Time \ 123

9: Shifting the Brain into Perspective \ 127
BrainShifting into Perspective \ 128

10: Perspective and Personality \ 139
Facets of Perspective on Personality \ 141
15 Lasting Attributes of Perspective \ 141
    Insight \ 141
    Wisdom \ 142
    Maturity \ 142
    Judgment \ 143
    Objectivity \ 143
    Empathy and Compassion \ 144
    Love \ 144
    Spontaneity \ 145
    Authenticity \ 147
    A Sense of Irony and Humor \ 147
    Creativity and Seeing Novelty \ 148
    Intuition \ 149
    Gratitude \ 150
    The Experience of Belonging \ 152
    A Happier, Peaceful Disposition \ 153

PART IV: The SatoriWest Method \ 157

11: Overview of the SatoriWest Journey \ 159
Recognize Your Tunnel Vision \ 162
Practice the Skills of BrainShifting \ 162
Practice Wholistic Life Wellness \ 164
Crisis as an Opportunity \ 164

12: Core Skills of BrainShifting: Notice Tunnel Vision and Split Attention \ 167
  SatoriWest Journey, Avenue One: Noticing Tunnel Vision \ 167
    Tips for Being a Tunnel Vision Detective \ 168
      Noticing Tunnel Vision When Attention Is Compelled or Freely Given Up \ 171
      Noticing Tunnel Vision at Times When Your Attention is Grabbed from You \ 171
      Noticing Tunnel Vision When Your Attention is Freely Given Over \ 172
      Noticing Tunnel Vision in Your Loss of Control \ 173
      Noticing Tunnel Vision as Being Less Aware \ 174
      Noticing Tunnel Vision in Being More Suggestible \ 174
      Noticing Tunnel Vision in Being Pulled into Your Imagination \ 175
      Noticing Tunnel Vision Driven by Ego \ 176
      Noticing Tunnel Vision in Distorted Thinking \ 179
      Noticing Tunnel Vision with Negative Emotions \ 180
    Noticing Tunnel Vision: Conclusion \ 182
  SatoriWest Journey, Avenue Two: Split Attention BrainShifting \ 183
      Example 1 \ 187
      Example 2 \ 189
      Example 3 \ 192

13: A Model for BrainShifting: What Shifts? \ 195
  The SatoriWest Model of the Brain as It Shifts Toward Perspective \ 195
  The Two Brains: Dominant and Nondominant \ 195
  Higher and Lower Brain Areas \ 198
  BrainShifting Brings It All Together \ 199
  Mindfulness: A BrainShifting Tool \ 203

14: More BrainShifting Skills \ 207
  Preparing for This Chapter's Exercises \ 207
  BrainShifting Part I: Awareness Widening \ 208
    The Body Scan Exercise \ 208

Brain Sweep, Phase 1 Exercise \ 212
　　　Brain Sweep, Phase 2 Exercise \ 214
　BrainShifting Part II: Detachment \ 217
　　　Breathing Flow Exercise \ 217
　Putting Them All Together \ 218
　A Daily Practice Suggestion \ 219

15: The Wellnesses and BrainShifting \ 221
　Indirect BrainShifting Through Wellness \ 221
　The Interconnectedness of Wellnesses \ 224
　　　Physical Wellness \ 224
　　　Mental Wellness \ 224
　　　Social Wellness \ 225
　　　Cultural Wellness \ 226
　　　Moral Wellness \ 226
　　　Existential Wellness \ 228
　Perspective and Wellness \ 229
　The Link Between Wellness and BrainShifting \ 230
　How a Shifted Brain Creates Wellness \ 231
　　　Physical Wellness \ 231
　　　Mental Wellness \ 231
　　　Social Wellness \ 232
　　　Cultural Wellness \ 232
　　　Moral Wellness \ 232
　　　Existential Wellness \ 233
　Key Wellness Strategies that Cause Your Brain to Shift \ 233
　　　Physical Wellness \ 234
　　　Mental Wellness \ 234
　　　Social Wellness \ 235
　　　Cultural Wellness \ 236
　　　Moral Wellness \ 236
　　　Existential Wellness \ 237
　Balance and Perspective \ 237

PART V: Blessed by Distress \ 241

16: Suffering and the History of Crisis and Opportunities \ 243
Blessed by Distress \ 243
To Suffer \ 244
Crisis as a Springboard \ 246
Not Suffering \ 247
Using Crisis and Hardship to Find Perspective \ 248
The History of Crisis as Opportunity \ 250

17: How to Use Crisis and Hardship as Opportunities \ 257
The Emotional Impact of Crises \ 258
The Four Factors \ 258
When Crises Wouldn't Work \ 269
The Use of Psychiatric Illness \ 269

18: Crises and Going It Alone \ 275
Professional Help \ 277

PART VI: Conclusion \ 281

19: Completing the Circle \ 283

Appendix 1: Questions and Answers \ 289

Appendix 2: Summary of the SatoriWest Method \ 297
Point 1: Recognize Your "Human Condition" \ 297
Point 2: Understand What Tunnel Vision Is \ 297
Point 3: Understand Perspective \ 298
Point 4: BrainShifting: The SatoriWest Method Journey
    to Perspective \ 300
Point 5: Use Pain and Suffering to Find Great Perspective \ 300

Acknowledgments \ 303

About the Author \ 305

Preface

The Story of SatoriWest and Me

It was a typically hot, muggy afternoon in 1972 in Miami Beach when, as I was sitting outside my high school reading a psychology textbook, my mind briefly but radically opened, and the trajectory of my life changed. The same thing could happen for you.

Here's what occurred. The textbook author posed a simple, yet mind-blowing question: "Isn't it something," he pondered, perhaps innocently, "that the human brain—ultimately, just a collection of chemicals—can wake up and know it's alive?"

Think about that for a moment.

Reflecting on that astonishing reality changed *my* brain. My mind drilled into what it meant that who I thought I was, was essentially a collection of inert chemicals experiencing this moment. More than that, these chemicals not only know what is going on but *know that they know*. That drew my attention inward, deep in. I became acutely energized and aware of my own aliveness. The world became vibrant. It was like low-definition TV becoming high definition. The experience lasted only a minute or two, yet it seared in me a desire to study the brain and consciousness.

That same year, I went on a tour of the *SS Hope* hospital ship at the port of Miami. As I gazed at its posters of excursions around the world delivering healthcare to needy, underserved people, I envisioned myself as a doctor, helping desperate people in difficult situations. Eventually, those two dreams came together, and I set off to medical school to be a psychiatrist. After medical school, I was accepted into a dual psychiatric residency/PhD program in neuropsychology to study the brain. More on that in a moment.

If you picked up this book because you are in distress, my high school realization may not seem relevant to you. However, I hope that by the time you finish the book, you'll come to appreciate my insight on a whole new level. An aspect of it lies at the core of the SatoriWest Method, the method you'll learn about in this book. The crux of it has to do with an intensified, inner-reflected awareness that changes how your brain experiences life.

It's a method that works. In recent years the SatoriWest Method was successfully used in a psychiatric and substance-use-disorder hospital and in a three-week outpatient program with many participants attesting to its healing and transformational potential. It's also accelerated my own psychological development, allowing me to wake up to the miraculous reality of my own brain and feel amazed at my own experiences. I am able to face life with greater equanimity and passion.

To understand the method and how it can help you, let's explore more about how it came to be. As I said, I enrolled in a psychiatric residency program with a parallel track in neuropsychology. Learning about neuropsychology involved studying and researching the brain as far as its impact on behavior and experience. I began to hypothesize about consciousness and consequently create a model that explained how awareness and "self"-awareness emerge.

It is important to point out that I put "self" in quotes because, although it's a common term, it technically does not mean awareness of an identity called a self. In other words, it doesn't mean I know I am "me." That usually refers to what people think of as being self-conscious. Self-awareness refers to an iterative, back-and-forth, inner-reflected awareness, a knowing that there is knowing—essentially, awareness of the fact that there is aliveness happening. We have that all the time. If I were to ask you if you are alive, you would reflect for barely a second before answering, "of course." That level of awareness is just in the background of our experience and the SatoriWest Method helps bring it to the forefront.

Early pieces of the SatoriWest Method were understanding what both awareness and self-awareness are. Although my theory of what in the brain creates awareness is not as critical to an understanding of the SatoriWest Method, my explanation of what creates self-awareness is. Let's explore that briefly, as it sets the stage for what came next in my life.

Awareness, plainly put, is knowing things. And, oddly, each "side" of the brain has its own *separate awareness*. This is fact, not speculation. It was shown in studies on patients with medically untreatable epilepsy who had to have the connecting tracts between the two sides of the brain surgically cut to keep the seizures from spreading. In those patients, for example, if the word "heart" was presented to a patient visually, but the "he" part of the word was sent to the side of the brain with language, and the "art" part was sent to the hemisphere that has no verbal language but is more artistically focused, the patient would verbally say the word was "art," but point to a picture of a man, representing the word "he."

In other words, each so-called "side" of the brain is really *a separate brain*. Each has not only its own awareness but a different way of experiencing reality. This, to me, was astonishing. *We have two brains in our head?* Why do we have two brains? The phenomenon has the quality of a hall of mirrors because we experience the world as if we have just one brain.

This is where the SatoriWest Method really begins. Based on that strange fact, my hypothesis was that *the awareness on each side of the brain can experience the other side*. That's what I believe "self"-awareness is and how it emerges. Self-awareness comes from each brain in your head being aware of the other. Amazing. In other words, it's an inner-reflected awareness going back and forth between the two brains. This means that we aren't just aware of what is happening in the world and inside ourselves, our bodies, and minds; we are also aware *that* we are aware. We *know* that we know.

That ability—already sitting there in your brain—can be honed. To the point that it can fulfill your potential to feel wholly alive, to feel that you're living your life to its fullest.

To get a handle on this is to understand this ability in practical terms. What *does* it mean to you right now to be aware of being aware? Basically, self-awareness tells you that you exist. Although other animals may have this ability to a small degree, humans have much more capacity for it. However, it's usually in the background of our experience. How much of your day are you consciously cognizant of being alive?

Understanding this core of what it means for us to be deeply fulfilled was, unknowingly, getting me closer to understanding why we are all so *unhappy*. Part of the reason for this is that I was learning to treat psychiatric disorders early in the process of creating the SatoriWest Method. I was getting to understand the brain when it was ill, during medical conditions that affect the mind.

My work on the SatoriWest Method continued after I finished most of the coursework for my PhD program. (I opted not to do the final dissertation research project because it was on an unrelated topic.) The model kept expanding because of my intense interest in self-awareness, which was shaped during the next phase of my life, when I became involved with Zen Buddhism.

My parents were murdered when I was 23, a year before I went to medical school. It was a time of indescribable pain and emotional turmoil. I felt untethered and disoriented. I returned to college a few months later to continue my path. A friend suggested that I might find solace by checking out the campus Zen Buddhist group. I took to it like a fish to water. It helped me immeasurably, both emotionally and intellectually. It grounded me and introduced me to my brain in a different way: experientially.

Thus, began a 40-year (and counting) involvement with Zen. This included daily meditation, attending multiple retreats, and reading books on Zen and topics in secular spirituality.

From hearing Zen talks and reading about spirituality, the idea of Enlightenment made me wonder why this peak human experience wasn't possible for everyone. Why couldn't all people fulfill the highest potential of their brain? Why can't we all feel the exhilaration and inner peace that comes from Awakening to what it means to be alive? I also wondered whether any degree of Awakening could be therapeutic. And, of course, I wanted to know what in the brain causes Enlightenment. (Note: we're capitalizing all words for Enlightenment, such as Awakening, Transcendence, Nirvana, Heaven Within, Transformation, and Cosmic Consciousness as a sign of respect for the singular importance of this level of development and to distinguish, for example, "spiritual" Awakening from awakening from sleep.)

The mechanism of Awakening became clearer and clearer. To put it simplistically, it happens when the brain comes to realize itself, that it is experiencing itself. As such, throughout history a small segment of humanity has been able to intensify an inner focus on aliveness while letting go of an outer focus on "things," objects, individual aspects of experience. This caused them to Awaken to the enormity of what it means to be alive—and to feel profound gratitude for their existence. To ostensibly fall in love with their existence, no matter what was happening.

How can we shift our brains in that direction? Studying the brain, and experimenting with my own, I realized what happens for that potential to be actualized; I came to call it BrainShifting. You'll learn more about BrainShifting in this book and need to hear about it now to understand how it became central to the SatoriWest Method.

In the neuropsychology program I came to understand that self-awareness was at the core of these so-called higher states. My growing understanding of the brain and my knowledge of Zen were informing each other.

I want to be clear that this book is not about showing you how to attain full degrees of Enlightenment, though that is certainly possible. It's mentioned because there are degrees of Awakening that you can instantly experience which can alleviate your suffering, if only for moments at a time. Even if you go only a short distance down the road we're taking toward your highest potential, it will be enough for you to find relief from emotional hardship and struggle. That's important to understand. The full potential of your brain and its greatest vulnerabilities are central to the SatoriWest Method, though the causes of suffering and Awakening are presented in simple, clear, and actionable language.

Forty years of meditation evolved into the conception of what goes into BrainShifting. But that was only the beginning of what I got from my investigations of the brain and Buddhism. To understand the whole of the model you have to know a bit about Buddhism itself. I became interested in the branch of Buddhism known as Zen at a time when Buddhism, which concerns itself with the direct experience of Enlightenment with an almost science-like objectivity, was just taking hold in America. Now Zen centers are almost everywhere in the United States, attracting people interested in Buddhism as a religion as well as people of different faiths and secular beliefs.

A few years before I started meditating in 1980, the practice of mindfulness was already being extracted from Buddhism and taught as a technique for stress reduction and relaxation. As you may know (and as we'll address here), mindfulness has mushroomed in popular culture. It's been researched extensively and found to be extremely efficacious for a number of conditions besides stress reduction. It's used by most psychotherapists and in medical hospitals, schools, and prisons, all for different reasons.

For years after starting to meditate, I wondered what about mindfulness itself, as it was commonly practiced, allowed for Enlightenment, not just stress reduction. I wanted to understand the Awakened state not just as a way to feel bliss and aliveness, but as an antidote for people's suffering. That meant understanding mindfulness in its larger Buddhist context.

I came to see mindfulness as an aspect of BrainShifting, as the first maneuver that shifts attention of the two brains in on themselves. This causes greater self-awareness. This defocuses them from the external. These are two important features of the SatoriWest Method and of BrainShifting's ability to end suffering and heighten aliveness. It answered the question why it was important to understand BrainShifting (including mindfulness) as a piece of a larger Buddhist approach and practice. That answer completed the SatoriWest approach, which began to take shape as a redefinition of the core tenets of Buddhism: the Buddhist Four Noble Truths—plus one, which became SatoriWest's five points.

Thus the two worlds of Western science and Eastern practice came together. The word "satori" was used because it's a Japanese Buddhist term for "Awakening," and "west" meant that Awakening was seen from the vantage point of neuroscience, behavioral science, and holistic wellness. In its totality, it was through the lens of this Western knowledge that the five points of the SatoriWest Method were described.

Drawing on my growing understanding of Buddhism as well as Western training, I was able to conceptualize each point in a clear, concise, and actionable way with great detail. This is why the SatoriWest curriculum is so effective in psychiatric and substance-use-disorder settings. It reframes what happens in the brain when you suffer and what happens in the brain when it realizes its miraculous aliveness. It's a "journey" to shift your brain from one side of the spectrum to the other. (It's a journey not in the sense of finding a better moment, with better things happening and better emotions, but a journey for the brain to discover itself just the way it is. That's why "journey" is in quotes.)

So how did the central aspect of the SatoriWest Method, the understanding of what suffering is, enter in? Because when it did, it began to explain a lot about mental health issues, and substance abuse and other addictions, as well as plain stress and distress. Even though the seed of the SatoriWest Method was planted the moment I had that epiphany in high school, in that fleeting, micro-Awakening, the Buddhist Four Noble Truths showed me that our potential can't be understood without grasping exactly what suffering is. In fact, it is said that the Buddha himself believed that Awakening was solely the relief of suffering (which itself is blissful).

As a physician, I began building a system that could help my patients, whether in psychiatric hospitals or in my private psychotherapy practice. I kept refining a way that was not only a shorter and more concrete route toward utter fulfillment but could be used to eliminate suffering as it shows up in our daily lives. That's what the SatoriWest Method became: a system for us to see why we suffer, so we can unwind it at every turn—in little steps and potentially much bigger ones.

The model describes the phenomenon of "Tunnel Vision" as natural brain hardwiring that causes us to suffer. That's where the brain focuses on external "things"—objects, thoughts, and emotions—so that knowing it is alive is tucked far away in the background. The method then describes an opposite brain posture with the term "Perspective," where the brain realizes its aliveness in a more profound way. Tunnel Vision and Perspective are not just opposite ways of experiencing the moment; they are ways of acting and thinking, of responding to each moment.

Understanding how Tunnel Vision and Perspective come about in the brain brought in the two last phases in my journey to create the SatoriWest Method: wellness and adversity.

We don't only suffer during times of crisis and extreme hardship. Most people suffer in milder ways every day. That's because suffering on any level, as you'll learn more about, comes from being in Tunnel Vision. Tunnel Vision causes the stress we face all day as we lead our lives. Whether we know it or not. The antidote is Perspective. So where does wellness fit in? Various wellness strategies become an indirect way to cause your brain to shift into Perspective all on its own. In other words, BrainShifting is not just a series of skills that you use to open your mind, heart, and brain to Perspective; BrainShifting happens on its own. The brain shifts into Perspective through normal aging, as well as by the practice of wellness, and, sometimes, by enduring trauma.

To understand my personal journey that brought wellness into the SatoriWest Method, we need to go back in time again, to when I was a kid.

My uncle suffered a severe mental illness, and my mother, in a desperate effort to help her brother, read about alternative and complementary ways of healing it. She eventually focused on diet and nutrients, including supplements, that affect mood and thinking. Although nothing stopped the progression of my uncle's hideous illness, the value of physical wellness was seared into my consciousness, especially as it relates to psychiatry.

I became a psychiatrist and began reading about natural physical remedies for mental illness. I eventually enrolled in another PhD program, in Natural Health Science. This time I did complete the degree. For my dissertation, I expanded the model I had developed in the neuropsychology program. It described what happens in the human brain as it goes from little to no awareness and automatic reflexes, all the way up to self-awareness and spontaneous ways of thinking and acting. It was the early version of the SatoriWest Method. It also informed my core understanding of what wellness really brings. That's because I had overlooked a crucial piece of understanding the brain.

The Natural Health Science program revealed an obvious gap in thinking that I overlooked when thinking about the brain: it is an organ, like the liver and heart. And every organ has needs that must be met for it to function at its best. The heart needs exercise and the right diet. The liver needs a clean body and to avoid excessive toxins. The brain, as a *biological* organ, needs all those things and more.

However, because it has a mind and sense of self, it's a psychological organ. Because it evolved to exist in specific social situations, it's a tribal organ. Because it is configured with extreme intelligence and creativity, can organize its environment and accomplish complex tasks, it is a cultural organ. Because it has a sense of right and wrong, it is a moral organ. Because, as we pointed out before, it can appreciate its own aliveness, it's an existential organ.

The human brain needs many different kinds of wellnesses to function at its peak. When it is given what it needs to enhance those six aspects—physical, mental, social, cultural, moral, and existential—it functions at peak levels and naturally becomes more aware of itself, as remarkable as that seems. So these became the six spheres of total wellness in the SatoriWest Method. Practiced together and with balance they cause the brain to shift faster, naturally. In other words, this kind of total wellness can be specifically aimed at the goal of gaining Perspective, of intensifying self-awareness, so that life has more meaning and suffering is relieved.

More than 30 years of working with psychiatric patients struggling with severe illnesses, of seeing others in a private practice grappling with stress and emotional distress, and of understanding myself better, helped me realize that to find a life of peace and inner contentment there must be a shift in how the brain functions day to day. And that this shift requires that you learn some skills (the direct *skills* of BrainShifting) and practice wellnesses in the wholistic way that will be shown to you ("wholistic" referring to being "whole").

So how did the subject of this book, the role of crisis and trauma, come in to the SatoriWest Method? As I worked with people with severe mental health issues and just plain life crises, while also learning about Zen and spiritual literature from the inside out, I came to understand the vital role of hardship. Throughout history, crises, hardships, and trauma have been useful, if not powerful, mechanisms to induce a brain to shift into Perspective—sometimes extraordinarily high Perspective. In this book, you will read about some of this ancient and modern literature showing how people find relief and sometimes great Awakenings arising from dark moments.

That was my "Fifth" Buddhist Noble Truth—the fifth point of the SatoriWest Method: crises can be opportunities, *especially if you're prepared for them.* That's the purpose of this book and the value of the SatoriWest Method: it shows how Tunnel Vision is the cause of suffering and addictions. It can be most clearly seen and felt in the gut during times when we suffer the most. That recognition shifts the brain. It's the road to Perspective, which ultimately means feeling a level of inner peace and contentment no matter what life throws at us.

I hope this book causes your brain to shift enough to at least find respite from life stresses and unhappiness. You may even come to realize the meaning of this precious, singular opportunity you have to be alive, the way to fall in love with *your* existence.

· · · · · · ·

I so loved my experience! Learning the SatoriWest Method has been an absolute joy, and mind awakening as well. I am walking away from this altogether extremely happy, confident, and knowledgeable.

—Develyn

Introduction

This book is a journey for you and your brain. This journey may feel like a rollercoaster ride as it takes you through the lows of life and all the myriad ways we accumulate stress and unhappiness. It then reveals what in the brain is causing all that stress and unhappiness (spoiler alert: it's Tunnel Vision). The journey then shows you what life can and ought to be when we fulfill our highest potential (which is all included in the simplistic term, Perspective). The journey then walks you through the details of how to stop your brain from bringing you down so that you can fulfill its highest capacity.

This is not a passive journey, though, nor will it always feel comfortable. To go from the lows to the highs of what it means to be you, you'll be asked to reflect honestly on yourself, to think about your life, and to understand a little bit of brain science. You'll be asked to do a lot of noticing and to change how you pay attention and to what.

To do all this, you'll travel through the five points of the SatoriWest Method: understanding the human condition, learning about Tunnel Vision, discovering what it means to have Perspective, taking the SatoriWest Method's journey, and then realizing how crises can be springboards to Perspective. I hope that by the time you finish reading this book, your eyes will be opened to how your brain functions, how it causes you to suffer, and how you can use it to bring you inner peace and ultimately find joy in being you. It's all there, right now, in your brain, waiting to be revealed.

The book is organized into five parts, based on these five points of the SatoriWest Method.

Part I ushers you into the human condition, the universal struggle, stress, and suffering that has befallen humankind throughout its existence. This is to get you in touch with the fuel you'll need for the trip. We all have negative feelings that we drag along with us through life. They can be strategically used to open you up, if they're not ignored, or if you don't work overtime to distract yourself from them. If you do, these universal emotions can cause you to feel alienated, like you're the only one struggling with them. They can make you insecure about yourself for having them. If you're in crisis right now, Part I will tell you that you're not alone in your struggles.

Part II reveals the actual reason for our human condition: we struggle with our minds, because they become warped though Tunnel Vision. This perversion of the mind is unique to humans. It comes from normal survival wiring in our brain.

In Part III we'll explore the heights to which our brains are capable of going, which are available to us right now. With just a subtle shift in our brains, we get Perspective, the opposite of Tunnel Vision. It opens our awareness, focuses us on the enormity of our existence, and gives us the personality traits that allow us to live our life at this peak.

Getting from one end of the spectrum toward the other, far enough to be relieved of our suffering, is the objective of Part IV: "The SatoriWest Method." It's about how to leave Tunnel Vision and find Perspective. This is where we'll explore the practices and skills of direct BrainShifting and the indirect, total-wellness aspects of BrainShifting.

Part V, the centerpiece of this book, takes up the issue of using crises, high stress, and times of suffering to propel us forward on the path to our best life.

Finally, the conclusion will look at the journey from a higher vantage point.

Keep in mind that the SatoriWest Method is not a substitute for professional treatment with medications and psychotherapy when a significant psychiatric or substance-use condition has been diagnosed. Even though the SatoriWest Method tries to increase your awareness of the moment as it is—to shift your brain toward acceptance and inner peace—there are times when pain or emotional hurt need to be removed right away. That's when professional treatment may be needed. Once the emergency is resolved, you can train your brain to accommodate the moment the way it is.

You might ask, then do you either engage in talk therapy and medications *or* practice the SatoriWest Method, but not both? No. They can and have been used together in a complementary way. Traditional psychiatric medications and psychological treatment, in the SatoriWest model, are integrated as important wellness strategies, as indirect ways of shifting your brain further along on the path to liberation, to your highest self. In fact, the SatoriWest Method has been used as professional treatment. It was the system of psychotherapy used inside a psychiatric hospital and in its outpatient setting, integrated with other psychiatric services.

As you read this book, you will be repeatedly reminded of this one essential fact: the goal of achieving Perspective, to feel liberated and manifest all the other traits that can arise with it, is not solely to replace bad feelings with good, happy ones. We need to establish this understanding from the beginning, and to reinforce it throughout the journey, so that you don't get off track. Because your brain and its mind, when caught in Tunnel Vision, will try to tell you that *is* what you want.

Likewise, learning about your Tunnel Vision is not solely about ridding you of bad feelings and replacing them with good ones. The method is not a "happy pill," in the sense of bringing about a static, unchanging state of positive emotions. The method opens up a window of opportunity for your brain to experience each moment in a different way, a way not typical for you. If you thought the SatoriWest Method was about a fixed, bliss-like state, that belief would direct your mind to constantly search for a future moment that is better than this one. That would land you in a different type of Tunnel Vision, and you'd wind up dissatisfied and frustrated all over again.

Reaching the heights of what it means to be alive means falling in love with our ability to experience the moment, exactly as it is. "Good" and "bad" moments. Thousands of years of human experience have taught us that being fully present and immersed in the Now is the gateway to our highest potential.

Wishing you good luck, strength, and persistence on your journey.

. . . .

I have been trying to get my mental illness under control for the last 20 years. I wasn't sure what to expect. Learning the SatoriWest Method has really opened my Perspective as to how to think about my mental illness. It has also helped me to be able to use my coping skills and ask myself what I need in that moment to break my Tunnel Vision and open my Perspective. The SatoriWest Method WILL be my bible for my mental illness.

—Michael

Part I

THE HUMAN CONDITION

1
Life Is Hard

You Are Not Alone

From the moment we are born, humans face an epic paradox. On the one hand, being human comes with the potential to be amazed by life—by all existence, for that matter. Only our species has the capacity to appreciate what it means to be alive, to experience equanimity and inner peace no matter what is happening, to have a passion for making a difference in the world. Taken all together, no drug high can really match this natural potential (or at least not for long, and not without side effects).

But there is a dark side to being human. It's found in this inexorable fact that has plagued every person who has ever lived, rich or poor, young or old, lucky or unlucky: human life is laden with suffering (until we learn to unwind it, that is). Sure, some of us are luckier than others. We inherited good genes or better life circumstances. And some of us are less fortunate, used to lives filled mostly with stress and trouble.

Yet deep inside *all* of us, at least when we're not distracted, we feel an incessant kind of suffering. Most of us feel insecure, frustrated with not having enough, a sense of loss, or disappointment with people and life. Human life is an emotional challenge. Navigating life's ups and downs is an emotional struggle for everyone. And even if you've been given a great deal in life, you may feel fear and distress at the prospect of losing it, whether or not you actually do so.

You'll learn in the next chapter that, for everyone except those who eventually learn to live otherwise, human life is a series of waves of small and big crises. You might be living right now in the shadow of a crisis. It could be a broken relationship, a family death, a health scare, a financial crunch, depression, or any number of other things. In fact, it's likely you are reading this book because you are hurting in some way, even if you're not in a crisis. That's because you've lived through a crisis of some sort before. And you realize, at least on some level, that another one is coming. That's part of the suffering that comes with being human.

Unless you're in crisis, these feelings can be so common that you may not even realize they're there. In fact, the emotional struggles that come along with waves of crises are so common, they've been called "the human condition." It's a term that reflects the universality of human suffering, stress, and dissatisfaction. The fact is that between those waves of crises the tide appears to be getting higher and higher. Check inside yourself right now and you'll see at least a couple of symptoms of your human condition—some anxiety, some sadness or emotional exhaustion, some frustration or anger.

One main problem is that we hide these feelings. We hide them from other people; we even hide them from ourselves. People who attempt suicide and survive commonly say they had all sorts of thoughts and feelings they thought were unique to them. If only they had known that what they were going through was not exclusive to them, they might not have attempted it.

Our culture tells us that crying or expressing anxiety or hurt feelings are signs of weakness. Our minds get the impression that our unique brand of human condition separates us from other people who we think don't suffer in this way. We get the sense that many people, in general, are much happier, emotionally stronger, or more "normal" than us.

That's an illusion. The vast majority of people are hiding their insecurities. They are masking the sadness and grief they hold on to. To the extent that they can, they don't let on how frustrated and impatient they feel.

I hope this and the next chapter will dispel the myth that you are beset with these issues and most others aren't. Because that illusion causes you to bury *your* negative feelings, to hide your insecurities. You're going to need those feelings as fuel for your SatoriWest journey. Also, trying to distract yourself from them with whatever will make them go away sets you up for even more negative feelings later. Choose your poison: excessive amounts of alcohol, television, movies, video games, sex, love-seeking, food, drugs, reading, focusing on other people's lives, working excessively long hours, even creating unnecessary drama in our lives are among the countless options at our fingertips that can make negative feelings disappear, at least for a little while, before they return with greater force.

What this means is that immediate pleasures or distractions often come with a price. Eating ice cream, no matter how happy it makes you, makes you gain weight. Going to a movie to escape your life does help you escape for a while. But when you come back to your life, things can feel even more stressful, because you haven't dealt with them. In that sense, using things that give you good, immediate feelings—besides having harmful aftereffects, like health problems, deteriorating relationships, or financial problems—can end up making you feel even worse when bad consequences start to kick in. That compels you to then dive into even more distractions that themselves come with more adverse consequences, and so on, and so on. It's a vicious cycle.

Enjoyable things are not bad in themselves. They become problems when we start to rely on them to feel the remotest bit of joy, or worse, to get us through the day or the week. They cause trouble when we use them to excess, or when they make it so that we don't deal with the source of our problems (which you'll learn more about in Part II).

As far as the SatoriWest Method is concerned, avoiding problems and the feelings that come with them has a potentially bigger consequence than not dealing with them: avoiding them closes you off from your birthright. It shuts the door to the highest capacity your brain is capable of. It keeps you from experiencing the exhilaration that comes from being alive, from appreciating what you have.

If something bad is happening in your life, feeling exhilarated is not exactly how you would describe your experience. That may in part be related to Tunnel Vision's blockade of Perspective.

Author's note: Although it may seem depressing, the SatoriWest Method starts off with this first point, the human condition, for very important reasons. If you are in crisis, it tells you that you have come to the right place. Your suffering is understood. You are not alone. You are not abnormal. This is the starting point from which to heal and grow. If you are stressed out or even just a seeker of higher states of being, it gives you a critical message, too. It tells you that you are not going anywhere in your psychological or "spiritual" development without fully accepting that you are mired in these feelings. Whatever your motivation for reading this book, whether you are in crisis, stressed out, or seeking Enlightenment, starting off saturating in the reality of life and how all the ways you feel makes it plain that you cannot avoid, suppress, or deny these feelings and that you will need them to serve as fuel for this journey. As you develop, you open up your awareness to radically accept each miraculous moment the way it is, which almost always includes some negative feelings. That's true even in so-called good times.

Fueling Up for the Journey

The human condition is dramatic and poignant in all our lives, coming in waves of crises and in the accumulation of difficult feelings left in their wake. We'll explore some of these crises in more detail in the next chapter. They include facing humiliations, dealing with aging, and suffering loss. Some can be so intense, they can take us down, leaving serious health issues or even suicidal thoughts.

Sometimes, though, crises force us to deal head-on with the cause of our unhappiness. That can be fuel for our journey inward to our highest selves. They can provide energy to change, motivation to do the work of self-discovery. Crises can serve as the catalysts we need to get off the treadmill of suffering and lead us to more fulfilling lives.

The title of this book reflects this paradox, represented in the ancient adage *People who suffer the most in life often have the most profound experience of what it means to be alive.* In other words, suffering can shake us up and out of our comfort zones. It allows us to be more aware of our Tunnel Vision (the cause of our unhappiness), so we can start making the changes we need. It can propel us forward in our development to become fulfilled, awake, and liberated. We're almost forced to face ourselves so we can come out on the other side.

Before this transformation can happen in our own lives, we need to understand the nature of our distress. We need to realize the universality of this rising tide of emotional unhappiness that comes from waves of life crises and the adverse toll left in their wake. Of course, we all experience this in our own way.

Your First Shift

The very act of realizing that you suffer from the human condition and accepting that it is universal shifts your brain toward its potential. If you've tried to do those things, congratulations. That's the true beginning of your journey.

Ultimately, accepting each moment, including the parts we don't like, which is considered a "radical acceptance," causes your brain to shift. This can be summarized by James Baldwin's quote "Nothing can be changed until it is faced." As your brain shifts to deeper acceptance of your human condition, you eventually experience a sense of belonging. You feel connected to everyone, even everything. It's like the transformation from driving on the road and feeling competitive and at odds with other cars, and then feeling part of traffic, where everyone obeys common rules and there's a coordinated dance of movement. That sense of unity is an experience of your human condition similar to that of every other person on the planet and everyone who has ever lived. It is normalizing to discover you're not the only one who is suffering. It evolves into a more radical belonging, an acceptance of the moment just as it is, good and bad, that you are part of. It takes witnessing the witnesser and everyone and everything all at once, just as they are, connected.

When adversity strikes, it is our default mode to feel more alienated, separate, strange, or different from everyone else. It is validating to understand that we are struggling with what everyone else is struggling with. Perspective is really getting—fully feeling—that you have the same affliction as all other humans, with maybe a different shade or manifestation. That confirmation, that we are not unusual, can be a powerful first step on the voyage to our best lives.

This book starts with the human condition or point one of the SatoriWest Method for an important reason: because our natural way to cope with difficult feelings is to stuff them down or push them out of our minds. Point one, though, helps us overcome any denial or shame we may have about suffering. It's meant to validate our feelings, to bring them out of the closet, so to speak. Ideally it helps us face ourselves and our lives and begin to change.

A Note About Suffering

Many people think of suffering as something someone does when they're in crisis. It conjures the image of someone writhing in emotional or physical pain. That same misconception can lead you to believe that because you aren't suffering, you're not terribly bad off emotionally at the moment.

So what *is* suffering? We'll address this a few times in this book. We'll define it specifically in Part II when we get into discussing Tunnel Vision as its actual cause. It'll come up again when we get to Part V and discuss crisis as opportunity. It's an aspect of the SatoriWest Method that may be confusing.

To begin, experiencing emotional or physical pain is not the same thing as suffering it. This may be hard to understand. For instance, we can feel sadness, anxiety, and anger—we can even feel significant physical pain—yet we can still feel grateful for our lives and what we have. That mitigates or eliminates suffering. Or, for example, some people have strong religious convictions that bolster them and lift their spirits, even in times of adversity. Some people can feel other emotions, like love, and other physical sensations, like softness, without focusing exclusively on negative emotions and sensations. That relieves suffering. When it comes to biological depression, some people can understand that their sad and anxious feelings are caused by a medical condition, so they realize it is not their fault or is going to pass, and so on. That's a classic way to diminish or alleviate suffering from the disorder.

Through the furthest reaches of BrainShifting, our brain can experience the negative information that comes with emotional and physical pain and turn it into the perception of energy, just different forms of energy. In a sense, that is what mindfulness-based pain clinics do. They change the information value of pain, from a matter of labeling and hating the pain to experiencing the changing sensations of bodily energy. That greatly alleviates suffering.

Feeling sadness, loss, grief, hostility, and fear is not the same thing as suffering them. Not even pain equals suffering. Suffering is a brain condition. Not suffering is a matter of Perspective. This is what the SatoriWest Method and learning to shift your brain is all about. A mind warped by Tunnel Vision causes suffering. The brain can change that experience.

Also, just because you are not writhing in emotional pain at this moment does not mean that you are *not* suffering. If negative feelings cause you to want to push them down, distract yourself from them, or do something to make them go away, you are suffering them. If negative feelings can drag you down and affect your appreciation of what this moment can be, then you are suffering. That's the SatoriWest understanding.

Conclusion

All of us are in the same boat, though some of us were dealt a more difficult hand in life. Yet we are all brothers and sisters in our human struggles. We all live our own versions of "the human condition." This includes even biological depression. It would be safe to say that most people on the planet, at one time or another, have had some symptoms of a major or minor (so-called subclinical) depression, whether it was officially diagnosed or not.

BrainShifting, as you will see, requires us to open up to the moment exactly as it is. If you are watching a horror movie, trying to not see the monster on the screen by closing your eyes or hiding behind the couch means you are actually paying more attention to it. Your human condition is like the monster. Seeing it in its fullest expression is an opportunity to learn about it and ultimately unwind it into greater Perspective.

It's in this spirit that we will be taking a deeper dive into your difficult emotions in the next chapter. Doing that, your every impulse may be to close the book and do something that makes you feel better in the short run. That is how people have coped with life since time immemorial. We are asking you to try a different approach, one that has worked for people who have discovered it throughout the ages. Similar to when you talk about your feelings in psychotherapy, the goal is not for you to suffer. Remember, delving into the things in your past and present that have caused you to suffer is in service to not suffering, to uncovering your best life and your highest self.

Of course, if you reach any kind of limit to what you can psychologically cope with, then the next chapter may be difficult to read. On the other hand, reading this book and embracing the SatoriWest Method can open your heart and mind so you can gradually develop greater and greater Perspective. Then crises, emotional pain, and hardship become incredible opportunities for positive change.

. . . .

The SatoriWest Method has shown me the pitfalls that plunge me into depression as plain as day. I feel as though my thinking has been drastically shifted away from misery and anger to a place of harmony and inner peace. I now have a strong grasp on how I should structure my thinking and behavior. I believe that anyone who engages with this material can learn valuable lessons on how to change their life for the better.

—Lucas

2
Surface Reasons for Suffering

Let's delve into the surface reasons why people suffer. It starts with the fact that people's lives are hard at each stage.

Author's note: It's worth repeating that this chapter might be hard to read and think about. It may bring up stressful and hurtful memories or feelings you might rather keep buried. For the most part, difficult feelings are already there. Bringing your attention to them is part of the process of using them to your advantage. Mentioning them would be hurtful and destructive if this book were not able to offer an antidote, which of course it does. I hope that you'll be able to stick with me and trust that there is a purpose to this exercise of looking at our lives. However, if reading the rest of this chapter becomes too stressful, skip it or save it for another time. You will still be able to gain substantial support in later chapters.

We'll begin at the beginning, at birth.

Birth

Our mother's womb was safe and comfortable, quiet and warm. We were free from anxiety. Being crushed through a narrow birth canal into a noisy, cold world is where your human story begins. Suddenly, you gasp and cry to take your first breath. You have to rely on someone to feed you when you're hungry. Your attention is required to get someone else's attention almost every minute for you to get what you need and want. It's the start of a lifetime of stress and focused attention on getting needs met. Welcome to the beginning of the human condition.

Childhood

Humans are highly sensitive and intelligent animals, hard to raise under the best of conditions. Most adults are not capable of raising children with the degree of sophistication and nurturing children fully need. It challenges most people to raise a puppy the right way; it would take a doctorate in child development to do it well for a baby, toddler, and child at every stage of development—and even then, there would be controversy among experts.

In addition, parents bring their own hurts and inadequate childhoods into raising their children. The upshot is that there are no perfect parents, and even the best parents are making it up as they go along. Most are far from perfect, some are unintentionally neglectful, some unknowingly hurtful, some downright abusive, some criminally so.

Even siblings pick on or reject each other: some of the most egregious examples of abuse come from the hands of older siblings. This abuse is commonly written off by the victims and everyone else as "just what siblings do."

School is often a competitive and anxiety-producing experience. Kids either struggle to fit in or deal with loneliness and isolation at school. Although children can be cruel to each other wherever they are, bullying is so pervasive in American culture that schools have bullying programs.

Of course, physical, mental, and sexual abuse are a nightmare. Some children witness or are victims of abuse by adults who are intoxicated or suffer mental illnesses. Others are living through the trauma of parental divorce or incarceration or overt physical or emotional neglect.

These Adverse Childhood Experiences (ACEs) were studied in 1997 in 17,000 adults. The study showed that 64 percent of adults surveyed experienced at least one of these difficult events, and some many more. The purpose of the study was to show the correlation between ACEs and the high incidence of mental and physical illnesses in adulthood. (Note: "Relationship of Childhood

Abuse and Household Dysfunction to Many of the Leading Causes of Death in Adults," published in the *American Journal of Preventive Medicine* in 1998, Volume 14, pages 245–258.)

Sure, children are resilient and find laughter and fun whenever and wherever they can. Yet it appears that the majority of adults throughout time, in different cultures and places, have poignantly painful memories of childhood. These recollections leave lasting emotional wounds, usually invisible to us and those around us, until someone or something sets off an emotional trigger.

> **Thought Exercise**
>
> Take a moment and think about your childhood. Scan your memory. Visualize your life until you were about 12 years old, the good and the bad moments. Did you have issues with your parents or the people who raised you? Whether you thought they were great or terrible, any negativity in their parenting caused some degree of negative feelings, which has stayed with you.
>
> How were you treated by your siblings? As a kid, did you have friends? Enemies? What were your school days like: filled with anxiety or with enjoyment? Now think about your childhood as a whole. How would you say your childhood was overall?

Adolescence and Late Teens

Throughout the ages and in most cultures, adolescence and the late teens has been considered a difficult time for people. Asserting ourselves as individuals requires that we separate ourselves from our families and leave our parents' control, security, and expressions of love. (Even if they were neglectful or abusive and ill-prepared for parenthood because of their own difficult childhoods, many parents still love their children without reserve.) Our drive is to connect more with our peers. It's liberating and it's scary. Powerful sexual hormones drive us to distraction. Our bodies are noticeably changing as we become acutely aware of how we look. Adolescents are fragile and self-conscious.

Cliques often form in adolescence. They force us to identify with one kind of group or another, feeling either left out, less than, or superior to others, none of which is a comfortable place to be. Put teens together with vulnerable peers and there can be dysfunction and cruelty, which can be dangerous, if not toxic, to our sense of self.

We will do almost anything to be accepted by peers, meaning we need to prove ourselves and try to fit into a group that has to prove itself. Looking back, it is a time of great anxiety, self-consciousness, and insecurity for us, as well as anger at our parents and society.

Thought Exercise

Visualize your childhood from ages 12 to 17. Remember how it felt emotionally to live through those times. How were your adolescent and teenage years? Were you "popular" or "unpopular"? What did that mean to you? Were you secure in your peer circle or did you feel like an outsider—or both? Did you feel secure? What was your body image like? What were your feelings about sexuality? How was your relationship with family? Were these overall good years, horrible, or somewhere in between? Why?

Adulthood

Finally, the day we've been waiting for arrives: we're grown up! Free—or so we think. With freedom comes responsibility and pressure. A lot of it. Whether we go on in school or not, our twenties and thirties are about accomplishing things. We have to pay for things. We have deadlines to meet. We have to compete for things we want. We feel compelled to be "successful," however we define that.

Being an adult in most societies is not just about dreaming about possibilities but also about fearing the opposite: failing. Can we find the right romantic partner to avoid being alone? Can we fit in with the right network of friends and community to stave off feeling isolated? Do we have what it takes to start a family and to do right by them? Can we find the right job or career to afford not only what we think are essentials but what we think will make us happy, and to avoid feeling like a failure or disappointment to others?

For many people, adulthood has a lot to do with raising children. This comes with the constant worry about whether we can keep them safe, whether we can strike a balance between discipline and nurturing, and whether we can juggle work, relationships, and child-rearing so no one feels neglected. It's a lot of pressure and stress.

We inevitably compare ourselves with other people we believe are successful. In some sense, we can never measure up, but we never realize that others are usually just as unhappy as we are, if not more so. This understanding is a major point of this chapter: we stress ourselves because of the distorted reality and mistaken impression that there are people who do *not* suffer the human condition, and so we endlessly strive to be as happy as we think they are.

A recent study showed that three-fourths of people in the United States and Canada, as well as in some countries in Western Europe and South Korea and Australia, say they feel stressed every day. Some describe stress that feels beyond their control. If we have a high income, we feel stressed by work. If we have low income, we feel stressed by lack of money. Long working hours, hard commutes, not enough time to plan and organize and recreate, too many demands, not enough time to unwind or do everything, and usually never enough money all put pressures on relationships, another source of stress. Studies show that stress is increasing in modern life. It links to increasing cardiovascular disease, inflammation, and other illnesses.

To underscore this aspect of the human condition, suicide is the second leading cause of death in people aged 10 to 34 in the United States (Suicide Prevention Resource Center, sprc.org).

> **Thought Exercise**
>
> There are different concerns and advantages at every age segment, particularly if you are 18-30 (early adulthood), 31-45 (middle adulthood), and 46-65 (so-called "middle age"). Whatever your age, think about these years, now and in the past. How stressed were or are you? What, if any, are your concerns about the following?
>
> - Global warming
> - Having children
> - Managing your time (having too much to do)
> - Child-rearing
> - Losing your looks
> - Losing abilities
> - Finding a spouse or life partner
> - Finding work that is aligned with your passions, talents, and skills

Aging

Up until about age 25, we see the future as endless. It is natural to deny that we are mortal. As a friend said to me recently, "Oh, people know they are going to die, they just don't believe it."

However, the unbelievable penetrates, sometimes slowly, sometimes in jolts of dawning realizations. This often happens after age 25, or sometimes not until our thirties. Part of the reason is that we have a visual image of ourselves that normally sets in in our early twenties. What this means is that when we think of ourselves and our identity, we think of ourselves from our twenties. Looking in the mirror as we get older, there's dissonance, because we don't recognize the image as us.

When we hit our thirties, we often begin to feel a gnawing angst, something akin to "Wow, I'm really 30. I actually am aging, and my time on Earth is limited." But because we are busy trying to succeed and avoid failure, it is relatively easy to ignore or laugh off that feeling. Hit 40, though, and start losing the looks and abilities we took for granted, and the angst we felt at 30 turns into a freak-out. Hit our fifties and the term "midlife crisis" exists for good reason.

Of course, in the United States we joke about men buying sports cars and women becoming obsessed with anti-aging remedies, but midlife can be a source of great misery and fear. Many men and women become upset at the rapid changes in their looks and abilities, their graying hair and wrinkles, sagging skin, slower cognition, and impaired memory. They may have difficulty running, lifting heavy objects, staying up as late, or sustaining sexual energy compared with their younger days.

If you think the midlife "crisis" is a modern condition of baby boomers, think again. Men and women have stressed about their midlives from early in human history. Of course, struggling for survival provides an immediate distraction from these lower layers of stress, fear, and grief.

> **Thought Exercise**
>
> If you are between 66 and 80, how are you dealing with this period? Are you often freaked out or do you feel happy to have reached these years? What, if any, fears or concerns do you have about aging? How do you feel when you look in the mirror?

Insecurity

Insecurity is a source of stress that can't be pinned to a particular time period of our lives. Starting in childhood and often carried throughout life, insecurity and low self-esteem affect the vast majority of us—even, and maybe especially, those who seem grandiose and overconfident. It's a chronic feeling of not being good enough, of being less worthy or even worthless, unworthy of love or respect. Insecurity drives people to seek approval or to fit in, to try to prove they are worthy of respect and love, to feel less anxious about being themselves. It often comes with a core feeling of shame, of needing to hide who we really are so people don't find out our "secret"—that we are not confident, we are not as emotionally well or happy as we project to the world. Not everyone has low self-esteem, but many people do.

Some people cover up these insecurities with bluster and arrogance, or at the very least by faking confidence. The feeling of never being good enough usually comes with the need to monitor actions and words to make sure they seem normal or competent. It's exhausting. That habit constitutes a quiet, background source of unhappiness.

Thought Exercise

Think about your level of inner confidence—not what you show the world, but how you feel inside. Keep in mind this is not necessarily related to being either an introvert or an extrovert. Self-confidence is not necessarily related to those characteristics. Many performers who appear outgoing lack inner confidence, whereas people who are unassuming can be inwardly confident. Keeping in mind that you may have a different level of confidence in different arenas of your life, depending on what role you are playing, consider the following:

- Do you hide your feelings (anxiety, anger, or sadness) to appear "normal" or calm?
- Do you go to some lengths to fit in, to look or act "normal," in public?
- Do you need to be complimented to feel a sense of achievement?
- What is your *overall* self-confidence like? Are you extremely insecure, do you feel inadequate, unlovable, and unworthy, or are you highly confident and secure in yourself? If you are somewhere in the middle, how would you describe that?

Illness

We all get sick at some time in our lives. Surely you've had a serious flu you thought would never leave. It can leave you feeling helpless and weak. Think about the thousands of chronic and acute physical diseases that exist. If we live long enough, we will likely get one of them, if we don't already have one. They can color any life with stress and hardship.

Then, of course, there are mental illnesses, which are becoming more prevalent. Perhaps they're related to the stress of modern living, or we are just becoming more cognizant of them as a culture. Dealing with a mental illness can make life intolerable.

On some level, many of us worry that if we don't already have a serious illness, we are going to get one. Besides the fact that they make us feel awful, illnesses can rob us of our autonomy, dignity, and livelihood, even of the things we used to do that made life fun and interesting. No one escapes having an illness. If we have so far, we know our time could come.

> **Thought Exercise**
>
> What illnesses have you had, or do you have? How much suffering does your illness cause you? Does it leave you frightened and in despair? Do you feel appreciative of illnesses for some reason? How do they affect you emotionally?

Loss

Though childhoods are often sad and difficult, they also often come with times of innocence, exuberance, laughter, and wonder. Many people are nostalgic about their past and happy times. This is why leaving our childhood home, city, or country, or even our childhood itself, can be a source of sadness or grief.

Life is filled with all sorts of loss, through either death or falling out of touch: missed times, cherished grandparents, parents, other family, friends, and pets, belongings, homes, you name it. Of course, we all know life comes with loss, but that doesn't make it any less painful. We accumulate this grief over years, one layer on top of another.

> **Thought Exercise**
>
> Think of the losses in your life. Consider relatives, friends, pets, places, times, or cherished things. How affected are you by these losses? Are you in active grief? When you remember these people, animals, places, and things, do you feel more grateful for having had them in your life than upset by their memory?

Old Age

A sense of mortality lurking in the background causes people to be more aware of the passing of time, to feel like they are running out of time. It's a sort of "time sickness." We are in a hurry to accomplish as much as we can before time runs out. When we are much older, we realize there is nothing we can do to stave off that denial; there are no items on our bucket list that we can achieve now. This realization can be a relief, but also the root of suffering in later years.

The sadness, dread, and fear that comes with the sense of mortality, the reality of which is clearly in our faces as we get older, is only compounded by being looked at and treated as feeble, as a stereotype of someone without the same needs and feelings as someone younger (which is not true). Being more incapacitated or incapable of functioning independently, giving up our independence or having it taken away, being forced to leave our homes, having to be taken care of, read to, and fed, often comes with some degree of condescension: we are essentially being treated like a child.

The longer we live, the more we will see our relatives and friends die while having to deal with our own impending death. The latter can come with some degree of resignation and relief, especially if we're in some pain, chronically sad, fearful, or even panicky.

> **Thought Exercise**
>
> If you are 81 or older, what is your experience with these years? Are you are stressed, demoralized, or fearful because of some aspect of being older? To what extent are you joyful and appreciative of having lived a long life?

Hopefully, the point came across: life *is* a series of waves of crises and hardships, and we carry the emotional wake with us. We accumulate more and more stress over our lifetime. This is the case for every human who has ever lived and was probably true for our pre-human ancestors. That is why it's been universally called "the human condition." Struggling with life, with this human condition, is part of what makes us human. Trillions of people have lived and died while accumulating heartache and pain, hurts and fears, anger and resentments, sadness and grief. We are brothers and sisters in our plight.

If this chapter depressed you, that was not its aim. Remember, the opposite of the human condition also exists—an extraordinary level of human experience, an advanced stage of development (for example, wisdom, maturity, authenticity, lovingkindness) that goes beyond where most people stop. That is also available to all of us. Yet we don't get there by ignoring or distracting ourselves or suppressing our discomfort. We have to use these feelings. This chapter allows you to engage the full expression of who you are, how you feel, and what you have been carrying with you and are likely trying to run from. That, as you will see, is an essential aspect of accepting and ultimately valuing each moment in its entirety, exactly as it is. Feeling all your feelings, in a way that is healthy and productive, is the first step toward feeling amazingly alive and exuberant about life.

. . . .

First of all, I came to the program because I was considering suicide. What I liked best about the program is that it is a step-by-step guide to work through problems in life. I had never seen another program like this and it made so much sense to me!

—Clara

Part II

TUNNEL VISION

3

The Human Brain–Tunnel Vision: Parts One, Two, and Three

If the ills and crises of life have gotten you down, this chapter will begin to turn that around by giving you insight and knowledge. It will reveal two time-honored truths. First, in spite of the universal human condition, suffering is not a given in life, in yours or in others'. In other words, it's universal, sure, but it doesn't have to be. That's why you're reading this book.

The second truth is related to the first and is of singular importance to the SatoriWest Method: all the reasons that we drilled into in the last chapter *are not the actual reasons why we suffer.*

That fact can be a real surprise. What we're saying is that we don't suffer from the "bad" things that happen to us or from missing the "good" things taken from us. We don't suffer from not getting what we feel we want, need, or deserve. We suffer for only one reason: our human brain is hardwired for suffering because of Tunnel Vision.

There's a lot to understand about Tunnel Vision, but one way of thinking about it sums it up. Tunnel Vision comes from focusing largely on getting what you want and then eliminating what you don't want. That means that when your attention is fixated in Tunnel Vision, besides all the other facets of it that are noxious to your happiness, you simply cannot be satisfied. It means that this moment cannot be good enough. It forces your mind to live in that reality. A brain with its mind in Tunnel Vision seeks a future moment that is better than this one, whether that future is now or at the end of your life. However, if you live your life in Tunnel Vision—which is what the chapters on the human condition were trying to tell you—no moment can ever be good enough. You can never be satisfied. There is always something more or better. This moment, this feeling, this experience is never enough—never.

It may seem like life has highs to it, unparalleled pleasures. Yet if those moments are obtained by or experienced in Tunnel Vision, they will be so fleeting, it will feel like they are yanked from you or you will feel they are diluted. You'll know it deep down, which will put you into even more Tunnel Vision.

However, human suffering, including its cause, Tunnel Vision, can be readily unprogrammed from our brain. In other words, every human has to endure suffering and stress until they learn how to do otherwise. We all have to face horrible life events that just happen. We hope and pray for the positive ones and try mightily to miss the negative ones.

But even though "sh** happens," it doesn't have to determine how fulfilled we are by life. Our experience of negative life events and even positive ones can change radically. Our human condition is not inescapable, a belief that is another reason why we suffer. The survival wiring of your brain warps your mind and causes what we're calling Tunnel Vision. Just understanding the parts and pieces of Tunnel Vision helps us see it for what it is. That's how we learn to unwind it and our suffering.

Let's explore how Tunnel Vision came to be in our lives.

The Brain's Survival Wiring and Tunnel Vision

Billions of years of evolution went into making the brains we have. Modern animals evolved to be survival machines, and human beings are at the top of the heap. Powerful, powerful programming controls what we do and how we experience reality life—even who we are.

So what is the key to survival? Getting what is needed for survival and avoiding what is a threat to that survival. Thus, when an animal needs something or needs to avoid something, its brain directs attention to it. It's pretty basic. Mechanisms in the brain direct its attention. These mechanisms focus attention on whatever object the animal needs or wants to have and needs or wants to avoid. In humans, this includes any thoughts and feelings associated with that object. That directed attention then sets in motion behaviors that move the animal toward or away from the object.

In this sense, if a cat sees a moving object, it automatically focuses attention on it. Say the object is a mouse. Whether it is hungry or not, the cat reflexively moves toward the mouse. Then again, if the cat is hungry, it will also pay attention, but this time focusing on its hungry feelings and memories about the mouse. It will scan the environment for either a bird or a mouse. If it sees another mouse, driven this time by hunger, it will be *even more* fixated on the mouse, tracking its every move until it pounces on it.

The same holds for any animal that is afraid of or repulsed by something. It will pay attention to the object and to the feelings, thoughts, or memories about it. For example, if a bird hears an unexpected noise that might be a predator, it will attend to that sound and its anxiety like a laser. It will often fly away even before it fully realizes what the risk is.

Survival wiring is powerful and hardwired. Those instinctual and reflexive mechanisms work well for other animals. There is a serious design issue, however, with those mechanisms in humans. We are capable of functioning at a higher level. That survival function acts like a defect that causes Tunnel Vision and creates the human condition.

Tunnel Vision is a design flaw in the human brain. There are many facets to it. You really need to understand them all. Recognizing each of these components will help you unwind them. Having acknowledged your particular brand of human condition in the last chapter, recognizing how your struggles arise in Tunnel Vision is central. This is the next step in the SatoriWest Method.

Recognizing your Tunnel Vision can be a challenge, as it is mostly invisible to us. Garden-variety Tunnel Vision, though the cause of stress and unhappiness, is so much part of a normal day, we don't see it. *Yet acknowledging your human condition helps make it more apparent; it crystalizes it in your awareness so that you can better see the Tunnel Vision that is causing it.* That's an important point to come back to over and over.

Let's explore Tunnel Vision in some detail. It affects your brain in eight predictable ways and, as a result, how you experience it and act. Even though Tunnel Vision isn't made of separate or sequential steps, we're separating it into different facets so that you can better understand it.

We'll delve into the details of Tunnel Vision in this and the next chapter. In this chapter, we'll cover the facets that are universal to all animals. In Chapter 4, we'll explore the facets of Tunnel Vision that are more uniquely human. Once you are familiar with the facets of Tunnel Vision and have begun to see it in yourself, they'll seem more obvious to you. Ideally, you'll then see how remarkable your brain and mind are, as well as how you can more readily maneuver them.

Tunnel Vision, Facet One: Attention

We said the facets of Tunnel Vision were not necessarily sequential, that they could happen one after another or all at the same time. However, this facet, attention, needs to come first.

To help you understand your brain and how it pays attention, we've identified three mechanisms of attention. We say it is either grabbed, compelled, or given up. This runs the gamut from mechanisms that are automatic, or unconscious, to those that seem more like a choice. Regardless of whether you're in control of what you pay attention to, the chain of events that follows leads to Tunnel Vision.

When we say your attention is grabbed, we are referring to the most reflexive version of this kind of attention. For example, if you hear an unexpected and loud noise, you will automatically focus on it and react in some way. Your head may turn toward it before you even realize it. When you focus on a ball someone suddenly throws at you, we say your attention was grabbed. Again, it is either a literal reflex or very automatic.

Anything unusual compels your attention. Anything that you may immediately be driven toward or away from will likely get you to pay attention in a more involuntary way. We can say It steals your attention or causes you to want to focus on it. You will exhaustively pay attention to whatever triggers your attention. For instance, if you unexpectedly see someone streaking naked outside your window, we say your attention is compelled. It's not a reflex, but it feels irresistible.

The third mechanism is when your attention is freely given over, such as when you scan a room of people to see who's attractive. It's not irresistible, it's not a compulsion to focus and act—although it may feel like it—because you still have a good deal of control. You give up your attention and focus attention throughout the day in many ways, such as reading, talking to someone, or searching the internet.

Of course, whether your attention is reflexively grabbed, irresistibly compelled, or appears to be freely given over to what interests you, they are all on a continuum. The reason, however, to delve into these mechanisms of attention is to make one singular point: *the more energy there is behind your focus of attention—in other words, the more drive there is behind it, whether grabbed, compelled, or freely given over—the more it locks your attention on the object. And the more your attention is locked on the object, the more Tunnel Vision is induced.*

> **Awareness Exercise**
>
> Every moment is filled with things competing for your attention. Obviously, you are reading this book right now and freely giving your attention to these words. If you were to put it down for a minute, you would observe the various things that take your attention. Each may last for only a few seconds. In a moment, put this book aside and see what grabs your attention. Don't control anything, just see where your attention naturally goes. Do you find that your attention is relaxed and that you are staring off or looking around and seeing things as a whole? Are you first pulled to feel things in your body, like hunger, or stiffness from sitting too long, or any emotions that may be waiting to be recognized? Or are you pulled into your thoughts and mental images? Attention is fleeting, so you'll need to work quickly. See what calls your attention. Try to do this for a minute or two.

Tunnel Vision, Facet Two: Control

You may or may not control what you pay attention to as much as you think you do. But once you pay attention, you don't control what you do or think next as much as you think, either.

There's a stimulus-response relationship between what we pay attention to and what happens afterward. Stimuli that grab our attention cause us to react on impulse instead of on knowing action. The longer we focus on the object, or the more intensely we focus on it—no matter how long that is—the more it controls us.

For example, if a bee were to suddenly fly in front of you, you would be compelled to act the second you locked your attention on it, by ducking, swatting at it (not always advisable), or freezing.

To help you understand the idea of Tunnel Vision's loss of control—to jump ahead for a minute—there is an opposite scenario: the Perspective scenario. If the bee grabbed your attention but you were able to quickly BrainShift—in this instance, meaning open your awareness—you might experience this differently and therefore act differently. You might calm yourself and move slowly or quickly but knowingly away rather than reacting out of impulse. You might repress the impulse to swat at it. You might even kill it if you thought that was the best action at the moment.

We respond with either some physical movement or by creating some idea or feeling. For instance, a loud enough bang could get you to run in the opposite direction before you even realized what you were doing. If you hear someone laugh unexpectedly in the next room, focusing on it could cause you to obsessively try to figure out what is so funny, which could distract you from whatever else you want to do. It's all survival programming.

This may seem like a good thing. Why wouldn't we want to react on impulse to what might be important? Because we want to be in control of what we pay attention to and how we pay attention, so that we don't, for example, do something dangerous that would be best to anticipate first, or jump to conclusions prematurely.

Here's a fascinating fact that seems weird, though it's not as unusual as you might think. It illustrates how we are controlled by what we pay attention to. In humans there's a phenomenon called "stimulus-bound behavior." It happens more obviously when the frontal lobes of the brain are impaired, because of either a brain injury or an illness like a manic state, catatonia, or autism. When someone is exhibiting stimulus-bound behavior, they appear to be bound or forced to interact with whatever potent stimulus comes into their field of awareness. For example, someone with stimulus-bound behavior passing by a light switch will be compelled to interact with it, either touching it or flipping it to the On or Off position—whether it makes sense or not, whether they want or need to or not. Catatonia is a condition that manifests in many ways, for instance causing the affected person to either not be able to initiate movement or to stop movement once initiated. (It's more than what people normally think of as catatonia, where they exhibit "posturing" or seem as stiff as a board.) People with catatonia also exhibit what is known as stimulus-bound behavior; they can't resist being triggered to act based on any compelling stimulus. For instance, if you put your hand out to shake their hand, even if you tell them to ignore your hand, they will shake it anyway. The point is that we're all "stimulus-bound" to one extent or another as part of being in Tunnel Vision.

Of course, the more our attention is taken or given, the more our brain exhibits the other facets of Tunnel Vision—in this case, the more we lose control of how we respond to what captures our attention. For example, you're on a strict low-calorie diet and some chocolate cake grabs or compels your attention. The more freely you give attention to it, the greater the likelihood you will wind up eating it, whether you think it's good for you or not. This also applies to stimuli that you imagine in your mind. Even imagining chocolate cake for long enough will compel you to go find some. If you are an alcoholic, and know you are, and you see a bottle of alcohol or imagine one, and it grabs your attention long or intensely enough, you will likely wind up drinking it or searching for it to drink.

As we said, the longer or the more intensely our attention is focused on something, the more we will be triggered to interact with it. It causes a functional stimulus-boundedness in us. If you are obsessed with looking at someone who is sexually attractive—even if you are in a committed relationship where fidelity is expected—you have a greater chance of acting on your sexual urges if the situation presents itself. This is survival programming that in people creates the conditions of Tunnel Vision.

Losing control because of Tunnel Vision also creates habits. Anything you pay attention to over time activates the same circuits in your brain. This creates patterns of behavior or thought that become habitual. For example, if you experience things the same way over and over, it will be hard to see them any other way.

Here's a fun example. You look at a random inkblot (as in the Rorschach test) and it looks like a butterfly or a particular face. The more times you see it, or the longer you look at it with that in mind, the harder it will be to see it as anything but a butterfly or that face. Over a number of years, this puts us into deep grooves of habit. It makes the way we experience the world and react to life stagnantly predictable. Since we're in Tunnel Vision most of our lives, the older we get, the more life can get stagnant and boring. We get set in our ways and become like prisoners of our conditioning, of our habits of experiencing, of our Tunnel Vision.

> **Thought Exercise**
>
> Think of times that you have either lost control or had less self-control. Have you done things that you knew you shouldn't during those times? What were they? Were they preceded by something that grabbed your attention? Was that something in the external world, in your body, or in your mind? Can you see the connection between how much it grabbed your attention—or how willing you were to give your attention over to it—and how much control it had over you?

Tunnel Vision, Facet Three: Awareness

This facet of Tunnel Vision, awareness, may seem obvious, but it's worth understanding in more depth, because it greatly affects our experience of life.

The more or the longer something grabs or compels our attention, or the more we choose to give our attention to it by locking our attention onto it, the more anything and everything else becomes blocked from our awareness. It stands to reason. If your attention is fixated on some object, you are not going to be aware of anything else.

By the way, this is an important point: when we say "object" of your attention, we mean not just something that you see, hear, taste, smell, or touch. It includes objects inside you, like feelings, thoughts, or mental images. In addition, and importantly, this includes the window of what comes with that object. So whether you are moved to pay attention to a sight, sound, smell, taste, touch, feeling, thought, or mental image, the "object" becomes *any or all* of those things, together. The window of your attention becomes a single "object."

And the more you focus on the "object" of your attention, the less you are aware of anything else. If you are raptly fixated on an insect crawling up your leg, you might not notice someone tapping you on the shoulder. Or say you are driving and see a super-attractive, mostly naked person. Staring at them, becoming acutely aware of their features and your sexual urges and fantasies, you might not notice what is happening on the road. Outside this narrow window of experience, your universe becomes increasingly hidden. I'm sure a number of summertime accidents happen with college students driving along beach roads, gawking at people in bathing suits.

Similarly, if you are afraid of needles and about to get a vaccination, your attention would be focused on the needle about to enter your arm, along with your fear, pounding heart, and thoughts about the needle. Depending on how scared you are, you might be aware of little else. You might not be conscious of the nurse trying to calm you or tell you to keep still for your own safety.

This third feature of Tunnel Vision causes our world to feel smaller. This can be serious when you are upset and hyper-focused on something that troubles you. You might not consider all the options when making choices. It could cause you to feel "painted into a corner" when you really aren't. You might miss slight but important bodily information, such as mild pain or abnormal sensations that can tell you that you have a brewing health issue. You might also overlook intuitions about people or events that could give you wisdom and insight. For instance, if you are focusing only on people's superficial attractiveness, you might miss other cues about their personality and morality.

This facet of Tunnel Vision has psychological repercussions. Paying attention only to what we are immediately driven toward or away from causes us to feel limited. The world seems smaller, caged in. People in Tunnel Vision have the subjective experience of being in a narrower world. People can feel really trapped. Tunnel Vision seems the likely mechanism behind claustrophobia.

You may think that a restricted experience of the moment would happen only when our attention is hyper-focused during an emergency or urgent situation. Not so. Humanity lives in some degree of Tunnel Vision all the time. It's just that Tunnel Vision is so normal, we don't notice how limited our experience is. That is why the human condition is so ordinary and pervasive. We miss the subtle and sublime aspects of each precious moment of our lives. It's usually only when we're in some crisis or extreme situation of Tunnel Vision that the experience of our world being small becomes more obvious. Think back on times that you were in Tunnel Vision during a crisis: do you remember how hemmed in you felt? Or maybe you feel like that now, because you're in a crisis.

One significant related problem with not registering a wider vista of experience in consciousness is that we miss out on things that would help us feel happy. These are less powerfully attention-grabbing things, things going on in our bodies and around us. For instance, just feeling the normal tingling sensations of our skin can feel good. Or traveling somewhere pleasant on vacation when we're already satisfied, our awareness might expand. We might take in more of the vista, more of each moment, noticing the subtle smell of rain, the sounds of ocean waves, and so on. These more subtle things can be sublime, such as the ordinary beauty that exists all around us all the time.

There is a Japanese concept, influenced by Zen Buddhism, called wabi-sabi. It is both a worldview and an aesthetic that recognizes and appreciates the beauty in the "imperfect, impermanent, and incomplete" in nature and in things made by humans. Objects and scenes that are asymmetrical, rough, simple, economical, austere, modest, and intimate are recognized for their beauty or elegance. For example, seeing the beauty in the colors and textures of a rusty piece of metal. It can be seen in the simplicity of a single drop of water as it hits a pool of water, sending out cascading, concentric waves that gently fade out. It can be heard in the symphony of sounds on a busy city street, especially if you are not used to hearing those sounds. These are things that we miss every moment we are focused on getting something to make us happy, every second we are trying to avoid some discomfort.

Wabi-sabi describes an appreciation that falls within the realm of Perspective that we will explore in Part III. The point here is that Tunnel Vision, both as a momentary phenomenon and as a way of living, causes us to miss out on the artistry and grandeur of the world. This is a source of stress and suffering that comes from Tunnel Vision.

> ### Thought Exercise
>
> Once again, in a moment, put this book aside. Then, for a minute or two, try to notice things that you would not necessarily notice. Things that are so insignificant, they wouldn't get your attention. Once you settle on one of those things and notice it for a while, see if it doesn't become more interesting or artistically appealing.

Point of Clarification

It sounds as if Tunnel Vision and Perspective are describing how we *experience*. Yet as you can see when we talk about the loss of control, it is not just about experience but about action—what we do, how we react, act, think, imagine, plan, and so on. So when you read the words "Tunnel Vision" and "Perspective," it is important to know that they are both a way of experiencing and doing.

Let's review what we have learned so far.

- To survive, animals pay attention to what they want and what they want to avoid. This includes desired and rejected things as well as the thoughts, emotions, and drive that come along with them.

- The more energy—drive or emotions—there is toward or away from some "thing," the more tightly attention is focused on it and the less the animal is aware of anything else. In other words, everything else is blocked out, denied, or ignored. When everything other than a narrow focus of attention is blocked out, denied, or ignored, the animal's experience of the world feels smaller, "boxed in," as if there are fewer choices.

- The more attention is grabbed, compelled, or given over, the less control the animal has over its behavior and processing (thinking for humans), meaning the animal is relying more on direct stimulus-response reflexes, unconscious instincts, or previously learned responses.

Ideally you can see your own Tunnel Vision at work in these three first facets that we explored. Can you see, for example, that the more you stare down some forbidden dessert, the more likely it is (magically) that you are going to eat it? Can you witness in yourself that the more you think about and focus on something, the more likely it is that you will lose control to it?

This is vital if you are an alcoholic. Thinking of or seeing a bottle of alcohol—even if you know you've had a lifetime of suffering from that—makes it more likely that you will drink it. Ditto for some object you see in a store while shopping: even if you realistically know it is not good to buy it, focusing on it means you are increasingly likely to buy it. The same holds for relationships. If someone compels your attention in positive ways—even if you definitely know they are not good for you—you are more likely to be involved with them in some way. Alternatively, the more someone compels your attention for negative reasons—say, by taunting you—the more likely it is that you will do something to them that you may regret for a lifetime.

Additionally, the more exclusively you focus on a problem, mulling it over and over in your head to the point that you are preoccupied by it, the fewer options you might be able to see and the smaller and more "claustrophobic" your experience will be.

. . . .

I worked through every facet of my mental health issues, and for the first time in my life I was able to see where I had Tunnel Vision and got stuck in my life. The program triggered things in me: things from my childhood, things from my family, and I was able to work through these things to see a way where we can live in our lives and just be better people.

—Clara

4

The Human Mind—Tunnel Vision: Parts Four Through Eight

Most of what was presented in the last chapter about Tunnel Vision applies to all animals, us included. Animal brains seek out and direct attention to what they want or want to avoid. Their attention can be instantly grabbed or strongly compelled.

I trained my dog to pay attention to me when I give commands. No one can be sure about the extent to which animals "freely" give over their attention to search for what they are interested in. Yet when they focus their attention *for whatever reason*, animals will cede control to events and stimuli. They can get stuck in habits of reacting, too. Their world can appear to be limited. A horse stuck in thick brambles with thorns in its side will kick and thrash—its world appearing to be smaller because it doesn't respond to soothing voices as it might have otherwise—even at the expense of causing worse damage. That's how its attention gets grabbed. The horse, in this instance, could be considered to be in some form of Tunnel Vision. And we're just another species of animal in these facets of Tunnel Vision.

In this chapter, we'll learn more about the features of Tunnel Vision that have to do with the human experience. In other words, what happens to the human mind in Tunnel Vision when attention is focused. Before first, it may be helpful to understand something about Tunnel Vision and its counterpart, Perspective.

Human Intelligence, Imagination, and Ego as Objects of Attention

It's impossible to know the extent to which lizards and cats have "thoughts." However, humans do, and that makes us astonishing animals. Our intelligence surpasses even our closest animal relative, the chimpanzee. Can you imagine a chimp driving a car on a highway, reading books, doing complex mathematics, performing classical music, or dancing ballet? Can you imagine many animals carrying around shame or a feeling of superiority their whole lives?

Three features of human cognition, of our minds, can also become a focus of our attention—besides the things in the world around us and within our bodies. These things that arise in our minds can steal our attention almost 24/7. They are our intelligence, our imagination, and our sense of self. These aspects of our minds can be both objects of our attention and facets of Tunnel Vision that get distorted in some way.

Even though it may be obvious what these features of the human mind are, let's explore them further to understand them in the context of this most important phenomenon: Tunnel Vision.

Human Intelligence

People use their intelligence every moment of every day. We listen to the news, think about our problems, get involved in our own and other people's stories and issues, and make lists of things to do. Thinking, doing, calculating, planning, and solving occupy our minds all day long. On crowded subways in Tokyo, Shanghai, and New York, almost everyone is on their cell phone playing games, talking, checking email, or searching the web. A few may be reading a book or talking to each other. Anyone else is lost in thought. We don't like doing nothing. We are obsessed with our own intellect. And it is a powerful draw to our attention.

To our primate brains wired for survival, any thought, and any plan, is treated as necessary for survival—as though we literally "need" to think about a movie we just saw, or we need to remember the winner of last year's Super Bowl. And with anything that requires survival comes stress. Only a blank state of just being is without stress. Thinking is a source of stress, to whatever extent, because it demands our attention. To that end, seeking pleasure with our intellect, planning for the future, and calculating how to avoid problems every waking minute is depleting and exhausting.

Human Imagination

Here's another layer to thinking: imagination. Imagination can be fun and the source of human progress and the arts. It essentially means fantasizing. It can be the part of our intellect that causes us to need things that are not immediately present or don't even exist yet. We can imagine ideal needs, like the best dinner, the perfect relationship, the best body, the most idyllic vacation, the ideal life (TV commercials and movies help us do that), and the best outcomes in life.

We can also fantasize the worst outcomes and dire consequences. For example, we might have an image in our head of what might happen when our teenager goes out on their own driving for the first time. Or what might happen if we get too close to the edge on top of a mountain. Similar to the stress of thinking and processing, "survival" feels like it's a matter of attaining these imagined "needs" and avoiding these fantasized "threats" to our existence. In a similar vein, we're driven by how things "should," "ought," or "must" be.

Here's the insidious facet of imagination: we are always imagining, whether we are aware of it or not. Mental images work in the foreground and the background of our awareness, coloring our experience. Our mind works 24/7, conjuring up the ideal and worst possible scenarios and outcomes of any action. It is continually measuring events for any risk associated with them or measuring them if they aren't going the way they "should." We can clearly see imagination projected onto reality in youngsters who dramatize and catastrophize every disappointment and setback. Yet adults do the same thing; we just hide it more effectively.

Many people rate every life situation, compare it with an ideal, and come up disappointed. How could they not, when competing with their imagination? They rate their family or life partner as "imperfect" or never "good enough," with traits that might not be that abnormal but cannot measure up against an idealized version.

Many people in developed countries believe that if their looks don't match the ideal seen in the media, they're inferior, for the same reason. In fact, even objectively attractive people don't often live up to the high standards of their own imaginations. "Body dysmorphia," which is experiencing one's normal body appearance as abnormal, is a psychiatric syndrome with roots in the facet of the human condition that causes us to focus attention on our imaginations.

We can even see what we fantasize as our own old age and dying, an otherwise normal process, as an unspeakable, unthinkable catastrophe; it conjures up fear and dread. It is not uncommon for young people to see a breakup with a boy- or girlfriend as an existential threat ("I can't live without him/her"), sometimes causing them to attempt suicide.

Struggling to fit our lives and everything and everyone in them into unrealistic and unattainable visions sets us up to be frustrated, disappointed, anxious, and fearful. That's because there is no perfect anything! The odds are that dreaded consequences are unlikely or not as bad as we imagine, yet pondering those consequences is the root of debilitating anxiety. Some depressions are caused by feeling we are condemned to inferiority, to having lost the chance to have an "ideal life."

This experience is connected to the notion of "time sickness," where we feel the passing of time as a stressor. This often-unconscious facet of our imagination causes us to dread the oncoming of our eventual death. Imaginings co-opt our attention. They make us oblivious to the reality that is around and within us, some of which is sublime and amazing but is always needed to make rational decisions.

Sense of Self

Here is a higher, even more abstract facet of our intellect *and* imagination: a sense of self. This is the "me" or "I" that tells us we are an individual, with a name, an identity, and a story, going through life. It's a way of perceiving that, like a magnet dropped into a random collection of iron shavings, orients all experience to the experiencer.

We can feel or sense our "self." We are so used to it that we cannot discern this awareness as a "thing." Yet if you were extremely self-conscious in front of a crowd, you would feel your sense of self pretty clearly.

It may be hard to believe, because it is such an ingrained experience, but this sense of self is a convention, an artificial construction of the human brain. It gives us a survival advantage in figuring out how to proceed in the future, based on previous experiences and memories. If an attacker started chasing us, it is a shortcut to imagine ourselves in various scenarios: running into a nearby building but having the attacker come in after us versus turning and fighting versus being killed. Obviously, imagining ourselves in different scenarios has survival benefits.

Yet this sense of self is not an objectively real thing. It gives us, for example, the false experience of being at the center of events we run across throughout the day, which is a form of self-consciousness. Oddly, it is also why we can feel excluded from events, like we don't belong, as if we are on the outside looking in at the perfect lives other people are living. Over-attributing things as about us or feeling artificially left out of things are features of an overactive sense of self.

Later in this chapter we're going to delve into aspects of a sense of self because it can be grossly distorted by Tunnel Vision. For that reason, the sense of self is perhaps the main cause of human suffering. Some aspects of sense of self are feeling inferior, ashamed, embarrassed, and humiliated. It includes feeling pride, dignity, conceit, self-important, vain, and superior.

Some of these aspects of a sense of self are useful, but only to the extent that they are not seen as so *real* we would die or kill for them. This sense of self feeds on approval, admiration, respect, even power. It wants to feel significant, like it has a purpose. It fosters the fantasy that it can live forever! It will also do what it takes to avoid disapproval, embarrassment, disrespect, and feeling insignificant. It wants to avoid death at all costs, including the existential death of insignificance and meaninglessness. Sometimes, the need to avoid insignificance (existential death) and actual death compete, so that people will sacrifice their lives to feel the immortality of feeling significant.

As we said, our attention can get grabbed, compelled, and freely given over. It can be focused on not only what we experience out in the world, and not only what is happening on and in our bodies, but also on our intellect, imagination, and sense of self.

Again, the goings-on in our head can be and often are a focus of our attention. In turn, our intellect, imagination, and sense of being us—our sense of self—all get warped by that focus.

Quick Recap

Tunnel Vision always starts when some object grabs, compels, or causes us to want to give over our attention. "Objects" include things we pick up with our five senses as well as aspects inside our bodies (like aches and pains, feelings, or drives), and minds (thoughts, imagination, and sense of self). What happens next in Tunnel Vision is not always a chain of events. They may all happen at once, one or a few at a time, and in no particular order. The next facet we explored was a loss of control, followed by a loss of awareness for anything else not focused on.

Now that we have more context to understand Tunnel Vision in human beings, let's continue exploring the other five facets of Tunnel Vision, beginning with suggestibility.

Tunnel Vision, Facet Four: Suggestibility

Suggestibility is a strange facet of the human experience. We think we choose what we believe, but what we accept as true is not as much of a choice as we think it is.

What the SatoriWest Method points to is that the more we pay attention to something, the more we accept as true whatever is presented to us, or whatever is in our mind at that time. For example, we may see a cloud formation that reminds us of a bunny rabbit. If that image grabs our attention, it will be hard to see it as anything but a bunny rabbit. If we focus on it longer, or more intensely, it might get to the point that we believe it is some weird kind of actual rabbit in the sky. Of course, most people wouldn't normally believe it's an actual rabbit. However, if the image were compelling enough and sufficiently attention grabbing, it is likely that more and more people would believe it was some sort of rabbit object posing in the sky as a cloud.

It's similar to looking at a random inkblot in the Rorschach test. To the extent that you see it as, for instance, someone's face, and that image holds your focused attention, it will eventually be hard to see it as anything else. In essence, anything that grabs or compels our attention will cause us to accept it increasingly as true. If we hear a noise outside our house at night that catches our attention, whatever we think that noise is at first blush would become a stronger and stronger conviction that we know what it is as we focused more intensely on it.

Likewise, any words that are "eye-catching" enough, like those of an empathetic speech or professional-looking poster, will cause us to be more accepting of their validity. Our suggestibility doesn't seem to matter *what* we are paying attention to, specifically. It appears that anything that compels our attention can make us more suggestible to either the object or anything else that comes along with it. That may be the strategy of advertising executives who try to catch our attention on a television or print ad that tries to sell us something. A giant dinosaur looking as if it is going to step out of the television screen can be used to sell car insurance, because the attention-grabbing image can cause us to accept as valid the information that this insurance company is trying to sell.

We could be enraptured by the flight of a beautiful bird, but if at the same time a random thought or idea were to enter our mind, we'd be more likely to believe it. This is likely the mechanism behind hypnosis. For example, if a hypnotist were to swing a pocket watch in front of your face while giving you suggestions that you are cold, you could start to believe you were cold—even if you are sitting in a warm room. You might even shiver and get goose bumps. This may be the way advertisers on television sell products: by getting viewers to pay attention to something weird on the screen—whether it's related to what they are selling or not—and then offering suggestions to buy their product.

The same holds for our intellect, imagination, and sense of self. *This point is very important.* The more we lock attention on the content in our own minds, the more we believe it. In other words, focus on your own self-talk long enough and you will start to believe whatever you come up with. Perhaps you've heard the saying, "Don't believe everything you think"? Well, focus on a particular thought long or intensely enough, and you'll believe it—even if it started off as an opinion. Inner concentrated attention renders us more suggestible to our own thoughts and beliefs.

If, for example, we hear that people of a certain color are one way or another, just having that thought and focusing on it enough will turn it into a belief. The more times we focus on it, the more likely it will turn into a conviction we would swear is true. Just the focus on a thought will turn it into what seems like a hardened fact we believe is absolutely true, to the extent that it captures our attention. So, the more we think something that might be true, the more we will believe it *is* true. People convince themselves of things this way all the time.

This is the same phenomenon that happens when we watch a movie. The more we give our attention over to the plot or the action of the movie, the more we believe what we are watching is real—even if our intelligence tells us otherwise. So, for example, if you are watching a horror movie or thriller and it grabs your attention, you will get as scared as you would if something frightening were happening in real life. Of course, that's part of why we go to movies. We love to believe what we are watching—to feel like the superhero, to believe in love. Yet the downside is that if our attention is captured completely by the plot—namely, it puts us in Tunnel Vision—we might not experience the cinematography of the film, we might not be able to judge the acting, or our anxiety or stressful feelings might skyrocket to the point that it gets uncomfortable and even traumatic!

This is very important. If your beliefs can be controlled by what grabs or compels your attention, you want to understand how that happens so you can—using the SatoriWest Method introduced in this book—learn to control your attention and keep your mind open. An open mind is objective, able to figure out what is true. An open mind is the mind of a scientist, and less inflexibly ignorant. It is a way to keep control of your thoughts and feelings.

> **Exercise**
>
> Think of movies you've seen. Some compel your beliefs more than others. Think of the cinematographic techniques used to capture your attention in suspenseful moments. We measure your beliefs in this case by how anxious you get. When the director is trying to increase your anxiety, a handheld camera takes over and gets close behind the actor on the screen, and eerie music comes on. Those elements control your attention and cause you to believe something bad is going to happen. Do you find that these techniques are effective enough to make you feel anxious? If you disengage from the screen or know those techniques for what they are, can that lessen your anxiety?

What comes next? What happens to the human mind in Tunnel Vision, when our attention is grabbed, compelled, or given over, after we lose some degree of control, after our world feels smaller and we become more suggestible? Could our reality be any more warped?

In some ways the warping of our reality has only just begun. Next, we'll explore how Tunnel Vision alters what we are aware of.

Tunnel Vision, Facet Five: Imagination

We spoke about imagination at the start of this chapter. We said that it could be the object of our attention, and it could be what Tunnel Vision warps. This fascinating facet of Tunnel Vision relates to the fact that, because we have an imagination, Tunnel Vision gets us lost in it. Our dreams, which form our imagination while we're sleeping, attest to this fact. At night we are lost in an infinite variety of scenarios and circumstances in our mind, with no awareness that anything else could be real.

Let's explore imagination while we're awake. One of the most common aspects of our imagination while we're awake is that we attach labels to our experience. We use words to describe what we are experiencing, and we experience those words as thoughts.

Thoughts focus our attention on what we want to be aware of or what we run across. Words describe what we perceive. Ideas and concepts tell us what is going on, carving up each moment of our experience. In that sense, our experience of reality is conflated with our imagination. For that reason, we practically live in Tunnel Vision.

For example, if you are staring at some delicious food when you're hungry, you might quickly begin by labeling what it is. Then you start thinking how you can get it, or that you shouldn't eat it, or that someone else would like it, or that it would go better with ice cream, and so on. Similarly, when paying attention to someone yelling at you, you start to think about that person, judging them, or assessing their risk of being a threat to you. *Focusing attention comes with activating your imagination.* The more your attention is fixated on something, the more your experience of the moment is colored by your imagination.

Think of someone focused on the image in their minds of their teenage child not coming home on time. Pulled into their imagination even further—into their head, so to speak—they fantasize about what might have happened to them or what they will say to them when they arrive. Conversely, if a loud bang were to steal your attention, giving you momentary Tunnel Vision, you would quickly describe the experience in words, causing that incident of Tunnel Vision to last even longer.

Being in Tunnel Vision causes us to experience the reality of each moment, in some part, with our imagination. In other words, in Tunnel Vision we color each sensory experience with own biases, beliefs, and memories. This facet of Tunnel Vision, like all the facets of Tunnel Vision, overlaps with the others because they are artificially separated for ease of digestion. As you'll see, each of the eight facets of Tunnel Vision are interrelated and really all one thing. If something draws you into Tunnel Vision, it magnifies your sense of self and distorts your thinking—both aspects of language and imagination. This is how our thinking gets distorted too, as we jump to conclusions about a situation, missing other information that doesn't fit into our partly imagined experience of the moment.

Remember, the extreme experience of our imagination is dreaming. Because we're asleep, the dream completely captures our attention. We are unaware of our bodies or what is happening around us; therefore, we experience dreams in Tunnel Vision. That's why we believe them, utterly. During waking hours, getting caught up in our head, we miss out on the subtle beauty and grandeur of the world in and around us that cannot be enhanced with our expectations or understanding.

This is jumping ahead, but many readers may be wondering whether it is possible to experience the moment without thinking or without applying language to our experience. The answer to that is that it is possible for brief periods. The more important question is whether it is possible to experience the moment without being pulled into Tunnel Vision. In other words, is it possible to have an open kind of awareness, where our attention is not pulled tightly into thoughts and mental images, without having conscious thoughts control how we pay attention? That more important answer is yes.

Exercise

Think of a time or imagine when an interesting or scary insect grabbed your attention. Besides focusing on the sound (like a mosquito) or the sight (like a big cockroach), can you see how that insect would also be projected in your imagination? Can you recall or now realize that you would be pulled into your head, imagining how to kill it, escape from it, capture it, or even observe how beautiful or interesting it is? In any instance, you are less in the experiential moment and more in your fantasies. Can you sense that the more the insect got your attention, the more this would pull you into your head, into using your thoughts and mental images?

Tunnel Vision, Facet Six: Ego

Remember, from the previous section, that a sense of self is a way of perceiving the moment that orients everything in its field to the experiencer; this is the facet of ego. It is the "me," or "I" that we live in relationship with every day. One measure of our relationship with our sense of self is self-esteem. Overall, we tend to love ourselves, like ourselves, just tolerate ourselves, dislike, or even loathe ourselves. We associate this personalized way of viewing the world with a personal history and a projection into what might happen to us in the future.

You may ask, related to whether the sense of self is even real, "What does that mean? I am real!" Let's put aside the question of whether the sense of being you is actually a real thing and not just part of our imagination (that is a discussion for those interested in the farther reaches of Perspective, in the spiritual realm of nonduality and ego-lessness). Most could agree that the sense of being you, the "I" or "me," is at the very least, flexible. There are times when you are more self-conscious, and times when you're not at all self-conscious. There are times when you are convinced you are right and no one need bother to present evidence to the contrary, and times when you have no vested interest in an outcome and have the ego of a scientific, objective way of experiencing.

This is the observation at this sixth facet of Tunnel Vision: it inflates the experience of your ego.

Let's clear up any misconceptions about what an *enlarged* ego is. The word "ego" is commonly associated in the culture with feeling overly important, grandiose, or narcissistic. And that is one way an inflated ego can look. Yet that's only a part of what we mean by an exaggerated sense of self. Here are several possible ways it could be experienced:

- *Self-consciousness:* We become increasingly self-conscious, feeling like everyone's eyes are on us, everyone is thinking about us or focused on us. For example, walking into a party we might feel like everyone is more aware of us than they really are.

- *Personalizing:* We take things personally that are not personal. For example, someone cuts us off in traffic and we believe they have targeted us in particular for disrespect.

- *Self-righteousness:* We stubbornly believe we are right, in the face of contradictory evidence, or refuse to hear contradictory evidence.

- *Feeling left out and isolated:* Seemingly the opposite of self-consciousness, this is where we feel left out of a situation, group, or segment of society, like we do not belong, or as if we are on the outside of some ideal life that everyone else is living. For example, we might see people at a café or bar who all seem to be having a good time and believe that, because we don't relate to their mood, they are "normal," and we are not.

- *Feelings of superiority:* This is the sense that we are inherently better than others we believe inferior to us. Some people, like royalty, were raised to feel superior. Others of us are just obviously grandiose or narcissistic; however, all of us inherently have prejudices that are a manifestation of this facet of Tunnel Vision. It's been the case since early in human history. This area of Tunnel Vision is so insidious, yet can be so invisible, that I feel it is important to call out several ways it can manifest in us: men feeling superior to women, women feeling secretly superior to men, younger adults feeling superior to much older adults, adults feeling superior to children, rich feeling superior to poor, poor but happy feeling superior to rich but manifestly unhappy, people with homes feeling superior to the homeless, people with an objectively beautiful appearance feeling superior to people with less attractive looks, intelligent people feeling like they are better than those with less noticeable intelligence, taller feeling superior to shorter, average height feeling superior to anyone outside the mean of height, spiritually evolved feeling superior to less evolved. I emphasize this point because it is so easy to consider only the most egregious examples of inferiority. Likely everyone has some aspects of this. Why is this important to understand? Spoiler alert: it is vital to understand and see one's Tunnel Vision to begin to relinquish it. That's the beginning of true Perspective.

- *Feelings of inferiority:* Everything I mentioned above is then foisted on us in the opposite, as we succumb to being judged by others. We feel a sense of inferiority for being who and what we are. "My car isn't good enough." "I don't look good enough." It happens more than we realize.

- *Self-blame:* This refers to feeling guilty for things we haven't done or aren't responsible for. For example, we might see a newsreel of hungry children and feel sad solely because we think we are personally responsible.

- *Competitiveness:* This refers to feeling the urge to compete. (Again, this facet of Tunnel Vision is both an experience and a way of acting.) For example, as drivers, we might focus on cars passing us on the freeway and have the sensation that we are falling behind and need to catch up or even surpass the other drivers. This can get so serious, it can not only cause people to get speeding tickets, but cause "road rage." Or seeing someone who is dressed better than we are might cause us to straighten out our clothing. Think about it and you'll see it isn't hard to find many examples of things that trigger us to compete.

- *Comparing:* Competing is triggered by comparing ourselves with others. An exaggerated sense of self—which is what this facet of Tunnel Vision is all about—compares itself with others. This might be a casual phenomenon, like walking next to someone who is quite a bit taller than us and noticing that in some exaggerated way. It might be more intense, like feeling under- or overdressed at a party and having difficulty letting that go enough to enjoy ourselves. (This facet of comparing is related to being self-conscious.)

- *Self-esteem:* We mentioned the emotional relationship with ourselves as loving, liking, tolerant, disliking, or loathing. This is similar but not exactly the same thing as feeling superior or inferior. When Tunnel Vision increases, the emotions we feel toward ourselves tend to increase with it.

Ego has been part of humankind, in human culture, going back as far as recorded history, and likely well before even that. Stories going back thousands of years are filled with tales of ego, which has likely been accepted as utterly normal.

Because all of us live our lives largely in some degree of Tunnel Vision, we are not aware of our egos being inflated (let alone created) by Tunnel Vision. For instance, most of us go through life self-conscious. We experience the magnified feeling of being looked at and judged when we're in public, so that we can't relax and be our authentic and natural selves. We often take things not related to us personally. For example, we can easily misinterpret even someone's innocent laughter while we're talking as being about us. We often feel left out, for instance, of a better life other people are living somewhere else.

We carry guilt or grudges based on perceived insults for years. We are driven by competitiveness, obsessed with comparing ourselves with what society says is normal or what we imagine is an ideal way to be. Even crying, a natural and healthy way to express emotions, can be a source of shame and self-perceived weakness, because we incorporate the stigma of mental illness into our self-concept. In that sense, our inflated ego doesn't allow for the acceptance of anything but what society says is normal behavior and emotional expression.

The point is that Tunnel Vision and the ego it inflates is part of the culture. It would not be surprising if there were evidence that cavemen and cavewomen were afflicted by ego. In other words, ego throughout the generations has been accepted as "the normal way people are." In our culture, Tunnel Vision that inflates our ego—although it hurts, can ruin relationships, and causes low self-esteem—is *invisible*. It has been and remains part of our lives. We see it in almost everyone else.

Yet this is one way that crises are opportunities. Because severely constricted Tunnel Vision magnifies our ego to abnormally abnormal extremes. To the point that it is no longer easy to dismiss as "normal." It is no longer *invisible*. A significant health scare, a dramatic humiliation, a significant death, a major life setback, even just a moderate blow to our self-image, like getting fired from work for the first time, can make our normal Tunnel Vision ego acutely visible. The sense of shame, the threat to our existence, the shaking of the foundation of our beliefs can expose our Tunnel Vision and its ego. The shifting foundations of our experience can sometimes cause people to let go of their ego-based reliance and surrender to a world of Perspective.

> **Thought Exercise**
>
> Think about how you feel about your sense of self. Do you love, like, tolerate, dislike, or loathe yourself? Does that increase when you are in Tunnel Vision, meaning when you are frustrated with a task, or being confronted at work, or feeling self-conscious at a party?

Let's return to the thought exercise we used in the last facet of Tunnel Vision—the focus on an insect. We said that when you spy an insect that grabs your attention, it pulls you into your imagination. Thinking about the effect on ego, say you decide (for the sake of argument, let's hope you aren't too much of a pacifist) to kill the mosquito. We'll say that mosquitos in your area have been linked to a significant viral infection. As you swipe at the mosquito and miss it repeatedly, imagining its demise, can you see how you would have a personal connection to killing it? It's *not* just an objective exercise in the best strategy to accomplish this goal. It's personal. You get upset when you miss the mosquito. Can you see how it can easily become something personal between you and the insect who you believe is outsmarting you?

Tunnel Vision, Facet Seven: Thinking

Quick reminder: all facets of Tunnel Vision are part of the same experience. In this instance, it would be hard to have an exaggerated ego and have that *not* change how you think and, ultimately, believe. That's because an exaggerated sense of self that is more suggestible will distort your belief system. You're going to believe your own thoughts more and more. For instance, you might believe you are right about your premature conclusions. (That's a form of distorted thought, as you'll see below.)

Here are some more common ways (from the field of cognitive-behavioral therapy) that a magnified ego changes how you think and what you believe.

- *All-or-nothing thinking:* This is where we believe that things have to be completely one way or it doesn't count or matter. For example, a student may believe that if they don't get an A on a test, they have not been successful on the test, or even that they are a failure.

- *Black-or-white thinking:* This is where we believe and then insist that things have to be one way or another, with no middle ground. For example, someone might believe that people are either good or evil, or that all people of a certain gender, race, age, or ethnicity are the same.

- *Absolutism:* This is when we insist that things "should," "ought," "must," or "have to" be one way, in spite of a more reality-based understanding. For example, someone may believe that men must act in a stereotypically masculine way or they are not authentically male. Or, after witnessing a crime, one believes that they should have stopped it from happening, even though they probably could not have done so.

- *Denial:* This is where we cannot experience an event that has happened or is happening because it is too painful or emotional. For example, someone may not believe that someone they loved has left them, so they keep insisting he or she is coming back.

- *"Painted into a corner":* We already mentioned this facet of Tunnel Vision earlier as a consequence of over-focused attention blocking other things out. I mention it again in this context because it affects our thinking. It may not even be a separate kind of thought distortion as much as it influences all the other kinds (though, honestly, many of them overlap in some way). It is not seeing options in times of stress. For example, a bill collector starts to harass someone and that person believes the only options they have are to leave the country or rob a bank.

- *Future certainty:* This means believing we know the future. For example, someone dealing with depression may believe they are always going to be depressed, or when preparing to deliver a speech, a person is certain they are going to mess up.

- *Jumping to conclusions:* This is when we make assumptions, based on little if any evidence. For example, seeing people talking among themselves at the office in a small group, one may assume there is trouble brewing for the company or the group of people is up to something bad.

- *Magnifying the negative and minimizing the positive:* This means giving more importance to bad events or mistakes than is warranted and/or neglecting or reducing the importance of positive events. For example, someone wins a well-deserved award, but feels they didn't do enough to earn it, so they minimize its importance. Or they rehash an error they made in their mind so that it takes on more significance than most other people believe it deserves.

- *Catastrophizing:* This is when we believe the worst will come of a future event. For example, a mother's teenager is late coming home and she imagines that her child is dead.

- *Rationalizing:* This occurs when we make a contrived excuse for misbehavior, and although the excuse is not true, we partly or completely believe it is. For example, someone may not report a crime because they say to themselves that reporting it doesn't matter, that there is so much crime in the world anyway and one more crime doesn't make a difference. The real reason, however, is that they are too lazy or don't want to take the risk.

- *"Mind reading":* Tunnel Vision causes us to believe we know what is in someone's mind when we don't. This happens because our mind makes assumptions and our ego believes them. For example, believing people don't like you even though they are actually just shy around you.

Understanding and observing your irrational thoughts and distorted thinking is the basis of the field of cognitive therapy. It points to how distorted thinking leads us to have negative emotions, whether we're unhappy, anxious, angry, sad, fearful, miserable, furious, even suicidal or homicidal.

Yet according to the SatoriWest Method, distorted thinking is just one of the eight interrelated facets of the mind warping that comes with Tunnel Vision. Recognizing your irrational thoughts can provide a clear window into the other facets of your Tunnel Vision, like your inflated ego and, as you'll see next, time distortion. Remember, just recognizing any facet of your Tunnel Vision is enough to begin to unwind it. That is crucial. See it for what it is.

Let's see if you can recognize distorted thinking in some of the previous examples of Tunnel Vision we looked at. Earlier in this chapter and the previous one we gave some examples of how Tunnel Vision shows itself in six of its facets. Let's expand on a few of those examples to show how we can recognize Tunnel Vision in the seventh facet, distorted thinking.

Thought Exercise

Take the example of an insect crawling up your leg. Besides causing you to be unaware of anything else, losing control and swatting it away, and feeling excessively threatened by it (ego dilation), you might have the distorted thought that insects "should" not be in your house (or on your lawn, or really anywhere you are). Thinking of that belief now, it may sound silly, but haven't you had a thought like that before? Haven't you asked yourself why mosquitos or flies have to be in your space? That thought can make you angry. That's an example of an "absolutist" belief.

Have you, deep down, had the absolutist belief that life *should* be perfect? That you *should never* (all or nothing) experience annoying things? Can you see how, if you didn't have those beliefs, you would face annoyances and even adversity with more equanimity, maybe even with a better sense of humor?

Let's take the example of staring at a scantily clad but extremely attractive person walking down the street.

Thought Exercise

With an exaggerated sense of self, can you see how you might have the distorted belief that that person would be attracted to you if only they could notice you? Or the opposite belief, that someone like that could *never* be attracted to you, because they could have anyone? Can you see those thoughts as examples of future-tripping and mind reading?

If you had low self-esteem as a manifestation of your ego exaggeration, can you analyze those thoughts as examples of rationalization? Meaning where you are finding excuses for not being capable or worthy, excuses that are not objectively true or proven by anyone?

We previously considered an example of someone yelling insults at you for making an innocent mistake. Let's explore that.

Thought Exercise

If the sight of that person yelling drew you into Tunnel Vision, focusing exclusive attention on him or her, can you see how you might feel hurt or get defensive because your sense of self got exaggerated? What thoughts might go through your head? How might you future-trip and catastrophize? How might you jump to conclusions? How might you magnify the negative and minimize the positive?

Exercise

To help you learn about the irrational thinking that comes with Tunnel Vision, here is a matching exercise. Match the statement in the table with the irrational way(s) of thinking, keeping in mind that some examples may fit into more than one category.

- All-or-nothing thinking
- Black-or-white thinking
- Absolutism
- Denial
- "Painted into a corner"
- Future certainty
- Magnifying the negative and minimizing the positive
- Jumping to conclusions

- Catastrophizing
- Rationalizing
- "Mind reading"

Here is a circumstance that could trigger these kinds of thoughts: You are in a less developed foreign country, traveling in remote villages. It's an incredible experience. Standing up in a crowded bus, you happen to check for your wallet. Normally deep in your front pocket, it is gone. You search everything you own to double-check for it. It's definitely not here. Your heart starts to pound. Anxiety wells up....

Example of Irrational Thinking	Category of Irrational Belief
"Oh my gosh. I'm screwed. I have nothing, no money, no ID. I'm never going to get home!"	**Future certainty**, because you don't know you're "never" going to get home **Catastrophizing**, because it is likely an outcome that is worse than what is going to happen
"Why do these things always happen to me?"	**Black-or-white thinking**, because of the use of the word "always"
Someone is disrespectful to you as a foreigner: "These people hate foreigners."	**Jumping to conclusions**, because you are making an assumption with insufficient evidence **Mind reading**, because you believe you know what is in someone's mind

Example of Irrational Thinking	Category of Irrational Belief
"I'm such an idiot. I should have brought pants with zippers on the pockets."	**Absolutism**, because thinking, "I should have done that," is less rational and forgiving than thinking, "It would have been better if I had."
"I hate this place. It's so dirty and backward. These people are devious and have no respect for people."	**Black-or-white thinking**, because you are making sweeping generalizations about whole groups of people
"Everybody's looking at me. I'm going to get attacked and robbed now that they know I'm a target."	**Black-or-white thinking**, because the word "everybody" is an overgeneralization **Future certainty**, because you believe you know what is going to happen **Jumping to conclusions**, because of the assumption that you know what people are going to do
"All my friends think I'm this experienced traveler. And now they'll think I'm naïve. I'll be humiliated."	**All-or-nothing thinking**, because likely not "all" your friends believe the same thing **Future certainty**, because you don't know if you will be humiliated **Mind reading**, because you believe you know what is in someone's mind

Example of Irrational Thinking	Category of Irrational Belief
"I shouldn't be such a nice person. It only gets you heartache. I need to be a badass so people are afraid of me."	**Absolutism,** because the word "should" comes with irrational expectations that take the place of "it would be better if…"
"All these people [on the bus] are looking at me and laughing to themselves, thinking, What a fool this stupid foreigner is."	**Mind reading,** because you don't know what other people are thinking

Whether or not you agree with the categorization of the above selections, the main point is to familiarize yourself with the types of irrational thinking, so you can recognize them instantly in yourself when they come up as a marker of Tunnel Vision.

Tunnel Vision, Facet Eight: Time

This facet of Tunnel Vision, time, is really an extension of the fifth facet, where you get caught up in your imagination. This is a special case, where we experience reality with the projection of past memories and imagined future, instead of being solely in the present.

Here are some other examples of how Tunnel Vision causes us to be stuck in the past.

- *Negative transference:* This happens when someone in our present mind reminds us of someone else—usually from our past. In Tunnel Vision we experience this new person as if they were the person from our past. We might dislike a friendly and kind boss because they look like a parent who mistreated us. Depending on how much Tunnel Vision we're in, we may or may not be aware of this.

- *Flashbacking:* This is when something bad that happened in the past is triggered by something happening now and we confuse the two experiences. This can progress to the point that we lose touch with any cues that tell us where we are in time and space. This is the classic understanding of a flashback, like a soldier who hears a gunshot and believes he is back in a war. Depending on how much Tunnel Vision we're in, we would or wouldn't lose touch with most of our sense of being here and now, so that we are just conflating the past and the present. For example, if someone survived childhood abuse and, now as an adult, is spoken to disrespectfully but not abusively, they react as if they are being abused again.

- *Time seems to pass slowly during stress and hardship:* For example, like the adage "A watched pot never boils," if someone is in a stressful situation while in Tunnel Vision, time will seem to go by more slowly.

- *Time feels short overall:* When we're not highly stressed, Tunnel Vision gives the perception that a longer time period has gone very quickly. For example, if we're in Tunnel Vision while busy with life, it may seem as if the years are shooting by quickly, without our having fully lived each precious moment.

After going through any traumatic or memorably difficult time in your life, this facet of Tunnel Vision can present itself differently. When something reminds you of what happened, you may experience it like an actual flashback, where you lose touch with reality and believe you are back in time. It can also be an emotional flashback, where you feel emotionally just like you felt in the past, even though the present circumstances don't justify it. For example, having been bullied by an older sibling, you might experience that emotionally abusive older sibling in anyone who has authority. They would have to remind you of your sibling in some way.

In recent years, behavioral health investigators have identified harsh and traumatic aspects of childhood that go on to have an adverse influence on the remainder of the person's life. A high percentage of people with mental health disorders, substance use disorders, and even certain chronic medical conditions have one or more of these so-called ACEs (Adverse Childhood Experiences).

If that is you, or if you have had the misfortune of having any trauma in your past, this facet of Tunnel Vision may be the most challenging one. Again, the premise of this book is that those who suffer the most in life can have the most profound experience of being alive—meaning Perspective—because of their struggles. Part V will address this core premise of the book in more detail.

> **Thought Exercise**
>
> Can you think of a time when someone's treatment of you caused you to feel like a kid again? This often comes up when adult children who have lived away from home return to stay with their parents. If you've had that experience, did you find yourself feeling the emotions of your childhood again—whether it was interesting and comforting or annoying and anger producing? Or has anyone treated you in a way that caused you to feel the powerlessness of your childhood (if you can see those feelings as that)?

The Eight Facets of Tunnel Vision

Here are the eight facets of Tunnel Vision: attention, control, awareness, suggestibility, imagination, ego, thinking, and time. They come from a brain that is controlled by what and how it pays attention. Over time, what we pay attention to becomes a habit. Tunnel Vision can become more and more invisible the more we experience life through it.

Although subtle in its mildest forms, Tunnel Vision manifests in many ways. Any one of its eight facets can be more or less noticeable or pronounced at any one time. That makes the condition hard to pin down as Tunnel Vision. It takes practice to recognize.

It is crucial that you remember, though, that these eight facets of Tunnel Vision are harder to recognize when they are present in less extreme circumstances. They seem so normal in our lives. However, they are definitely more visible in extraordinary situations.

This book is a wake-up call to see your Tunnel Vision for what it is, while you can. Better to see it when it is mild, so that when your brain gets taken over by a crisis, you can see what is happening to your mind that much more clearly. In those instances, you can even use your Tunnel Vision to your advantage to find extraordinary Perspective. But in any case, one thing is certain: Tunnel Vision negatively affects the direction, fulfillment, and meaning you can experience in life. Hopefully, this chapter gave you enough familiarity with each of the eight facets to be able to start to see them for yourself. Look for them.

The next chapter will show how unwitnessed Tunnel Vision is never static. If you don't learn about yourself by seeing your Tunnel Vision, it will likely worsen as a pattern or go out of control in a particular crisis situation.

. . . .

This was a great program and I am glad I went through it because I can definitely see a difference in my overall mental health. I came here because of my high stress levels and anxiety, and now I can feel that both of those have rapidly declined. I feel much more content and at ease. I think this program helped me a lot because breaking scenarios down and discussing how I am feeling emotionally really helped me put things into perspective. [BrainShifting] was definitely a key component as well.

—Anne

5

The Downward Spiral of Tunnel Vision

Whether we know it or not, we lead our lives like Tarzan, swinging from one vine of Tunnel Vision to another. Most of the time, we grab another vine while still holding on to the last one. Sometimes we let go and are propelled through the air of Perspective, right before we grab on to another vine.

However, one episode of Tunnel Vision is not separate from the next. If you notice a three-inch stain on your carpet and it pulls your attention (quick review), it can cause you to feel compelled to deal with it. You may block out anything else about the carpet, believing that the stain won't come out, that leaving it would be a stain (pun intended) on your reputation as someone who can afford to have clean carpets. You might believe that carpets in people's houses *should* (absolutism) *never* (all or nothing) be stained, and so on. A stain on a carpet can become a stressor in your life. And what if you try to clean the stain and it doesn't come out? That additional focus can really stress you out, causing your thoughts to become even more negative, e.g., "I have to hire a professional carpet cleaner, or replace the carpet, or put something over it."

At that point, you might start dwelling on thoughts of unfairness and have feelings of frustration or anger beyond just being aware of the spot. That becomes a new episode of Tunnel Vision. (Noticing a spot on your carpet with Perspective, by the way, is a very different experience, one we'll explore later on.) If you were already stressed about other issues, the Tunnel Vision about the stain could devolve into a mini-crisis. In that sense, an episode of Tunnel Vision can become a chain reaction, linking to a deepening continuous episode. In other words, Tunnel Vision leads to more Tunnel Vision.

It is important to add that chains of Tunnel Vision can happen over years. We develop patterns or styles over time. These amount to the negative aspects of our personality, traits that can get worse with age. That's how people become more rigid in their views, where their self-esteem gets lower and lower, or they get more and more arrogant. People can become more reliant on habits, even desperately addicted to certain pleasures, anything from admiration and dependent relationships to that drink in the evening, to having more and more to feel complete. We'll explore the immediate payoffs of Tunnel Vision in the next chapter.

It stands to reason that anything that causes you to focus your attention is going to distort your mind in those eight ways that Tunnel Vision manifests. Any one of those eight ways, or all of them together, alter your mind in a way that causes you to feel bad sooner or later. Feeling bad, you're going to be susceptible to even more frequent and tighter (meaning more constricted focus of attention and hence more severe) episodes of Tunnel Vision.

It's very important that we see how our Tunnel Vision can become a chain reaction, one that not only stresses you out but causes you to do things that are bad for you. It can also make you susceptible to Tunnel Vision branching out into other areas.

Here's another example. Say you are triggered into Tunnel Vision when someone at work tells you about a genuine mistake you made—you forgot to return a phone call—but they tell you in a demeaning way. You may not notice any of the eight facets of Tunnel Vision, but they can manifest like this: at the moment your coworker is snidely telling you about the mistake, your attention starts to focus on them and on visualizing the mistake (focus of attention gets exclusive). As your reality warps, you start blocking out anything good you did in that instance (lowered awareness). You start to believe the mistake was as bad as they say (suggestibility). You become extremely self-conscious about it (ego expansion). You think things like, *The client is probably so angry, they'll tell the boss. I could get fired. I am a terrible worker. I shouldn't make mistakes like this. I should have been careful to not miss a phone call.* (These are distorted thoughts of magnifying the negative and minimizing the positive, future-tripping, mind-reading, absolutism, and so on.) Any of these facets of Tunnel Vision could cause you to focus even more tightly on the situation. It can feed off itself and put you into even tighter Tunnel Vision, warping your reality even more.

This downward spiral of Tunnel Vision is shown in Figure 1. After capturing our attention with an emotion, the downward spiral warps reality and causes us to feel even worse, which captures our attention and then warps reality even more.

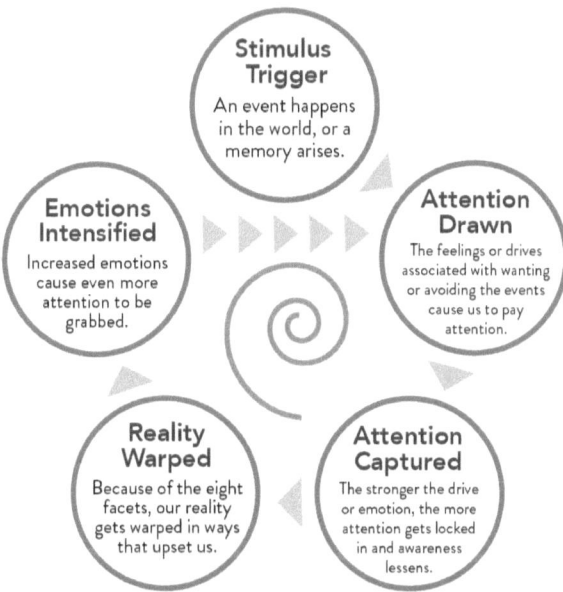

Figure 1. *Downward Spiral of Tunnel Vision*

If we don't find a way to put the brakes on this cycle, a slightly difficult event can be magnified into one that feels much worse.

We can turn a very bad event into one that feels unbearable. One chain of Tunnel Vision could ruin your day. It could even spiral into a crisis.

And that episode can branch out into other episodes because you're more sensitized. For instance, now that you feel like you are a bad worker for missing that call, the next person who offers feedback—even if it's constructive feedback about another matter—could spark another episode of even worse Tunnel Vision in you.

That "bad day" at work can cause you to find relief by purposely focusing on something else that creates another type of Tunnel Vision. For example, if you come home from work upset about the criticism you received, you can find temporary distraction by watching television or drinking alcohol. You might overfocus on managing your children, go shopping for status items, have sex with your spouse to distract yourself, or eat sweets. You can even use religion or spirituality as another form of Tunnel Vision to try to relieve the previous episode of Tunnel Vision. Many episodes of Tunnel Vision feel good at first, that is, until they cause negative consequences.

Any of those things could set you up for frustration and negative reactions from others, because they are being done in Tunnel Vision. Any seemingly positive aspects of life can be used as distractions from the control that Tunnel Vision has over you, turning them sour and causing more Tunnel Vision. We can get trapped in many different cycles and levels of Tunnel Vision, for example by addictions, in the coarsening of our personality, or in desperate attempts to feel better, such as eating ice cream, causing more Tunnel Vision as a result.

This is why we say that, with few exceptions, everyone lives in some degree of Tunnel Vision. It can ensnare us if we don't know what it is and how powerful it is. We can get preoccupied with ourselves, with achieving something, comparing our looks and abilities with those of others, getting enough things done, appearing competent or normal, all driven by, or at least worsened by, episodes of Tunnel Vision that have left traces of emotional hurt and pain.

Downward spiraling chains and branching of Tunnel Vision can clash with other life difficulties, like losses, setbacks, illnesses, aging, and harassment. As we'll practice in subsequent chapters, your SatoriWest task is to recognize the many ways your Tunnel Vision can look before it triggers multiple chain reactions, like a domino effect. Before you waste precious years of your life having your joy chipped away and your natural Perspective cloaked. Before you wind up increasingly and desperately unhappy.

To help you further recognize some of the ways Tunnel Vision can show itself, the next chapter will discuss the various ways Tunnel Vision can manifest.

. . . .

In a moment of crisis I would start thinking that I would never get over the situations of the past, I'll never get over crying, I'll never get over being distraught. It was just totally opposite from Perspective. I was distraught. I'd look at other people and think, Oh, I used to be like that, why can't I get back to being like that? It was the feeling of grasping at straws. At home here my husband, with his encouragement, would keep me going and living, but it was a struggle. It was just a struggle mentally to be in that place, and that was terrifying to me. I just felt like it was going to engulf me.

I was just fearful the bipolar would come back and engulf me. I would think of different fears, things that I wouldn't be able to do. I'm an artist, and I'm very involved with crafts and I had this fear that I'd never get that gift back. That I would be robbed of it.

[With the SatoriWest Method] I was able to take away those fears and stand back and say, "I still have that gift, it's still there, I'm going to be able to do the things." And I was able to do that

applying the SatoriWest Method of seeing the Tunnel Vision and then get back to Perspective again. And it was so enlightening, I just felt exhilarated again to do crafts like I had before.

Perspective just gave me the realization that I'm vital again. I have all those things to look forward to, which I thought I was robbed of. I have a wonderful husband, and we have so much to look forward to, and our retirement, and our two beautiful daughters that bring so much joy to my life, and my grandchildren. I've got that confidence now that I can be to them what they need me to be. And it just is basically fulfilling.

—Debbie

6
The Immediate Rewards of Tunnel Vision

If Tunnel Vision is so negative, if it's the source of so much unhappiness and misery, why can't we see it? Most people know their ego is toxic. Most of us are aware we can be gullible and easily influenced. We know we project our biases on the world and have distorted thinking, jumping to conclusions too easily. We know we bring our past into the present, and not usually in good ways. These and other facets of Tunnel Vision are known to us. Religion has repeated this over and over in literature and sermons. The field of psychology has shown this; we see its warnings in self-help books and articles.

There are many reasons why Tunnel Vision can hide from us. The first and most obvious reason is that we don't know what we're looking for. That's the purpose of this book and the SatoriWest Method. However, even if you do know what you are looking for, Tunnel Vision can still hide itself. It does that because it is so rewarding and so familiar (familiarity is rewarding in itself), we don't recognize mild instances as a problem. Let's explore these two insidious aspects of your brain's survival wiring. We'll start with the rewards of Tunnel Vision.

The Rewards of Tunnel Vision

Make no mistake, Tunnel Vision does not always come with bad feelings. Not at first, anyway. It can hide itself in being powerfully gratifying. It can feel so good that it seems like a method of self-treatment, like sex or a glass of alcohol when you're feeling down. If you're held captive by some difficult event that happened at work that day, and then the idea of ice cream enters your mind, it's more likely than not that you will wind up eating it. That can be seen as a self-reward. It's relaxing and stress-reducing and makes you feel better in the moment.

Remember the metaphor of the frog sitting in a pot of water that's slowly being heated? The frog doesn't notice the change and may even feel good to a point and so doesn't jump out, and eventually is cooked to death. One big reason the frog doesn't jump (as far as I'm concerned, stretching the metaphor a bit) and why we get cooked with stress in our lives, is because Tunnel Vision comes with such immense immediate pleasures.

To understand this, it's important to remember that Tunnel Vision is survival programming. You see something to eat, you focus attention on it, you eat it, you feel good. You see something that scares you, you focus attention on it, you escape it, you feel relieved. It's animalistic. We don't often experience higher ways to get what we want and avoid what is bad for us. We don't know we can literally shift our brain (BrainShifting), causing it do otherwise. We don't know there are higher ways to get what we truly need, and to avoid what we need to avoid, without giving in to urges and impulses. For example, we teach children to not grab what they want out of someone's hands and to not scream and hit if there is something they don't like. We tell them to ask calmly and to use their words if they are not happy. It takes some BrainShifting into some Perspective to do those things. Similarly, adults want to be happy and feel at peace, and they want to avoid stress and heartache, but they don't know how to be happy and avoid stress. Why? Because they are using Tunnel Vision to accomplish their ends.

Being in Tunnel Vision means we are being victimized by environmental conditioning and our physiology. For instance, getting what we want in the moment, like ice cream or a compliment, conditions us to seek it again and again. In technical terms, it's reinforcing. How is it reinforcing? In the SatoriWest model, whatever we want or don't want controls our attention. And grabbed, compelled, or given over attention causes us to lose control and go after our immediate wants and avoid what immediately makes us uncomfortable. Desires and fears compel our attention, causing us to seek satisfaction again and again—whether we know it or not. Once you eat ice cream as a way to reward yourself after a tiring day at work, it is likely to enter your mind the next day. This time it will come into your mind as an even stronger pull at your attention. And down the road to Tunnel Vision you go. In the same way, avoiding discomfort—like escaping the feeling of loneliness by watching TV, or averting the feeling of social anxiety by drinking alcohol—can cause you to seek that relief again and again. It controls your attention and practically forces you into Tunnel Vision.

Although we will address BrainShifting in a later chapter, you'll learn that the first task of BrainShifting is to recognize your Tunnel Vision. The trick, for example, is to recognize how you pay attention to food and its immediate pleasures even when you're not actually hungry. Or observe yourself shopping for new things when you don't really need them. Or see how watching television, obsessing about getting affection or validation from your partner, being preoccupied with approval at work, or even creating unnecessary drama in your life are controlling your attention. See how all these things and many more create the circumstances for Tunnel Vision. Notice it in how it affects your attention and in all the other seven facets that show themselves with it.

One of the first therapeutic tools in the field of cognitive therapy is to take a baseline. The therapist asks the client to notice and record themselves, in this case their irrational thoughts and negative emotions, without changing anything. This is similar to the first aspect of BrainShifting. (In fact, the SatoriWest Method incorporates aspects of cognitive therapy.)

Each episode of the old *Mission: Impossible* series used to start with a recording of a voice talking about the seemingly impossible mission being assigned to their agent Jim Phelps: "Your mission, Jim, should you decide to accept it, is…" Well, again, your mission, should you decide to accept it, is to recognize your Tunnel Vision in all its infinite manifestations, but especially when it is so immediately satisfying. It's not an impossible mission, but it can be very challenging. The rewards of Tunnel Vision are seductive.

Like the task of taking a baseline, in using the SatoriWest Method there's no need at first to force anything to stop. All that is necessary is to notice. Noticing itself takes at least a bit, if not all, of the intensity out of the attentional pull of the object, which unwinds Tunnel Vision. It may even instantly short-circuit it.

Notice any and all of the eight facets of Tunnel Vision, whatever shows itself to you the most. For example, the first facet of Tunnel Vision is that your attention is given over to something. So witness the pull on your attention by something, some object, like alcohol, chocolate, or sex, even though they feel so great at first that you won't want to see that as Tunnel Vision. (Remember, an "object" is not only a single thing, like something you detect through your senses; it can also be a thought, mental image, or emotion.)

The second facet of Tunnel Vision is loss of control. Observe how immediately anesthetizing and comforting it is to indulge yourself in it as you give up control to it.

The third facet of Tunnel Vision is lowered awareness. Observe how the object causes you to block out other things, especially unpleasant things you don't want to see, like things in your relationships, your work, or your life that aren't fulfilling.

The fourth facet of Tunnel Vision is being more suggestible. So witness how you can convince yourself that what you are doing (eating, drinking, shopping) is right or good.

The fifth facet of Tunnel Vision is increasingly using your imagination to experience the moment. Recognize how much you use your imagination to fantasize about getting what you want or to try to enjoy what you are doing. See how in some way you conflate your imagination with reality.

The sixth facet of Tunnel Vision is that it inflates your sense of "I." So note how what you are doing exaggerates your ego. See if the ice cream, or the activity that you think will bring you a compliment, causes you to feel better about yourself, ashamed, or both. In some ways, the fact that grabbed attention inflates your sense of self could be its most compelling aspect—better even than the taste of the ice cream, for instance. It can be a real high to be admired by someone. The fact that the ego rewards of Tunnel Vision are so motivating can be hard to notice, because society says it is okay to be competitive without considering others' feelings, to look down on someone who disagrees with you, to indulge your vanity, to insist on being praised for what you do. Getting complimented or attaining a position of status at work really does feel great, because it feeds your ego's need to be liked, feel important, or be respected. All those aspects of ego are tempered with Perspective. They are perfectly fine if they don't drag you into Tunnel Vision so that it controls you and sacrifices your wellness.

Your job is to notice this. See if you can even feel the everyday pulls and even addictions of these culturally sanctioned objects of Tunnel Vision that offer a powerful payoff. That can be hard, as we said, because it may seem paradoxical, or it seems healthy right up until you realize it isn't. We'll address this issue of society's role in Tunnel Vision in the next section when we talk about cultural Tunnel Vision.

Even when it gets inflated by Tunnel Vision, ego can be hard to see when it affects your motivation to see it as dysfunctional. You might feel justified in what you are focusing on and in what that causes you to subsequently do. For instance, if you're feeling unhappy and can't stop thinking about improving your body or facial features, your ego can convince you that you have to make yourself more attractive and desirable to be happy. That becomes hard to notice as Tunnel Vision, particularly when actually improving your looks winds up feeling so great for a time—before it insidiously moves into more Tunnel Vision. (Keep in mind, there is nothing whatsoever bad about grooming or wanting to look good. The problem is when it is done in Tunnel Vision as a way to distract yourself from other Tunnel Visions.)

Witness also how your object of immediate gratification changes what you think. This seventh facet of Tunnel Vision, distorted thinking, is also a challenge, because your ego compels you to insist you are right. On this same issue, *your Tunnel Vision will make you more likely to believe your rationalizations about your behavior:* "I can eat ice cream because I will exercise the weight away tomorrow."

Try to notice this facet of Tunnel Vision, even though it can be tricky to do so. See your thoughts about how things *should* be. Catch yourself being certain you know what the future holds. "If I eat that ice cream, it's gonna make me a happier person." "If I get my coworker to pay me a compliment, she'll like me more." (Again, the pleasure of eating ice cream or being complimented is not the issue. The problem is doing it *in* Tunnel Vision to cure another case *of* Tunnel Vision.)

The eighth facet of Tunnel Vision is time distortion, which is just plain hard to see; it's not impossible, just challenging without taking a minute's worth of introspection. Eating ice cream or getting complimented sends you back to a happier time.

Some combination of those eight facets of your Tunnel Vision will appear to you as you allow Tunnel Vision to take hold of your mind. They will feel familiar, pleasurable, compelling, and irresistible at times. They will tug at your motivation to witness them. At times, they will cause you to feel like you're being dragged along by a tsunami, and witnessing them will be a challenge. At other times they will not occur to you as being Tunnel Vision until they have progressed for a while. You may even become aware of having been in Tunnel Vision *after* an incident is over. That's still very useful. In other words, being aware of Tunnel Vision is more useful than not being aware of it, whether in its early stages, later, or even afterward.

You unwind Tunnel Vision by noticing it when it's visible. Without judgment. Judging is likely just another form of Tunnel Vision. The trick is to recognize Tunnel Vision that compels you toward some immediate gratification when the "water" is not that hot, when it's even seductively soothing. Then, you'll be more ready for it when the water starts to scald you. See it for what it is. That is the first and most important step in the SatoriWest Method's journey, the first act of BrainShifting we will review again in Part IV.

> **Thought Exercise**
>
> Let's explore detecting Tunnel Vision that serves as a distraction. First, check in with your human condition. That's what drives you to seek objects of Tunnel Vision that can distract or temporarily take away its negative feelings. Then ask yourself what you have recently done to distract yourself from the feelings of your human condition. What have you allowed yourself to be pulled toward, or what have you sought out that furthers how others see you for ego gratification reasons? Have you been posting something on social media that others might envy? Are you writing a book, hoping readers will appreciate you for it? How many conversations have you had today where you changed what you said to get someone's approval—or to avoid disapproval? Did you shop for things that might impress others, such as clothes or a car? Did you put on facial creams or go to the gym to work out so you will look good for others? Did you focus on something not good for you in the long run and wind up consuming it anyway? Are you thinking of something like that even now—vacation, sex, food, shopping?

> Ask yourself if you can see how these things control your attention. Can you see how they may have, even subtly, distracted you from appreciating what you have, from having Perspective? This is not to say that you shouldn't seek to impress others, want to look good, or eat dessert. Doing those things *with* Perspective is a different situation. You can do that. Then they become icing on the cake and not the cake itself, so to speak.
>
> Ask yourself if you actually believe you need immediate pleasures to be happy inside and feel complete. Or flip the question around: can any pleasure that is taken away, such as love, status, and wealth, take away your basic happiness and satisfaction with life? If you answer with anything other than a belief that you can find, in yourself, a place of gratitude for the gift of your life, then the chapters on Perspective will be essential to you and your fulfillment in life.

In case you weren't already painfully aware of this, paying attention to things that bring you immediate pleasure just feeds on itself. It has its own downward spiral, causing you to want more to get the same temporary high. That's the same whether you are satisfying a physical urge, like eating salty popcorn during a movie to shake off the day's stress, or engaging in activities that satisfy your ego. Things that help you feel important, feel that you belong, or feel "normal" to distract yourself from feeling irrelevant, alienated, or abnormal.

Hopefully, you didn't suffer serious childhood or adulthood setbacks, insults, or traumas. Yet as discussed in Chapter 2, almost everyone carries some scarring from childhood, adolescence, or adulthood. Past stress and traumatic episodes are not forgotten. We remember them even if we aren't consciously aware of them all the time. They are imprinted in our brains and prime us for Tunnel Vision in the future.

Author's note: It is important to repeat this clarification: just because Tunnel Vision drives you toward immediate pleasure and away from immediate pain, it does not mean that you stop seeking or avoiding things. It just means that when you seek from a place of Perspective, when you already feel grateful or have a sense of humor about life, or you have a good attitude about yourself, you won't be seeking based on being an artificial "need." You won't be driven to do what is not in your best long-term interests of gaining even greater Perspective. You already feel complete.

The "Cultural" Rewards of Tunnel Vision

The other reason why Tunnel Vision is hard to see is that everyone you know, and likely will ever know or hear about, suffers the same condition. It's hidden inside our popular culture. In its seemingly most benign form it's what we call cultural Tunnel Vision. The aims of cultural Tunnel Vision are widely believed to be "normal," part of what it means to be human. Of course, what is considered normal is a matter of who determines it. Is it normal for the interests of creating a consumer environment for the benefit of the economy or normal for one's personal development?

We mentioned how each of the eight facets of Tunnel Vision can hide themselves because they are in some way rewarding. For example, they can feel so familiar that they are not recognizable as negative, or they can fool you into thinking that their result is healthy, such as believing that routinely drinking alcohol after work is "therapeutic." Ultimately, if you are aware of them, the eight facets of Tunnel Vision will be seen as largely unhealthy and self-destructive. (That is, unless you choose to give them your attention, like when you are watching a movie. In that case, hopefully you have enough BrainShifting skills to draw your attention back if you don't like what you're seeing.)

However, certain facets of Tunnel Vision may be even harder to recognize. That's when society, our culture, says the effects of Tunnel Vision are the best way to be or to experience life. For instance, capitalist societies promote getting ahead financially as a way to be happy instead of fostering Perspective. Society unintentionally promotes ego in an us-versus-them mentality under the guise of national pride, team spirit, or doing what it takes to get ahead.

Corporations, in trying to maximize profits—a reasonable objective for a company—may take their promotion of consumerism to extremes, to the point that they ask people to waste resources or feel shame for not having what everyone else has. Of course, it is also up to you, as a consumer, to learn to BrainShift so that you aren't unduly influenced by media or popular culture.

All these cultural values promote Tunnel Vision. Keep in mind, there is nothing wrong with these attributes—such as getting ahead—when they are experienced with Perspective. It's just that we wind up judging our very happiness by the external measures of financial success, an enviable mate or family, popularity, power, and possession of status symbols.

Can you see how believing these cultural rewards as the way to find happiness surreptitiously promotes Tunnel Vision? For instance, the rewards promote ego to the point that we become self-absorbed, feeling separate from and competitive with other people, even our loved ones. This robs us of the Perspective that could bring us inner happiness. Most of us understand that when we realize there are others in the world worse off than us, rather than being solely focused on ourselves, we feel grateful for what we have.

If this facet of Perspective were widespread, it might adversely affect the economy. It makes it harder to sell things that people don't absolutely need. It makes it harder—but not impossible—to sell what is naturally available to them, like love, fresh air, even healthy food they can grow themselves. (In essence, that's what this book is doing.) The marketing of that kind of consumerism—creating "needs" for, say, whiter teeth, better technology, or status symbols—makes it more difficult for people to appreciate what life has given them naturally. Can you see how it may cause chronically irrational beliefs about your life and yourself—that you are *not* as lucky as you think you are, for instance, or that life is inherently unfair unless you have what others have?

> **Thought Exercise**
>
> Can you see how affected you are by the culture? Do you see the messages you received from childhood to be "normal," to attain a certain level of education, to achieve a certain level of financial success, to be gender or sexually normative? Which of these objectives are in service to your highest emotional development? Which aren't? Do you think you may have Tunnel Vision based on achieving these ends?
>
> Do you feel the subliminal and conscious influence of consumerism on your values? Can you sense the power of what you see on commercials or in other media on your desires? Do you think that may influence the development of Tunnel Vision based on achieving these ends?

The Familiarity of Tunnel Vision

One immediate reward of Tunnel Vision often alluded to in this chapter is familiarity. Tunnel Vision, even when it has harsh side effects, like when it harms our relationships, is familiar to us. Some people, believe it or not, depend on the misery and drama they were raised in as children to feel good. Tunnel Vision, whatever the type of suffering it causes, can be perversely comforting.

We have been trained and have been training ourselves to be in Tunnel Vision since we were children. It feels recognizable and predictable. Familiarity is comforting. In simple terms, even though we are miserable or unhappy in our Tunnel Vision, that recognizability brings about an odd sense of reassurance, a security. We gravitate toward and feel safe in our habits of doing and experiencing.

You might ask how we can feel comfortable with our ego while feeling alienated and lonely, taking everything in life personally, being easily insulted and holding grudges, or feeling shy and trapped in unassertiveness. It feels awful, yet it is easier to be who we have known ourselves to be than it is to take the risk to be open to the moment, unprotected, and authentic. If you feel trapped in your personality that is protective of your ego, it's because your brain is seduced by Tunnel Vision. Even though we may scare ourselves by imagining the worst things that can happen in life or with loved ones, even though we know wanting more things and money is destroying our happiness, it is easier to let ourselves get trapped than to overcome those mindsets. All these things and thousands more that ruin our lives are strangely compelling because they are what we know well.

As familiar as we are with this aspect of our Tunnel Vision, that's how unfamiliar we are with Perspective, especially wide Perspective. It must feel strange to not get insulted or take things personally when we are clearly being insulted. It's got to feel odd to want what we have, instead of incessantly wanting something new and different. Being moved by gratitude in difficult times instead of being compelled to immediately be somewhere better or be doing something better probably feels weird to us. For many of us it's foreign to not want to be busy every free second. Freedom is scary. Surrendering our ego feels risky. True inner peace (not just temporary relaxation), true contentment and joy (not just immediate pleasure), is foreign territory. We need to understand this. Otherwise we may face a resistance to letting go of our ego. We might sabotage our SatoriWest Method journey despite its validity.

Thought Exercise

To the extent that you can now recognize Tunnel Vision in yourself, can you sense how familiar it is? Can you feel how that familiarity is rewarding, or at least comforting?

Conclusion

Almost all of us latch our attention on to whatever helps us escape an unpleasurable or painful moment, to find a better moment. Perhaps by the end of this book, or at least before the end of your life, you'll come to accept this moment as having a perfection to it—as odd as that may be to hear. That's the difference between temporary pleasure and pain and the fulsome fulfillment of which your whole brain is capable. As a thin minority of people throughout the ages who have achieved it attest, it happens when our brains shift enough for us to experience the gift of *this* moment.

. . . .

I've just felt so much desire to get back [after finishing the SatoriWest partial hospital program], and so much anticipation to be back in my routine, back in my normal life. I've just had all the desire, you know, to be able to get back into life, and apply the things [I learned about the SatoriWest Method]. Cause I've always had low self-esteem. And I've been able to restore a feeling even better than I was before, that I could be creative. The creative thoughts have started coming, creativity in my crafts have started coming. Anticipation of being able to see my family through situations instead of having to just be the one that everyone had to help. It's bad that my family had to go through what they had to go through. But I was able to let go of that and just feel like I have a direction that I didn't have even before I was able to be in the program.

—Debbie

7

Traversing Levels of Tunnel Vision

As we mentioned in the last chapter, Tunnel Vision can be hard to see, sometimes impossibly hard. That is one of the main purposes of this book and the SatoriWest Method. That's because invisible Tunnel Vision is harmful and sometimes dangerous to our mental health, people we love, the environment, and society.

There are many reasons why Tunnel Vision is hard to see, even if we are familiar with it. One reason is that it can feel so wonderful so quickly. It's like that tasty piece of chocolate when we're depressed. The effect of reinforcers on our brain is powerful. Plus, unfortunately, the very nature of Tunnel Vision makes it hard to see *it* and its consequences. We are either not capable of being aware of what is going on in and around us, because the neurophysiology of Tunnel Vision blocks awareness, or the power of the immediate payoffs causes us to not want to see anything else. It's like being in denial, where we're so focused on getting ahead at work that we may not see—even though we know on some level—that our family life is falling apart.

Another reason why Tunnel Vision is so hard to detect Is that our society sees lesser versions of it as normal, even good. Most cultures, for their own purposes, reinforce certain facets of Tunnel Vision that are immediately rewarding. These can seem valid on the surface, like achieving financial success, status, or admiration. They are difficult to see as problems because our acquaintances, our friends, and our family members are all motivated by them.

Also, the media, whether overtly or covertly, shows these cultural values to be equivalent to inner happiness. They aren't. We called this cultural Tunnel Vision.

Of course, religions, spiritual movements, and wise individuals throughout the ages who have attained high degrees of Perspective have warned against these kinds of rewards. They exposed them as ephemeral sources of unhappiness and pain. It's just that, even for the religiously observant and spiritually attuned, it is difficult to resist society and the forces of one's own brain.

Remember survival wiring? The forces in your brain that create Tunnel Vision? Chocolate, amphetamines, and alcohol all have a similar drug-like effect on us, as does getting praise and feeling important. From the beginnings of life on this planet, animals have focused both on what they needed and what they needed to avoid simply to stay alive. These same forces cause humans to focus attention on what they physically need and what they physically need to avoid to actually survive, and also, as we said, to focus on what they imagine they "need." This has a lot to do with ego needs.

Our egos tell us what we must have to feel complete, to feel happy, and to avoid feeling unhappy, scared, and bored. But our egos are misinforming us. Egos are magnified out of proportion to reality in Tunnel Vision. Getting status, getting recognition, being admired, and having power over others can be highly rewarding, at least at first. Sometimes it's only for a matter of seconds, sometimes it's for years. Yet as we said, the consequences of Tunnel Vision eventually show up. The effects of status, wealth, admiration, and power can't substitute for the simple yet mind-blowing reality of the fact that we exist *as us*. Drugs, possessions, and movies won't substitute for true and unconditional love. Even seemingly loving relationships that induce Tunnel Vision can't substitute for relationships that exist within the context of the love that emanates from Perspective.

Degrees of Tunnel Vision

The one common denominator of the cultural values we just mentioned is that status, admiration, wealth, and power are reinforced in the society you live in from the time you are very young. Yet if they take control of what you pay attention to each day and in life overall, they can make you chronically unhappy. Tunnel Vision that comes from seeking cultural needs can, and usually does, slowly (or quickly) spiral downward into life crises—midlife crises, the empty nest syndrome, even adolescent and young adult crises.

Before we explore more about cultural Tunnel Vision and the role it plays in crises, it's going to be helpful to identify different degrees of Tunnel Vision, besides cultural. That's an additional way to self-monitor your Tunnel Vision besides just knowing you are in Tunnel Vision. We'll divide the experience of Tunnel Vision into three levels of severity, from loose to tight focus of attention caused by the pull of the object of attention. Of course, Tunnel Vision starts with what grabs your attention. However, the degree of Tunnel Vision includes any or all of its eight facets, individually or all together. For instance, there can be less and less self-control or more and more suggestibility. We'll call these levels "cultural," "toxic," and "crisis" degrees of Tunnel Vision.

We already discussed cultural Tunnel Vision, and we will add more about it later in this chapter. Again, it comes from our own ego desires that are encouraged by society. This so-called "normal" Tunnel Vision is relatively undetectable. It so pervades the culture that people might wrongly experience the consequences of it in themselves or others as "just the way life is." "Life is a rat race," they will say with a shrug.

Toxic Tunnel Vision is a way of experiencing that might or should lead someone to seek counseling or therapy. That's because they feel acutely unhappy, anxious, or angry, and the consequences of the Tunnel Vision are more acute. For example,

Tunnel Vision can be considered toxic if you overuse things that bring pleasure to the point that you struggle with your impulses—for example, regularly overeating or over-shopping as a way to self-soothe. These examples of toxic Tunnel Vision come with serious weight gain or significant financial problems.

Toxic Tunnel Vision can also mean having such an inflexible or difficult personality that people have a hard time being in a relationship with you. It can also cause you to make the same mistakes over and over—for example, marrying more than one abusive spouse—so that you start questioning your own sanity. It could look like wanting to get ahead so badly that you commit acts of immorality, such as being unkind, dishonest, or untrustworthy.

Crisis Tunnel Vision is extreme. It warps our reality so much that our normal way of being in the world is very different. It distorts our sense of reality, ourselves, and our thoughts to the extent that we can become a danger to ourselves or others or to our health. These are instances when some event causes us to go into such constricted Tunnel Vision that the eight facets are grossly distorted: we lose a great degree of self-control, become so suggestible, or have such a distorted ego and thinking that we contemplate or actually do things that we would normally never do. This could look like road rage, attempting suicide or homicide, getting into fights, or committing crimes.

Here are a few fictitious examples of getting stuck in different degrees of Tunnel Vision.

Cultural Tunnel Vision (Attention Is Not as Constricted)

Nancy is a 78-year-old African American woman who raised four children with a husband who died 30 years ago. Nancy recently retired after working in a clerical position. Her children are grown and have moved away. Nancy often feels weary dealing with sexism and racism. She's engulfed by it in that she has let it define her. That's why she focuses her attention on it and is self-conscious in white neighborhoods. She feels a bit beaten down by it all, but it's been part of her life for so long it feels mostly normal. The stress of life makes her tired, though she's not usually aware of it, again because it feels normal. Yet she is still a loving, relatively content person. She focuses on getting old, as if she will be glad when her weariness ends.

Toxic Tunnel Vision (Attention Is More Tightly Focused)

Robert is a 26-year-old single white man. He works in the IT department of a large shoe company. Although he's a nice-looking young man, he feels that he isn't as attractive or as tall as several of the salesmen who work in the sales department. A well-dressed, fast-talking crowd, they make the same base salary as Robert, but can also earn large commissions, which means they can afford more than Robert can. Robert is friends with a few of these salesmen, and they often go out for drinks after work and hang out on weekends.

Robert has been on a few dates in the last few years, but when he has, he can't help thinking about and imagining his friends. He is acutely aware of not being as smooth with words as they are, not as sophisticated in his dress and mannerisms, and not as well built or tall.

In the last few months he has been dating Jill. He is starting to really like her, and when he is with her, he finds her captivating. He sees her as exceptionally beautiful, perhaps almost perfect. She seems to like him, too, but he imagines she is comparing him with his friends, so he feels jealous and insecure at times. He even feels inferior and self-conscious when he's with his friends. His relationship with Jill will likely not last because of his toxic Tunnel Vision.

Crisis Tunnel Vision (Attention Is Very Constricted)

Ted is a 48-year-old gay Vietnamese American man whose parents emigrated to the United States before he was born. He was married to a woman for 20 years. They had two children before his urges to be with men, which started when he was 16, overwhelmed him and he broke his marital vows with another man. After the divorce, he and his boyfriend were together for eight months before they broke up. Now Ted, whose ex-wife hates him and who is distanced from his children and his family—the latter because of his homosexuality—feels alone. Ted believes he is destined to be alone, that no one loves him, that he is an inferior person, and that his family would be better off without him. He feels suicidal, with no other options.

These are three examples of literally billions that could represent these broad classifications of Tunnel Vision. Remember, there is a smooth continuum from severe crisis to subtle cultural degrees, just as there is within Perspective, as you can have mild, great, and so-called spiritual levels of Perspective.

The Name of the Game: See Cultural Tunnel Vision in Yourself

Therapists who use mindfulness-based therapies—or any kind of therapy, for that matter—can help people who are in crisis and toxic levels of Tunnel Vision find relief. The problem is that they get back to a cultural level of Tunnel Vision and see it as normal. A place that is familiar. A way of being in life where they are coping well enough to function as they had before, or as society tells them they should. It's a life where the degree of desperate unhappiness is tamped down to manageable levels, where the human condition is interspersed with moments of immediate pleasure that serve as pacifiers.

That's not what this book is about. That is not the opportunity the title of this book suggests you take, where you use your suffering to evolve your brain and transform your life and your personality. Noticing Tunnel Vision only occasionally, perhaps when you are stressed, is not the fullest use of the SatoriWest Method, either. Really evolving your brain toward its peak capacity and having an exceptional experience of life takes strategically using crisis and adversity to Awaken you out of cultural Tunnel Vision. Of course, noticing your cultural levels of Tunnel Vision is very important as well. It's just incredibly powerful to notice it during crises. In that way, you'll open your Perspective enough to be truly happy and deeply fulfilled.

To do all that, let's drill more into cultural Tunnel Vision. Getting better acquainted with it will give us a better sense of what adversity helps reveal, so we can find our highest selves.

Cultural Tunnel Vision starts in childhood. As the human condition begins to take hold, we are rewarded for whatever removes it. For example, one way it starts is staring at candy or a toy we see advertised on television, when it's all we can see as a way to be happy inside.

What is not emphasized enough or at all in schools or in many homes is that our truest happiness is not found outside of ourselves. We can't find it from owning or consuming things. Not only is this not taught, but it isn't exemplified, either. We personally know few role models who epitomize the truest joy that is found in the experience of just being alive. Judeo-Christian and other religions do tout versions of this in their own ways. Yet the obvious fact of the miracle of our existence is a hard enough lesson for an adult mind, let alone a child's.

So we dream about an ideal life. Most people do. Anywhere you go in the world, people are visualizing the greatest life they can have for themselves and their families. This is not about not having enough to live reasonably well, whether it is food, clothing, or shelter. It's about wanting an ideal. The very best.

The most. Because of Tunnel Vision, we are continually driven for "more" and "better." We rarely stop to feel satisfied with, let alone love, what we have.

Remember, not having Tunnel Vision doesn't mean you would necessarily stop dreaming about the future. It just means that dreams don't control your attention. You can balance being completely present and grateful for your existence with the fun—but not necessity—of striving for some better future.

> **Thought Exercise**
>
> Do you see the dissatisfaction with where you live, your job, your friends, your family, your relationships? Take this moment to look around and feel inside yourself. In what way is your life about relieving something, gaining something, or accomplishing something? Can you sense how that grabs your attention? Can you notice any dissatisfaction at this very moment? Can you also sense that you are alive and what that really means? Can you feel the importance of being given the gift of life?

As we said, cultural levels of Tunnel Vision are invisible in part because they can be so rewarding. For example, being highly identified with our role makes us feel like we are stable and belong in society. Whether we identify with what we are at work (for example, an executive or an assistant), in our family (for example, the dad or the child), or in society (for example, a man or woman, a southerner)—good or bad—it makes us feel solid, like we know where we fit in. It seems so normal to be strongly identified with a role that it is hard to recognize it as a form of Tunnel Vision. Yet it also makes it hard to be flexible. It pulls us away from the healing and simple joy that comes from being in the present.

Author's note: I take a lot of pride in being a doctor and a psychiatrist. Yet if my self-esteem depends on that, I'm going to be at a loss until everyone at a party knows that fact. Or I might feel defensive, angry, and controlled if someone pokes fun at psychiatrists.

Overidentifying with a role is one way that cultural Tunnel Vision is limiting, sometimes to the point of being suffocating. Men who overidentify as masculine might suppress their "feminine" side. To avoid appearing weak and emotional, they might swallow their feelings and not allow themselves to cry. They might also suppress their creativity or flair for the arts, let alone the full expression of their real emotions. A person who identifies as "poor" might not feel entitled to abundance and might sabotage their success, although even that identity can provide comfort. It's like Tevye, the father in the musical *Fiddler on the Roof*, who dreams of being rich but bases his friendship with his God on the identity of being a poor milkman. Yet even though strongly or overidentifying with a role can be stifling, it gives us something to hang on to.

Cultural Tunnel Vision is also invisible because not having Tunnel Vision seems abnormal. For instance, if you were insulted, people would expect you to get angry and take the insult personally. If someone with Perspective were insulted, others might see them as weak, weird, or even as a strangely exceptional human being for just laughing off the insult or even feeling empathy for the person insulting them.

Cultural Tunnel Vision is also invisible because obsessively pursuing pleasure is the norm. It is typical to hear people talking incessantly about their next meal, who is sexually attractive, some romance they saw on TV, or their vacation dreams rather than appreciating what they have. It doesn't make for great banter at work to talk about your actual feelings of sadness. It would be odd to share your feelings and thoughts about your human condition, which is part of why we bury them inside ourselves. It would be odd to hear you voice appreciation for yourself the way you are—even for the traits that society derides, like being emotional or insecure.

It is possible to value a job you don't like even if you want to change jobs. It is possible to appreciate your health no matter what shape it's in, because the body does deteriorate with age, even though we can take better and better care of ourselves. Cultural Tunnel Vision is also hard to see because it's also the norm to avoid anything uncomfortable, any disapproval, any disappointment. It's the exceptional person who willingly faces disapproval from family or friends by telling them truths they would rather not hear.

> **Thought Exercise**
>
> Cultural Tunnel Vision is hard to see, in part because it *works in the short run*. It gives you immediate pleasure and helps you avoid immediate pain. Let's see if any of these examples help you see your culturally acceptable ways of being in Tunnel Vision.
>
> - Do you deal with frustration at work by routinely having a drink afterward? If that works, do you find you need progressively more alcohol to get the same effect?
>
> - Do you avoid feeling low self-esteem by fantasizing about shopping and buying a great outfit or new whatever? Do you find that you're doing a lot of shopping to feel emotionally buoyed?
>
> - Do you feel any level of genuine enjoyment for the work you do, or are you there solely for the pay, a chance at promotion, or the position's status? If the latter is the case, do you find the work is getting tedious or emotionally draining?

- Do you seek out sex to satisfy a deep yearning for love and deep connection? Is that as satisfying as having both?

- Do you avoid social situations so you don't have to face social anxiety, causing you to miss out on the benefits of being with groups of people? The idea is that without Tunnel Vision telling you that you had to be or act or look a certain way, confidence in social situations would not be as important as feeling natural no matter who you are or how you act.

The invisible, slowly heating water of cultural Tunnel Vision is harmful precisely because it appears to be so normal. It's part of most human cultures today and those in the past. With the advent of technology and corporate marketing, the pull of the social norms that create cultural Tunnel Vision seems to be increasing.

Of course, modern technology comes with great advantages, too. There has been an essential evolution of society in terms of its Perspectives on human rights and dignity. That point cannot be overemphasized. Society, and the technology that transmits it, are also forces for good.

Yet there is a concerted effort in market economies to foster Tunnel Vision, to convince people that achieving outer sources of pleasure is the way to find inner and lasting happiness and relief from pain. Marketing companies spend billions on research to convince us of that. Corporate marketing induces us to see people with material success or who appear beautiful—with whiter, straighter teeth, straight hair, or better skin—as truly happy. That's why people wind up obsessively seeking a "better" life, all the while feeling increasingly limited, unhappy, and out of control. We wind up trying our hardest to avoid looking stressed, to appear only happy. We try to avoid the signs of aging and physical imperfections. When someone casually asks us how we are, most of us say "fine," but we don't literally mean it.

The Downward Spiral from Cultural to Toxic to Crisis

Tunnel Vision can turn from cultural (chronic and uncomfortable) to toxic (more acutely painful) to crisis (dangerous) if something doesn't stop the cycle. Over the years our "human condition" can ferment into something that is unbearable in middle age. At that point we can't drink enough alcohol to douse the feelings, we can't make enough money, we can't find the "perfect" enough in anything—spouse, children, job, meals, and so on. Deep grooves of habit set into that survival wiring. We really can get stuck, no matter how much Perspective we have at times. We really can feel helpless to change our patterns of behavior. We can feel victimized by our own personalities, our way of seeing and being in the world.

This pattern of cultural Tunnel Vision being solved with more Tunnel Vision is at least partly why people become alcoholic or morbidly obese, go into extreme debt, or wind up alone or in one destructive relationship after another. Our personalities do not seem to get more flexible the older we get. We often get stuck in habits that rob us of self-control. We just cannot see or understand how we or life could be any different. We move from crisis to crisis until we understand what is happening to us.

It is important to say again that Perspective naturally increases with age. That might indicate why aging is associated with more emotional freedom. However, Tunnel Vision also hardens with age. Where you fall out depends on how caught up you are by Tunnel Vision of any severity or type, cultural or otherwise.

Life can get more vapid and unfulfilling the more we get caught up in this downward spiral. That warm water actually can get uncomfortably hot early in life, as early as adolescence. Yet we don't know how to jump out, precisely because we can't see the role Tunnel Vision plays in our often "secret," and sometimes not-so-secret, unhappiness. However, what would happen if the water heated up very quickly or very noticeably? That's the goal of this book that we'll dive into in Part V.

What is this Perspective we've been alluding to? What is this natural force of human development that can counter the survival wiring of Tunnel Vision? Part III will explore this amazing side of us and of our astonishing brains.

· · · · · · ·

I was very anxious. I was shaking and wanting to take medications...[The SatoriWest Method] really helped me listen to myself and feel more at peace with myself and my mind...Yeah, it works.

—Anonymous

Part III

PERSPECTIVE

8

The Core of Human Potential

In Parts I and II we discovered the difficult, harsh, and destructive aspects of having a human brain. When it's pulled into Tunnel Vision, that is. Yet as we've been saying, our brain also has an opposite aspect. On a day other people would find stressful, you could be naturally at ease. While others feel that they are not accomplishing enough or are not enough for the people in their lives, you could feel content with who you are and what you are doing each moment. When others believe the adage "Life sucks and then you die," you could feel utterly fulfilled—no matter what you were doing!

Your brain is capable of all this. It can feel moments of natural bliss. It can live in deep tranquility. It can, as we have alluded to, give you a sense of amazement at the fact of existence itself.

It can even feel an intimate connection with the entire universe. Your brain can be resilient to even the worst disaster. This is all because the object sitting in your head at this moment is the most complex structure in the known universe.

What is it about your brain that makes it so miraculous? In the Preface we learned that what gives the human brain, your brain, this extraordinary gift is not its extreme intelligence, or its imagination, or its sense of self, as astounding as those attributes really are. It's that it has the potential to know on a profound level that it is alive. This feature is almost formed in other animals' brains, but it's taken to a vast new dimension in humans. And it's based on the fact that we don't have one brain sitting in our head—we have two.

Remember that we mentioned studies of people who have had the connecting fibers between the two "sides" of their brain completely severed to reduce intractable seizures from spreading from one side of brain to the other? What was revealed was the surprising fact that each "side" has a *separate awareness*. Without those connecting tracks of fibers, each side would be relatively unaware of what the other side knows. In other words, you use two brains every moment, not one.

As we also said, like having two eyes that see the same objects gives depth to vision, two brains give depth to experience. Having two brains allows for awareness to reflect on itself, giving us so-called "self-awareness." This amounts to an awareness of being alive.

You might still be wondering what the big deal is. We all know we're alive. Of course we do—on some level. But that experience is vague. It's in the background of your everyday experience. You take it utterly for granted—like a fish takes water for granted. Tunnel Vision robs us of that full realization. It puts the depth of the experience of aliveness in the background as achieving things takes over the foreground. It's no wonder people wind up asking where the years went and why they didn't appreciate them more.

> *The most fortunate are those who have a wonderful capacity to appreciate, again and again, freshly and naïvely, the basic goods of life, with awe, pleasure, wonder and even ecstasy.*
>
> —Abraham Maslow

When the two "sides" of the brain are trained on each other—which is part of what BrainShifting is—the objects that create Tunnel Vision are released to the background. Your brain begins to focus *in*. It zeros in on the monumental fact that that you exist. That experience can help you truly know what it means that you got to be born, that your life is a gift and each moment truly extraordinary.

The more power and energy to that deeper realization, the more life changing it is. It alters our view of life and ourselves, as we'll show. In short, a brain trained primarily on its existence and opened to the wholistic view of each moment is the polar opposite of Tunnel Vision. That's the core of Perspective. Let's get more specific about what that means.

Defining Perspective

Perspective is the opposite of Tunnel Vision. For instance, whereas Tunnel Vision pulls your attention into objects and into your mind, so you don't pay attention to the fact of your existence, Perspective allows a widened awareness of the world around and within you.

And yes, you can have Tunnel Vision and Perspective in any one moment about one event at the same time. You might react childishly to something and know that you're doing so at the same time. You can have Tunnel Vision about many different issues, such as your teenager's abhorrent behavior, but have tremendous wisdom, humor, and Perspective about life in general.

Let's explore what the opposite of Tunnel Vision might be like. We'll first review each of the eight elements of Tunnel Vision, then consider what the Perspective version might be. And then we'll show a few possible immediate benefits of this element of Perspective. (Please remember, like in Tunnel Vision, these are not really separate elements. They were artificially separated out to illustrate the principles.)

Facet One: Attention

Tunnel Vision
Attention is pulled or freely given to a single subject or event. This includes whatever related thoughts, inner images, and feelings may come with it.

Perspective

Awareness is kept open, although it can be directed toward one thing. In other words, with open awareness, attention is not exclusive, it's *inclusive*. It takes in the focus of attention and other unrelated aspects of your experience that aren't focused on. This means you experience what your mind pulls you into and other things going on in the same moment. What other things? It depends. Oddly, with Perspective your brain will just process what else it is aware of, the other second-tier stimuli that might enter its awareness.

Think of your brain as being like a room with various closed-circuit TV monitors capturing different images in different locations. Your mind—motivated by your ego—is pulled into the activities of one of the monitors. That's Tunnel Vision. However, the brain can process much more than whatever we are paying attention to each moment.

The strategy behind Perspective is to access more of your brain. In its most basic and easy-to-understand form, that strategy, which we call BrainShifting, is simply to be aware of whatever scene your mind pulls you into and something else that is unrelated to it. It's that straightforward. The instruction is to use an "and" way of experiencing, not an "or" way of experiencing.

Immediate Benefits

One benefit of being more aware of what is going on in the moment than what your mind and ego are driving you to analyze, accomplish, and control is that it allows you to experience the subtlety of each moment. To be aware of not just what you may believe you need to do or see, but the ordinary, nonessential things. In Japan, there is the notion of wabi-sabi. That means to experience "the beauty of things imperfect, impermanent, and incomplete; the beauty of things modest and humble; the beauty of things unconventional" (Leonard Koren, *Wabi-Sabi for Artists, Designers, Poets & Philosophers* [Berkeley, CA: Stonebridge Press,

1994]). This can be likened to a photographer's eye, or someone who can find art in the most mundane objects and moments. It's an "and" way of experiencing. This facet of Perspective, widening awareness, opens your eye up to this kind of recognition.

Another benefit is that you are better able to be aware of what is happening around you, for safety's sake. Think of someone who knows they are going to be attacked at any moment from any angle. This facet of Perspective is infinitely practical in that you have more "eyes" around you open at the same time.

Facet Two: Control

Tunnel Vision

There is a stimulus-response connection between what is experienced and the action it induces. This causes impulsive actions, thoughtless reactions, and in general, less and less self-control.

Perspective

A more open way of experiencing lends itself to not only greater self-control, with less reactionary behavior, but also to greater executive control. This means that the brain is allowed to use its vast amount of unconscious processing to "decide" what to do and how to do it.

Immediate Benefits

This amounts to the ability to use nonverbal intuition—a gut sense—to process a situation. Although intuition is not perfect, it can be invaluable at times. That's because our attention is driven by an ego that wants what it wants right now. That kind of attention may overlook internal warning signs, the thoughts and feelings that say, "Don't do it." The ego also wants to keep itself from being hurt or embarrassed, which can be stifling and excessively risk avoidant. This facet of Perspective allows the thoughts and feelings that may say, "Just do it."

Facet Three: Awareness

Tunnel Vision

When your attention is exclusively focused on something, it stands to reason that you will not be aware of anything else. Of course, the degree to which other things are blocked out depends on how focused your attention is.

Perspective

When your attention is not exclusively co-opted, it opens up your awareness to things that may not be immediately relevant to getting your needs met. For example, say you join a meeting of people you don't know. If your attention is exclusively focused on the words being said, you may miss subtle cues in participants' body language or emotional intonation that can tell you a lot about the meeting.

Immediate Benefits

In addition to the above example, where you might get more information and context about a situation, this aspect of having a brain in Perspective is also the antidote to denial. We've all experienced denial, blocking out what we don't want to see. People can be in denial about their loved one's misbehavior or about our adoration of public figures as well. In the chapter on cultural Tunnel Vision, we mentioned a scenario where a person focused on the ego gratification of work might be so fixated on their job that they might not notice their relationship or family life falling apart. Not so when enjoying work in Perspective.

Perspective's ability to counter denial will not only save you grief and heartache but is practical and can help you be more effective in how you relate in relationships, to scientific inquiries, and to life problems in general.

Facet Four: Suggestibility

Tunnel Vision

Focused attention seems to make people more apt to accept ideas as true, whether they are or not. The full force of this believability can fly in the face of a starkly different reality. As was said, it has a hypnotic level of suggestibility. We gave the example of telling someone whose attention is compelled or given over that they are freezing cold, and they show visible signs of being cold, even when the room they're in is hot.

A quick anecdote. It is said that famous defense attorney Clarence Darrow put a wire in his cigar so that while delivering his closing argument, the ash from his cigar grew to unusual lengths, catching the jury's attention. Other attorneys have employed similar attention-grabbing tactics. The goal is to catch the jury's attention and help persuade them to accept the lawyer's argument, regardless of whether they fully believe it.

Perspective

This facet of Perspective primarily means that you would be less suggestible. The wisdom and insight of your Perspective would make you a more discerning person. You would be better able to sniff out falsehoods. You would be less apt to follow the crowd and better able to think for yourself.

Immediate Benefits

Not being suggestible would make you better able to make independent and wiser decisions. It would prevent you from being persuaded to do things that are not in your best interests or those of your loved ones. If you had a good deal of Perspective, you would not be susceptible to Darrow's tactic of trying to convince you of a guilty person's innocence simply by causing you to focus on his long cigar ash.

Facet Five: Imagination

Tunnel Vision

Any narrowed attention causes the brain to use its imagination more and more to analyze and process what is happening each moment. The common way of saying this is that you get more and more lost in your head, and less and less focused on the present, sensory world.

Perspective

Having mental images and thoughts is part of being human. Getting caught up in them so that they seem as real as what is going on in reality is a recipe for problems, if not disaster. With Perspective you would not allow your imagination to take control. What you imagine is clearly separate from what is experienced in your sensory world. With great Perspective there is even a radiance to the sensory world, as you experience it as raw and unfiltered.

Immediate Benefits

Keeping in mind that this facet of Tunnel Vision puts you in your head more than in the world of reality, in this facet of Perspective your thoughts and imagination are less of a filter of the present moment. In other words, you aren't projecting your biases, wants, and preferences onto the world, so you can be in the world in a fresh and novel way. With Perspective, your attention, which is usually but not always driven by ego, is freed up to be aware of things that are unique about the moment.

For example, in your head, your memory and imagination color what you hear, see, and feel. The more Perspective you have, the less you filter through the lens of your past experiences or your imagination, and the better able you'll be to hear what someone says without as much bias. This allows you to see people for who they are in the moment, not what you want them to be, not what you have experienced them to be in the past, not what you predict they will do in the future. This lets you better connect with them, to know them better for what and who they are right now. It allows for more intimacy. That's because people are seen and validated for who and what they are right now. Of course, with Perspective you are aware of your memory and intuition that tells you whether what they are saying and doing is truthful or trustworthy—or not. It's just that it's not dominating your reality.

Facet Six: Ego

Tunnel Vision
Your sense of self becomes exaggerated. This can take many different forms. For example, you take things personally that are not about you. Or you feel isolated from others and/or like to be the center of attention. You can feel superior and/or inferior to others. You get overly competitive and obsessively compare yourself with others.

Perspective
Your ego is tamped down so the world is experienced through less and less of a personalized lens.

Immediate Benefits
Less ego means you would worry less about others' opinion of you and not seek approval or compliments as much, if at all, from others. This might look like being able to be your authentic self without caring as much about whether people were paying attention to you because of it. You would feel an easy sense of belonging with others you cared about or with humanity in general, but without feeling better than anyone else, and certainly not feeling less than others. The immediate effect of these benefits is a feeling of liberation, of freedom from the oppressiveness of worrying about what people think of you.

Facet Seven: Thinking

Tunnel Vision

Your thinking gets distorted because of the inflation of ego and other factors related to Tunnel Vision, such as being more suggestible and being more lost in your own inner world (in your head). For instance, you would be more inclined to jump to conclusions, making assumptions without enough evidence. You would insist that things are either black or white, all or nothing. You would be certain you knew what the future holds to the point of catastrophizing. You would magnify the negative side of life and events while minimizing the positive. You would also insist, believing it fully, that things, people, and events "must," "should," "ought" to be the way you believe they must be.

Perspective

With Perspective your thoughts become less egocentric and more reality based. It is the opposite of the way thoughts get distorted in Tunnel Vision. For example, you would not jump to conclusions based on preconceived ideas; instead, you would be better able to discern what is true by objectively putting together all the pieces of evidence you have, but in any case, waiting until you'd received enough information to hypothesize what *might* be true. You would intuitively discern that few things are all or nothing, that most things come in shades of gray. You would be less certain about what the future holds. In any case, you might even have a fresh interest and curiosity about what the future holds—even in the next second. Instead of insisting that things, events, and people must be the way you think they should be, you would frame this as things "would be best," "would be nice," "would be good" if they were one way or another.

Immediate Benefits

Warped thinking, or so-called "cognitive distortions," are ways that we make ourselves unhappy. Reality-based thinking, being rational and reasonable, feels like a relief. People, things, and events don't have to conform to your preconceived ideas; they are what they are, so you can experience them more fully and appreciate them more completely for their uniqueness. That means you are not upsetting yourself, which means you are happier. It also means that you have a better understanding of how the world works, including the people, things, and events that make it up. That is a much less frustrating way to go through life: you aren't facing the consequences of frequently misinterpreting things. *Perspective makes you functionally more intelligent.*

Facet Eight: Time
Tunnel Vision
The experience of time can also get distorted in Tunnel Vision. This happens largely because we are lost in our minds and memories in Tunnel Vision and only partly experiencing the present moment while partly experiencing the past, and at times, the future. For instance, if you were treated badly by a man in your past, you might carry that memory into your relationships with men in the present. In other words, you might conflate or confuse an innocent man with one who hurt you in the past. Similarly, expectations of the future might color your present world so that the way you treat people is in response to how you assume they are going to treat you in the future. For example, we assume someone is going to criticize us for something we are about to tell them, so we approach the encounter feeling defensive and being snippy with them from the get-go.

Perspective
With Perspective, experiencing is firmly grounded in the present. In that sense, you are also more reality oriented, as you were with reality-based, Perspective-based thinking.

Immediate Benefits

Being grounded in the present moment is a touchstone for feeling safe, centered, in control, and fully appreciative of whatever you are aware of.

It helps you feel safe, because not being lost in the past and future allows you to best discern the singular and unique requirements of the moment. In other words, you can face the exigencies of whatever arises each moment with a clear, objective mind that is fully taking in the circumstances, so you can respond appropriately.

It is centering or anchoring because you are fully feeling the moment with your senses, as opposed to experiencing the moment by screening it with your thoughts and mind. You are in better control for many reasons, the most obvious of which is that you are clearly discerning situations, people, and things—and you know you are. When we use Tunnel Vision and insist that the moment *must be* or *is* one way or another, we feel deep within ourselves that we have less control. We feel more vulnerable. That's because either we know we are not accurately discerning the moment or we have butted up against our mistaken ways of interpreting things in the past.

Later we'll move from the details of Perspective and their immediate benefits to the longer-term benefits of Perspective on your personality and ways of being in the world. Even seeing its immediate benefits, you can see that Perspective is the very definition of mental health. It's the aim of what human emotional and psychological development should be. It is a state of experience that is deeply fulfilling and liberating, which radiates happiness itself.

· · · · · · ·

My approach to the temporary problems of life is less about responding to rooted fear. I recognize and acknowledge Tunnel Vision thinking and have gained a broadened and expanding Perspective; a calmer sense of self prevails. I respond to the difficult moments in life with some space, with Perspective. I find that solutions appear with the lowered resistance and fear that I learned with the SatoriWest Method.

—Dee Dee

9

Shifting the Brain into Perspective

Because we took some time to explain Tunnel Vision by delving into the survival wiring mechanisms that create it, we'll also present a brain model that shows how Perspective is created. We'll begin to answer the question "How *do* we shift into Perspective?"

Perspective comes from what the SatoriWest Method calls "BrainShifting." In this chapter, we'll describe BrainShifting in more abstract terms. In Chapter 14 we'll lead you through a few BrainShifting exercises more methodically.

Spiritual master Tony Parsons calls what I consider BrainShifting "as easy and natural as breathing." In general, BrainShifting is a shifting of attention, like the adjustment of a camera lens. When you adjust a camera lens, you switch foreground and background. In the brain, the foreground is normally focused on all the individual elements of your experience that allow you to accomplish goals, such as objects, thinking, and sense of self. This way of focusing attention on identified objects and events is the mechanism that creates Tunnel Vision. Yet as we develop our brain, we don't need to exclusively focus our attention, because we can use a higher, inclusive way to accomplish tasks. In the background of our brains is the ineffable knowing that we are alive.

BrainShifting on purpose is usually, but not always, a gradual process—a switching of foreground to background, and vice versa. It's learned as a series of skills. It can also happen to your brain on its own indirectly, where your brain shifts automatically through total wellness and by being traumatized. We will explore these two aspects of BrainShifting in Parts IV and V.

The diagram gives an overview of the SatoriWest Method. It shows the ways you can shift your brain so that extraordinary Perspective is revealed. It presents a map of how Tunnel Vision becomes Perspective, involving wellness. It can also be looked at as a diagram of the components of the SatoriWest journey, i.e., to recognize Tunnel Vision and Perspective whenever you can, practice direct BrainShifting—practice wellness. We left crisis and trauma off this particular diagram.

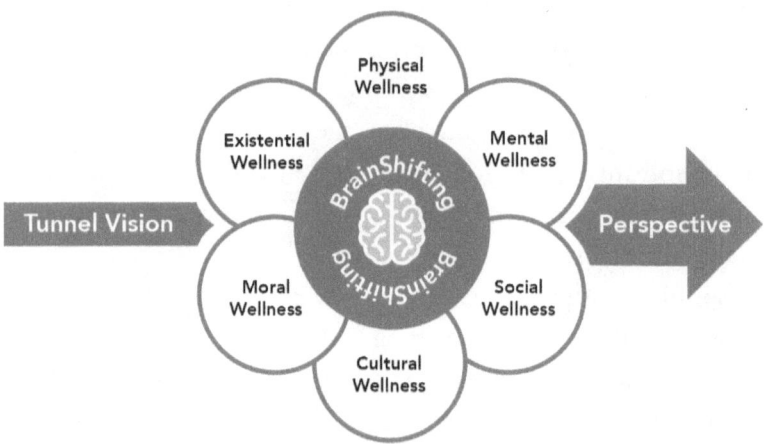

Figure 2: *The SatoriWest Method*

BrainShifting into Perspective

We've artificially divided BrainShifting into several parts. There is, however, one basic shift that happens in your brain. It amounts to perceiving a greater internal sense of being alive while experiencing a widening and detaching awareness from everything else.

> **Thought Exercise**
>
> Imagine walking up to a viewpoint that looks out over a beautiful mountain range. In one scenario, you try to capture the moment, telling yourself how beautiful and memorable it is, describing the scene to yourself, breaking it down into words, or thinking how you wish someone else were there to see it. In the other scenario, the visual scene, the scent of the air, the emotions of the moment, the sensations of your body, all are allowed to *come to you* while you focus in on the feeling of being alive in that unique moment. The first scenario was Tunnel Vision. The second was an experience of the moment where BrainShifting allowed Perspective.

As far as the sense of being alive, remember, your brain already knows it alive. It's in the back of your experience. Yet it's a realization you can call on at any time. And there are ways to intensify that awareness. Here are a couple of thought exercises you may be able to relate to.

> **Thought Exercise**
>
> When you woke up on the morning of any of your birthdays, or on a particularly important birthday, did you have a slight rush of energy at the magnitude of that day? Can you see that as feeling more alive? You might have noticed this feeling of energy. Perhaps you experienced the feeling of greater importance of each moment, maybe even how that came from a deeper place inside you. At whatever moment you

> had the strongest sense of that energy, of the significance of that day, did you notice that you paid attention to that feeling more than whatever you happened to be looking at or hearing in that moment? Or at least that it made everything seem more vibrant and clear?
>
> Or think of any singularly important moment in your life, perhaps your wedding or the birth of your first child. You may remember feeling a greater sense of aliveness that was not necessarily there on the so-called "ordinary" days. (Ordinary was put in quotes because with wide Perspective you are aware of the extraordinariness of every day of your life.) These moments might have an energy, like being excited about something. This internal sense of aliveness is, in many ways, separate from *what* is happening.

Author's note: An example of having both comes to mind when I think about a typical moment at my job. As of this writing, I am the chief medical officer of a hospital as well as a psychiatrist who sees patients there. I am very busy. My inner clock is always running (a time focus ripe for creating Tunnel Vision). There are many things being asked of me at any one moment. Unfortunately, I allow myself to live in a degree of Tunnel Vision in that position—trying to please others, show up on time to meetings, complete administrative tasks, help the many staff I supervise, and win approval for doing a good job. Most of which I often do in Tunnel Vision, the cause of stress.

Yet when speaking to a patient who is struggling, my priorities shift. Perspective is allowed to emerge. My heart opens. My sacred and ethical responsibilities to my patients are clearer to me. Even if I am acutely aware that I may be paged or that I have a meeting soon, I will listen to any patient I think needs more time than I have allotted until I feel that they have been sufficiently helped. That is Perspective happening alongside—perhaps even overshadowing—Tunnel Vision. Moreover, there are many moments when I feel a great appreciation for my job and the fact that the SatoriWest Method is being implemented there and helping so many people. Those moments are more purely Perspective.

Exercise

See if you can mimic the sensations of those important moments in your life. Relax your body and allow an excited energy to flow into your head behind your eyes. Of course, that sense of being freshly alive is more than energy; that energy goes along with a feeling of what it means to be alive at that moment. What you just did, without even trying very hard, was to BrainShift a bit. If you take up a daily ritual of BrainShifting, which you will learn in Part III, it will come to you, probably when you least expect it.

The second facet of BrainShifting is the opposite of the main survival brain mechanism of Tunnel Vision. It's the opposite of having attention pulled into things. It's the widening of awareness. This is the facet of Perspective that is easier to experience right away. It is the experience of one thing or a group of things that catch your attention *and* anything else unrelated to it, usually mundane things, like the sensation of parts of your body you aren't usually aware of.

Widening awareness is really that simple. What may be confusing is that normally, whenever we are aware of anything, our mind attaches words to the experience to capture the moment. Words and concepts meld various things into one "thing." For example, if you are looking at a table and a chair in a living room, your mind may be focused on the "table" or the "chair," but not on both. Or, if you are more directly focused on both of them, then you're not focused on the sense of the room. Yet after applying the word and concept "room," you might expand your awareness to the experience of the "house." Words coalesce what you pay attention to, limiting what you notice to the boundaries created by the concept in your mind. That creates Tunnel Vision.

When our minds try to capture our experience by labeling it, it seemingly makes it easier to focus attention in each moment. Yet labeling with words *limits* our awareness to one identifiable concept at a time, no matter how small or wide that word or concept may be, such as "a bug," "a mountain range," "the universe." The Tunnel Vision created by this limited kind of attention distorts the mind. That's the glitch in our survival programming.

This may seem counterintuitive. It seems like being able to focus attention is a good thing. Yet being more generally aware of the moment—while, if need be, also being more aware of one aspect of the moment in general—is a more advanced way of experiencing. For example, if while doing homework you can be aware of your level of tiredness, and maybe even the sounds around you, and maybe even the sense of the importance of this moment in your life, you might do better with the homework.

Parents might argue with this point, as they believe their teens are not able to concentrate when listening to the radio. However, multitasking may decrease your performance if there are multiple kinds of Tunnel Vision going on. Yet that is not the same phenomenon as perceiving with Perspective. With Perspective, you may be intensely aware and even concentrating your awareness in one direction, but not exclusively on one "thing." For example, what is in your mind and imagination, what is in your sensory field, what is going on in your body. It's an inclusive, as opposed to exclusive, way of perceiving things.

Tunnel Vision seems so natural, though. That's because language and concepts are so easily used to define our experience. Yet again, by allowing our words (our thoughts) to dictate what we are aware of, we limit our experience to one thing at a time. *Remember, our brain is capable of taking in many things at the same time.* In fact, it is taking in a huge amount of information every moment; we're just not aware of it because we're in Tunnel Vision.

It feels less natural, but not difficult, to allow our awareness to take in more than one "thing." Again, that awareness can involve whatever is inside us, around us, in one or more of our senses, in our thoughts, even the sense of ourselves. We do this by relaxing our brain to the extent that it loosens itself from an *exclusive* focus on singling things out and opens to an *inclusive* kind of awareness. It's a process of more and more widening.

For instance, with Perspective, using the example of the chair again, we see the "chair," but can widen our awareness to see the "chair" in the context of the "room" it is in. If we then focus too much on seeing "a room," we could also experience the sense of being in the room in a "house." If we get stuck in experiencing the "house," we could also be aware of the sensation of our toes while in the house.

It's a loosening, a widening, a relaxing of awareness. Again, attention switches from being exclusive to being inclusive. You can still direct awareness toward a few things at a time—for example, to the room and house we were talking about before. It's just that when your brain is BrainShifted, it takes in more than what is called for.

Eventually, labeling experience—which is the main reason to pay exclusive attention to a single thing—becomes unnecessary. *We don't need to label to be able to experience a moment.* When that level of Perspective happens, we are in the moment as it is, just as it is. The opposite is going into Tunnel Vision. That's where, besides separating out individual parts of experience, we are triggered to try to grasp the object, own it, change it, believe it, take it personally, hold on to it forever, or get rid of it.

Here's another common example of the widening aspect of BrainShifting. You probably experience it when you watch a movie. When our awareness is widened, it keeps us from getting completely lost in the plot. We could be somewhat immersed in the story, but we might also notice it as cinematographic art, even as light moving on a screen. Now, I realize some will say that watching a movie being BrainShifted, with Perspective, could ruin the fun facets of Tunnel Vision. Possibly. However, many people can immerse themselves in a movie while also noticing its contextual aspects, such as the quality of acting and directing. Our attention would be wider than just on the plot being played out in our minds.

I know what some of you might be thinking right now: "But it's so much fun to be in Tunnel Vision during a movie where you get lost in the action, where you almost completely believe that what you are seeing is real." The answer is that with Perspective, with a modicum of BrainShifting, you might find yourself enjoying more than one dimension of the movie—as an actor's art form, as a directorial accomplishment, as a cinematographer's experience—and less as a way for your ego to pretend it's someone or somewhere else. Yet as we'll repeat in this book, it's totally fine to let yourself get swallowed in Tunnel Vision by being absorbed in the plot of a movie or story, as long as you know how to come out of it if the plot or the images become frightening or distasteful to you.

So far, we have discussed two brain mechanisms of BrainShifting: the enhanced sense of aliveness and widened awareness. The last brain mechanism of Perspective we'll discuss is really not different from widening awareness. That is because it happens at the same time we widen awareness. It's *detachment*. The word "detachment" does *not* mean to *not* be aware of something. For now, it is easiest to think of detachment simply as objectivity, like stepping back. Seeing things intensely, but dispassionately, from a bit of distance. When it comes to our ego, detachment means not taking a situation personally. Being de-identified.

There are many ways to experience detachment. We would experience detachment from our child or spouse if we really wanted to see them for who and what they are, and not what we want or believe them to be. By seeing them more completely at that moment—without the Tunnel Vision of taking them personally—we can react with wisdom, compassion, objectivity, and maturity. The same holds for seeing any place, thing, or person for what they are.

Detachment is having the awareness of a scientist who is objective, open, and curious. But that doesn't mean you are stoic and unfeeling: detachment often gives you greater appreciation for what you are witnessing. You can also witness your own negative reactions and feelings about situations from a place of objectivity. This is important to know, because witnessing your own depression or mental health symptoms with detachment would keep you from making them worse. You would see your illness as a brain condition and stop personalizing it.

Detachment is also a way to experience our own movement. For example, we would be detached if we watched our fingers automatically button a shirt. Or when we typed on a keyboard or played a piano without being aware of or trying to micromanage what our fingers were doing. Our brain can step back and experience things from a still, inner reference point; it is witnessing from an objective inner place. That's how we experience flow or spontaneity.

Here's another way to relate to detachment. Imagine someone is looking at you with disgust, then calling your name, almost yelling, and telling you that you are a horrible person. To detach from them means to see them for who they are. Rather than get hooked into Tunnel Vision—focusing on them exclusively, carving them out of everything else in your experience, and taking them personally and getting angry—detaching means that instead of taking them personally, you see them for who they are: someone directing anger at you.

As we said, detachment takes some widening of awareness, and vice versa. To detach, it helps to see that "thing" (person, place, object, event, thought) as part of the whole moment.

The thing to look for when your brain shifts to Perspective—when you more fully realize you are alive, and when your awareness is more widened and detached—is a certain amount of change in your bodily energy. Remember, we spoke about that energy when we mentioned your birthday or some other significant life event. There's an ever-so-subtle or very noticeable surge of alertness and energy as well as a relaxation of mind and body.

Sure, when someone is upset or angry, they feel a surge of energy, but it's not the same kind of energy as when you have Perspective. Perspective brings a calm, heady kind of energy—like when we're feeling peacefully happy and carefree, but not giddy or wildly euphoric. It's the same energy as when we looked out over the scenic mountain range and felt more alive. The feeling is pretty common. It happens when we're having a really good day, maybe feeling good physically, rested, and healthy, feeling a settled maturity, centered, and good about yourself—not because someone complimented you, or you won something, or you are doing something special, but because you're just feeling good inside. There's nothing in particular stressing you out.

Intentionally BrainShifting can get you to that place of widened and detached awareness, where you experience more explicitly being alive, regardless of what is happening in your life. Practicing wellness within all the spheres of wellness can also get you to that place. And being in that place, you feel energized, alive, relaxed, and deeply content. Again, it happens when your brain is in touch with the reality of being alive while having a widened and detached experience of the moment.

Now that we recognize these three basic mechanisms of BrainShifting, let's continue to explore the longer-term benefits of Perspective.

. . . .

The Satori West Method shows how one can transform their way of thinking, in opening up the world to a much bigger place. It has opened my awareness to the shallow way of thinking I have been doing for many years. I am looking forward to practicing these skills to open up my world and become much more adaptable when things don't go quite as planned.

—Daren

10

Perspective and Personality

Perspective uses your brain to its fullest capacity. That's why it leads to amazing experiences that have been written about for generations. The epitome of Perspective offers an intense experience of being alive, so that the moment takes on new meaning. Nothing is taken for granted, and the value of your life can be seen as inestimable, beyond words. People who have been able to achieve great Perspective have described themselves as bursting with gratitude and joy. They describe it as life altering.

But do we need a great amount of Perspective to be happy? Judge that for yourself. Is it enough to feel centered and able to effectively express your feelings when other people seem to lose self-control in difficult situations? Is it enough to feel slightly more appreciative than critical in any given moment?

Since Perspective comes with some degree of widened and detached awareness, it gives you the ability to see multiple sides of an issue at the same time. Is it enough to be someone who can see more than one side of an issue? What is the value of fostering Perspective in yourself so you can see more than one side of people? For instance, instead of a teen seeing their parent as just "good" or "bad" in any one moment. Instead of seeing a parent seeing their teen as "mature" or "immature," they can see both aspects.

Even a moderate degree of Perspective is life altering if your life was heading in the wrong direction. A reasonable degree of

Perspective can help you see the context in a difficult situation. For example, when facing a grim financial decision, instead of personalizing it and adding that stress to the moment, you're able to discern why it is happening, experience your emotional reaction and intuition as information, and then make an objective decision about what to do. One of the benefits of Perspective is increased wisdom and good judgment.

Perspective does expand into levels of experience that are known as "spiritual." These so-called ecstatic or spiritual states are, according to the SatoriWest Method, part of a direct progression of Perspective to its highest levels, a progression that really has no end. Unless you run into a degree of crisis and trauma that provoke it, evolving yourself in that direction involves a regular practice of learning to BrainShift and taking care of your wellness. If an extraordinary degree of Perspective were to happen, that would be great, yet even modest amounts of Perspective are healing.

In fact, in Buddhism, to just stop suffering is considered the definition of Awakening. It's a relief to stop torturing yourself with Tunnel Vision ways of experiencing. For example, ego inflation comes with feeling alienation and separation from others, even from the world. Perspective allows you to stop being angry and disappointed by people so that you can feel more connected with them. It gives you the feeling of belonging, like you are a member of a close-knit tribe. That may progress to feeling part of the human race.

Tunnel Vision's egocentric distortions of your belief system have been proven to be self-destructive and cause misery. Even a small amount of rationality in the face of those distortions would be a lift. Small achievements at Perspective are nothing to discount. Anything that brings respite from the worst facets of Tunnel Vision can be enormously valuable.

Facets of Perspective on Personality

Remember how we said that Tunnel Vision can affect your temperament in any one situation, but that it can also cause a chain reaction in a way that could shape your personality? It's the same for Perspective.

Perspective is about more than temporary ways of experiencing and acting. It is a way of being. It determines who we are and whether we will ever be the best version of ourselves that we can be. Keep in mind that Perspective is not a recipe for a cookie-cutter personality. There are some commonalities that we'll address here. However, as you'll see, Perspective makes you more individual, more authentic, more immersed in and responsive to the uniqueness of each moment. It's the opposite of Tunnel Vision, where it is easier to see personality types and disorders.

To more easily digest the personality attributes we would have if we more fully integrated Perspective into our lives, we'll separate them into 15 key attributes discussed below. Keep in mind, they all overlap, some quite a bit.

15 Lasting Attributes of Perspective

Insight

The widened and detached awareness of Perspective gives us insight, which is the ability to understand a situation or moment objectively without personal biases getting in the way. Here's an example of insight. Say you were a visitor at a workplace and sitting in on a meeting. If before the meeting started no one was talking to each other, and you accurately got the impression that people were unhappy with their jobs because the company's culture was regressive, that would be insight. You might even infer that the employees' dissatisfaction is related to their not feeling valued. I realize this example may seem like a stretch, but some people have that much sensitivity, that much Perspective.

Really insightful people can pick up a lot of information with widened and detached awareness that reads their gut reaction as much as what is happening around them.

Wisdom

Wisdom is the facet of Perspective that uses insight in the service of reaching the greater good for ourselves and others. Wisdom helps us understand the root of issues so that we can do what lifts us and others toward greater and greater Perspective.

Having insight, but not using that knowledge to do what is beneficial for everyone, is not wisdom. In the example from the previous attribute, we would be showing wisdom if we somehow tried to contribute to a healthier workplace culture, whether or not it immediately benefited us to do so.

Maturity

The maturity part of Perspective can be thought of as being less reactionary, more stable, and less judgmental. Although being less judgmental necessarily means that it takes more to get us angry, with the exception of righteous indignation, a mature person will take action if necessary to protect himself or others.

To clarify, being reactionary means being impulsive, reacting without a wider comprehension of what the moment requires, reacting from Tunnel Vision. On the other hand, maturity means (rapidly or slowly) assessing the situation inside and outside yourself, and then taking wise, decisive action.

Maturity clearly runs alongside the insight and wisdom of Perspective. Along with many other facets of Perspective, it has a good deal to do with morality. In a disaster situation like an earthquake, where other people are reacting from emotion (probably to their ultimate detriment), a mature person is able to control what they pay attention to. This is because of widened awareness and detachment. Using the insight and wisdom that arises to understand the nature of the earthquake as well as the psychology of the people around them, they can determine a good outcome for all involved. People tend to gravitate toward people with mature Perspective for leadership.

Judgment

Some attributes of Perspective overlap quite a lot. That is the case for judgment, as it is similar to maturity. Judgment, a term psychiatrists are called on to determine in every patient we treat, has more to do with the mechanics of decision making. It is the ability to use widened awareness to methodically or quickly think through a course of reasonable action before initiating it. For example, someone with good judgment who can assess risk may parachute from an airplane but not run toward the edge of a mountaintop. Again, this may involve raw intelligence, but that intelligence would be useless without the widened and detached awareness that allows intelligence to be used toward good judgment.

Objectivity

Objectivity is the direct effect of detached awareness, allowing us to experience ourselves and situations with some distance. With objectivity, to whatever extent we have it, there is very little "ego" at stake in life. We take almost nothing personally—neither perceived insults nor attempted compliments nor situations that actually have nothing to do with us but in which we might otherwise mistakenly insert ourselves. Someone with objectivity who was fired from a job or failed at a business would not take that experience personally, but rather as an opportunity for learning.

Empathy and Compassion

Objectivity allows for empathy. Putting ourselves aside when listening to or watching someone enables us to put ourselves in their place, to see life through their eyes. That almost always generates compassion for that person. Connecting with someone's humanity almost always allows us to not hate them, regardless of how they behave. Sure, you may hate their behavior, but you wouldn't hate them. Here's an example. Say your spouse or partner was yelling at you. While witnessing them with widened and detached awareness, generating great Perspective, you might hear their words—perhaps some are valid, perhaps some are not—but you also feel their anger, using the understanding of insight and restraint of wisdom, and see the pain that lies at the core of their outburst.

Love

The brain, not the heart, is the seat of love. When awareness widens and detaches that allows the brain to experience all of itself in a new way, and not just in limited parts—that's Tunnel Vision. As Perspective dawns, a feeling of love emerges. This so-called "heart-mind" connection that happens when Perspective opens up has been written about for thousands of years. It has to do with the feeling of empathy and compassion for ourselves and others. It also has to do with being unblocked from self-interest so that we experience people, places, times, and things as amazing, with such gratitude that we feel an upwelling of love for them, for the incredible uniqueness they bring to the world.

Let's continue with the example of your spouse or partner berating you. If you see beyond the adult attacking you personally, perhaps you can better see the hurt child inside them acting out their pain. That may cause an outpouring of compassion for them. If, with this heightened degree of empathy, you can reconcile your relationship, that's great. Your relationship will be stronger for that. If reconciliation is not possible—perhaps it is too toxic at this point, and change is not going to happen—at least you draw that conclusion out of insight, wisdom, and maturity instead of resentment.

Of course, with Perspective comes a great capacity to better feel and accept people's praise, approval, or love. Although I am not dedicating much time to this facet of love, the importance of happiness and soaking in love that is being directed toward us cannot be underestimated. Tunnel Vision blocks people from feeling and acknowledging love. Perspective heightens it. Combined with the unity experience of Perspective—basically, the feeling of belonging and connection—this is part of what gives Perspective the reputation for inducing bliss.

Spontaneity

Perspective is not just a way of experiencing, but also a way of acting—an unself-conscious flow of movement, thought, and emotional expression. It comes from widening and detaching our awareness to the point that it includes a sense of ourselves. What happens next is that our brain is liberated from having to act from conscious thought and sense of self. Actions then flow from a deeper part of ourselves, from an unconscious center that integrates information quickly and more creatively than our conscious mind can.

Not acting from conscious thought may seem like a bizarre idea or something extreme, unlike anything you have ever experienced. Not so. It is far from weird or unusual. Here's what I mean. Imagine you had to walk along a high ledge that is five inches wide. Try it and see. To do it well, you'd have to trust your body to take over. *You can't think your way into balance.* Your brain would need to wake up and be present. It would step up its energy and concentration. To allow your legs to walk without looking at them and without overly instructing yourself, your brain would also need to widen and detach its awareness so that it is more aware of its body, mind, and surroundings. Widened awareness can include thoughts and anxious feelings. However, to maintain your balance, they must be included equally in the totality of awareness so they don't control you.

Author's note: Here's a personal example of the spontaneity that comes with Perspective. Years ago I was doing something unusual for me: playing a video driving game. I was trying to do laps around the virtual track as fast as I could. I was frustrated because I couldn't keep the car on the track. It kept crashing. I realized I had Tunnel Vision in how I approached the game. I was overthinking the driving and getting frustrated with myself for not improving, so I decided to try what I now call BrainShifting.

I opened and detached my awareness. I allowed the entirety of the experience—the screen, my hands on the wheel, my feet pushing on the pedal, my thoughts and sense of self—all to come into view as a totality, the best I could. That's when I noticed a pronounced shift. My hands, feet, and eyes seemed to take over. Indirectly observing the car on the screen so my focus wasn't locked on it alone, giving myself a bit of distance, my brain seemed to drive the car, smoothly pursuing the road, anticipating curves without thought or hindrance. It felt liberating! The car was lapping the road without careening off. My score was shooting up. You could say it was a change of Perspective on how to drive on a video game. It was more than a way of experiencing; it was a way of moving. Of course, at that point, I wanted to see how high my score could go. I began to focus on the score and the car, and Tunnel Vision set back in; of course, my driving ability worsened again.

This "open state" is what Eastern martial artists try to attain. Stepping back and being aware of their surroundings and inner experience, heightening their awareness of possible surprise attackers or sneak attacks, allows their body to respond spontaneously, free of anxiety or excitement.

Authenticity

Being authentic overlaps with spontaneity, free-flowing movement, thought, and emotional expression. It reveals who we are, our personality. Authenticity—born of being BrainShifted into Perspective—entails being our true selves without the veneer of social conformity. There is an element of being socially fearless. Keep in mind that Perspective makes us more loving and moral, so we're not fearless because we don't care about other people; we just don't care whether they approve of us.

Most of us who live in a more ego-controlled and self-conscious Tunnel Vision cannot see that we act in ways we believe are "normal" but are really stilted and inauthentic. We are inhibited from being ourselves for many reasons that have to do with Tunnel Vision's effect on our ego—making us careful about not fitting in, not looking abnormal, weird, childish, or vulnerable to judgment. That typical level of Tunnel Vision control is invisible, yet it takes a toll on joy and peace.

With true Perspective, being deeply BrainShifted, we can come to the liberation of self-expression. This may mean expressing anger, sadness, and fear as well as love; however, whatever emotion is felt is expressed within a context of wide awareness. That awareness, remember, lends itself to wisdom and judgment, insight, empathy, and compassion, so anger might look more like assertiveness and vociferous honesty than aggression, or a single self-releasing scream; sadness, for instance, could manifest as a "good releasing cry."

A Sense of Irony and Humor

Have you ever laughed at yourself? Maybe at an innocent mistake you made that struck you as funny? Have you ever remarked on how ironic someone else's behavior was, maybe because they said or did something that was hypocritical? It is Perspective that allows us to appreciate these things. Whether we know it or not, it comes from expanding and detaching our awareness beyond our normal sense of self so that we don't take ourselves or anything else so seriously that it stresses us out. That's how we are able to laugh at ourselves and maybe even certain kinds of adversity with a sense of good-naturedness—to be amused with our own foibles, to deflate our stifling egos with self-deprecating humor, to laugh at all! We need Perspective for that. The ability to laugh without being cruel or mean-spirited—like many of the other parts of Perspective, like love, gratitude, and amazement—is what gives spiritual Awakening (i.e., extreme Perspective) its reputation for bliss.

Creativity and Seeing Novelty

Liberated from its reliance on conscious, thought-based control, the brain is free to be not only spontaneous and authentic but more creative. That's because creativity happens below the level of awareness. Given the right circumstances, it emerges. Highly creative people often say their moments of peak creativity occurred when they were not trying to be creative. In other words, when the ego falls to the background, creativity emerges.

This spontaneous creativity doesn't just happen to artists; renowned scientists describe mulling over a complex issue, only to have the solution come to them in a moment of unexpected insight. Perspective allows insight to dawn more readily.

Perspective also means that our brain is allowed to open to each moment with fresh eyes. Where Tunnel Vision is a means of fitting each experience into the lens of a past experience, Perspective allows the brain to notice things about each moment that may be different, new, relevant, or interesting, and possibly fascinating.

Author's note: Once, when visiting New York City for a conference, I was walking to my hotel when it started to pour down rain. After a minute of getting drenched, I took cover under a storefront canopy.

It was late, I was tired, and I was frustrated that my clothes were wet and I couldn't get to my warm, dry hotel room. A couple of minutes standing there seemed like a long time (the time distortion of Tunnel Vision), and I was getting more frustrated, sad, and angry.

The suffering of that moment caused me to think about and start what I now call BrainShifting. (This is one of the benefits of suffering that is the premise of this book.) I widened my awareness and detached a bit. I relaxed a bit and let in more of the experience. Instantly I heard the rain on the canopy top as if it were a percussion concert. More than that, I saw neon lights reflected in the puddles of water around me like a psychedelic visual display. An oil slick on the surface of one of the puddles looked like a subtle but beautiful rainbow that was being broken by each raindrop into a magnificent kaleidoscope of colors. I was spellbound, amazed my brain could perceive such beauty. I felt much happier and relaxed. Although I was aware of being cold, it didn't bother me as much, as the chilly air on my face felt refreshing.

Intuition

Intuition is a gut sense, an unconscious integration of present thoughts and feelings with past experience. It emerges more clearly with Perspective. That's because mixing thoughts, feelings, memories, and momentary information requires more intensive and rapid processing than our brain can hold in our awareness. Focused awareness is too limited and, frankly, slow. There are millions of pieces of information in our memory and in each moment, too many to be processed consciously.

For instance, our intellect may tell us that someone is trustworthy. Maybe they fit all the normal criteria for a trustworthy person. For example, they are an older, majority-race woman (a little old lady). Perhaps they even tell us they are trustworthy. Yet with heightened Perspective, we can pick up subtle cues in their facial expression, pupillary dilation, slight movements, changes in voice inflection, and rate of breathing that only lie-detecting software could pick up. Our unconscious brains can often pick up on these cues; they can be processed with our emotions, even though Tunnel Vision would have us deny them. Perspective allows these subtle signals to be brought into some level of awareness or spontaneous expression.

Gratitude

Gratitude is the core of Perspective, the epitome of being BrainShifted. (In the wellness chapter, under what we call "existential wellness," we'll purposely cause gratitude to emerge by doing gratitude exercises. It's the inside-out and outside-in aspect of the SatoriWest Method.) "Spiritual wellness" or "spirituality" are much more popular and recognized terms than "existential wellness," but the latter is preferred here because "existential" refers to insight into the meaning and significance of one's existence. Of course, it begs the question of what created us or anything else. But appreciation of existence at all is the core of what we think of as "spiritual" or even "religious." That meaning and significance has clearly been in the realm of spiritual and religious teachers, yet it is a fairly self-evident insight.

Gratitude is a central aspect of feeling euphoric. Of course, we can be grateful for many things, and ultimately for everything—good and so-called bad—but at its heart, it is a clear seeing into the magnitude of our existence!

Here's a review of how this usually works. When awareness widens and detaches, it can do so to the point that what we are aware of opens up in scope. That's when the contents of our consciousness—the things, the information—that fill up each moment fall to the background. As this happens, the new foreground of our experience opens up. In the new foreground is a sense of presence, the "here and now" you've likely heard about. The appreciation of being here, being alive, is always there—it's just previously been invisible, in the background of our typical experience. It's relegated there by Tunnel Vision grabbing most if not all of our attention. Once Tunnel Vision is relaxed, it allows the fuller magnitude of our existence to come to the foreground. It brings the fuller reality of being here, now, into focus.

Thought Exercise

Let's try to get a better sense of what it means that you got to be here right now. We'll do that by exploring a bit of the science behind the miracle of your existence.

First, the universe had to come into existence. No one said that the Big Bang that birthed the universe *had* to happen. Then, after eons of explosions forming increasingly complex atoms, stars and planets came into being. Then this perfect planet formed with oceans of a scarce molecule, water, the right mix of organic chemicals, all just the perfect distance from its star for liquid water to exist. Then those chemicals mysteriously joined to form complex molecules that not only carry the blueprint to build cells, organs, and bodies, but are also capable of replicating themselves.

Chemicals that "know" how to re-create themselves are astonishing. If that were not inconceivable enough, those molecules evolved by way of trillions of accidents to such complexity that the human body and brain, with its awareness and intelligence, came into existence. When contemplated, this expands the mind well beyond the ordinary.

Then all of your ancestors had to meet, and out of all the people in the world who've ever existed, your parents had to meet. If all of that weren't unlikely enough, that one sperm out of millions had to hit that one egg out of hundreds, and you were born. And here you are, right now.

Your birth defied astronomical odds. It defies logic. It is like the odds of randomly picking one specific grain of sand from all the beaches in the world. The fact that you are alive, as a human, can be described as a miracle. You won a cosmic lottery.

The outcome of this astonishing fact is that this moment of your existence, of your life—right now—is precious beyond words and will never happen again. If you truly comprehended that simple fact, you would be lifted closer to the very height of Perspective. You would have a feeling of euphoria, a humbling appreciation and devotion to whomever or whatever you believed made this possible, and an intense gratitude for your existence.

The Experience of Belonging

The essence of Tunnel Vision is that it causes people to feel cut off from others and from the world around them—the universe, really. This is a manifestation of their egos taking prominence in their experience of the moment. This leads to people feeling alienated. The core sense of "I'm on my own. No one can really relate to me. I'll die alone." This happens even if they have close relationships. In its other manifestation it causes them to feel different from other people, which is one of the reasons why we feel insecure and troubled. It leads us to worry that we'll be rejected or ridiculed, which is the result of an even greater ego influence on our experience.

Perspective is the experience of connection, of unity. It helps us feel a sense of belonging to people in our lives and to society in general. It is a feeling of love and affiliation. So many individuals and families feel alienated and lonely that this facet of Perspective is valuable beyond words.

However, more than that, Perspective gets very, very wide—to the point that it is possible to experience being part of everything, not just with people, but with the environment, even the universe. This so-called non-dual experience is a fairly advanced state of Perspective. In it, the world is experienced from a silent, still, empty reference point, where there is no tangible sense of self, so that there is no separation between "me" and the rest of the world. Again, this is an advanced brain development that we are not necessarily shooting for in this book.

A Happier, Peaceful Disposition

Taken together, all the attributes mentioned for Perspective make us more joyful people, deeply at peace and fulfilled in life. Again, it often gives us those positive emotions. And Perspective also allows us to be fully expressive of so-called "negative" feelings, such as anger, fear, or sadness. Perspective allows for these emotions out of a sense of love, concern, context, and maturity.

Again, these 15 facets of Perspective are not separate. Like sides of a prism, they emphasize different angles. And like Perspective itself, there are degrees of each.

Because this question comes up for people learning the SatoriWest Method, it is important to point out again that the picture of Perspective painted above does give the impression that it is a one-size-fits-all, static state, where everyone acts and reacts the same way, where people are perfectly evolved all the time. That is not the case.

First of all, because of the survival wiring in our brain, we will always be drawn toward Tunnel Vision. With enough Perspective we can find creative ways—sometimes with humor, sometimes employing wisdom about ourselves—to unwind it. There are no superwomen and men. There are degrees of Tunnel Vision, there are degrees of Perspective, and there are countless moments throughout the day when one or the other predominates, from figuring out the answer to a crossword puzzle to a major revelation about one's life.

The balance between Tunnel Vision and Perspective can change in a moment, based on circumstances. We may have more Perspective at work than we do at home. We may be more spontaneous around certain people than others. We may be approval seeking around our parents and fearless about disapproval in public. We can be full of the mirth and irony of Perspective one minute, then doleful and sad the next because Tunnel Vision sets in. It can depend on how we're feeling physically in that moment if we're not mindful.

There are also specific Perspectives, like a creative idea. There are general ways to have Perspective, like someone who is good-natured. And we can have overall Perspective but get triggered into Tunnel Vision about certain things. For instance, we can be philosophical about life, but get anxious and driven into Tunnel Vision when it comes to money. That's because Perspective, like Tunnel Vision, can change second to second. We might have a moment of awareness and clarity of purpose in one situation—say, when telling ourselves that eating late at night is not good for us—but then get worn down when our spouse starts eating chocolate cake right in front of us.

Perspective does tend to chain and branch to higher levels when given the chance, just like Tunnel Vision does in the opposite direction. We might consider ourselves a good parent, taking little personally, taking things in stride, taking pride in being wise, loving, even-tempered, and even-handed, and then lose all that objectivity when our daughter starts dating a new boy. Don't be fooled into believing someone with wisdom and Perspective is going to be that way all the time in every situation.

People do, however, have traits of Perspective that are stable over time. As we said, moments of Perspective chain and branch, just like Tunnel Vision. Mature ways of dealing with one situation lead to more mature ways of dealing with other situations. Finding contentment in one difficult moment will lead to finding contentment in other hard situations. Finding seeds of appreciation during times of stress will lead to finding gratitude in other difficult moments. It's the same with being loving, authentic, and in good humor.

The greater the Perspective we have on the whole, the more our lives will feel meaningful, fulfilling, happy, and peaceful.

． ． ． ． ． ． ．

Perspective is getting to basically the end of a problem where you've really opened up your thinking and allowed other alternatives in your life. And for me that's really a fantastic place to be, that I'm not stuck in my life and I can look at a lot of other opportunities. I have never had a program that has shown me how to do this!

—Clara

PART IV
The SatoriWest Method

11

Overview of the SatoriWest Journey

How *do* you go from Tunnel Vision to Perspective? Is it done as we orient to each circumstance, each moment, or is there a general way to open to life overall? That's what the SatoriWest Method will address in this part of the journey. We must do both—notice our Tunnel Vision and the degree of Perspective we bring to each situation throughout each day while routinely practicing the SatoriWest Method as a lifestyle.

We've alluded to the overall approach throughout the book in discussing the skills of BrainShifting: feeling a sense of aliveness, widening our awareness, and experiencing detachment. We specifically mentioned one strategy for widening awareness by using an "and" technique. We also showed that these direct skills of BrainShifting are supplemented with indirect ways of causing BrainShifting by employing strategies from all six spheres of wellness.

Part IV of learning the SatoriWest approach is the how-to section. The previous parts have been more educational and theoretical in nature, although we've presented Thought Exercises throughout. Yet an intellectual understanding of the fact that you are caught up in the human condition, just like everyone else, is not enough to actualize that sense in order to lift you out of it. Knowing that your Tunnel Vision is ruining your happiness and hurting others and the environment is not enough to unwind it in difficult and challenging moments. Intellectually understanding that Perspective embodies everything you want in life but think you are searching for outside yourself is not enough to really embrace Perspective in moments of Tunnel Vision. You need to start building a daily and life practice.

This is arguably the most important goal you can have in your life. It is more important than making a name for yourself in the world, or getting rich, or finding an ideal relationship, or creating the perfect home life, or even having a mission to change the world. The evolution of your brain must come first, or at least parallel your own personal development, for anything else to be effective and not about your ego.

Just as you are not alone in experiencing the human condition, you are not alone on this journey. However you may label it—as a religious, secular, or psychological quest—there is a sea of humanity taking it with you. We all want to be happy and to feel like we are fulfilling the incredible gift of life that we embody. However, understanding that this is a brain evolution quest seems to be crucial. Knowing that the brain goes into Tunnel Vision can keep you from looking in the wrong direction for solutions. Knowing that Perspective resides with each of us does the same thing. Knowing that our brain, in all its complexity, needs care and maintenance is essential. Otherwise it's like taking an automobile across country without servicing it or even knowing it needs gas.

As you know, the SatoriWest Method is based on the time-honored Buddhist path, only clarified with a modern understanding of brain functioning and the behavioral sciences, all seamlessly integrated with wholistic wellness. We'll now dive into the mechanics of how it all works. Once again, the diagram presents the how-to aspects of the SatoriWest Method. It shows how Tunnel Vision, when exposed to the SatoriWest Method—the BrainShifting skills accelerated with six spheres of wellness—comes out as Perspective.

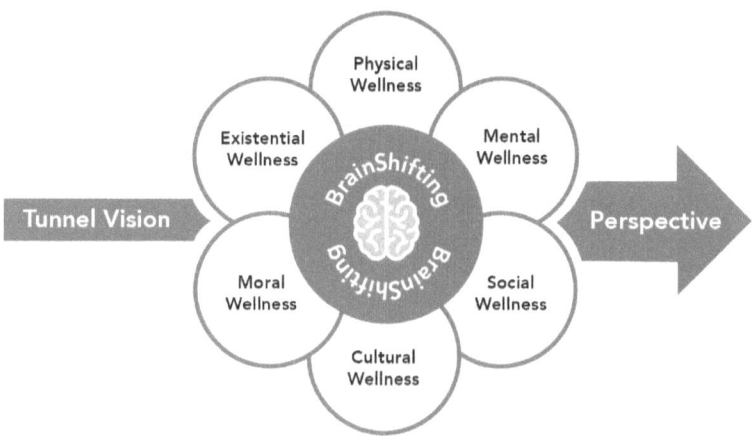

Figure 2. *The SatoriWest Method*

As you are now aware, the wheels of the SatoriWest Method need to be turned continuously over a lifetime. Tunnel Vision will become less and less tight, and Perspective will grow wider, greater, and more profound. And as you'll see in Part V, moments of trial and struggle can be springboards to propel you forward.

Because there are five points to the SatoriWest Method, it can be confusing to figure out what is responsible for the transition to Perspective. Understanding and getting familiar with the human condition with Tunnel Vision and with Perspective causes a shift in your brain. Both reading about them and doing the Thought Exercises shifts your brain. Merely knowing that crises and times of grief and trauma are opportunities prepares you for them and allows you to use them to gain even greater Perspective when they happen.

As far as what you can do daily to shift your brain, to BrainShift, there are four main avenues to this timeless SatoriWest journey. We'll summarize them here and delve into each.

Recognize Your Tunnel Vision

Recognizing your Tunnel Vision is the most important of the four ways of discovering the best life you can lead. In previous chapters we pointed out the "anatomy" of Tunnel Vision—the eight ways it manifests in your experience. They are 1) the extent to which attention is grabbed, compelled, or given over; 2) blocking your awareness of everything else; 3) lowering self-control; 4) making events and thoughts appear more believable; 5) causing your imagination to be more and more real than reality; 6) exaggerating your sense of self; 7) which distorts your thinking; and 8) distorts your sense of time. The flip side—which, paradoxically, is harder—is to also recognize Perspective when you have it.

Remember, recognizing Tunnel Vision is itself Perspective. It has an effect on your brain that strengthens the circuits that allow it to shift.

Practice the Skills of BrainShifting

BrainShifting is what your *brain* does to get Perspective—not *you*. In other words, you can try to have Perspective by doing something, usually thinking, but your brain has to change for the clarity of understanding and emotional changes of Perspective to emerge. This is an underappreciated point. Your *brain* must shift for you to have Perspective. *It* must change for you to see things differently. Sure, you can work to find infinite gratitude in each moment, for example. That's one of the existential wellness strategies that amounts to a passive or indirect way to BrainShift, a way to cause your brain to shift on its own. Yet whether you are using direct skills or allowing wellness to take over, your awareness must widen and detach, and you must be at least somewhat anchored in the present for you to realize anything.

BrainShifting is represented by the large inner circle in Figure 2.

BrainShifting can be accomplished on purpose, and when it does, it is identified as the "skills of BrainShifting." We previously presented three of its parts: widening, detaching awareness, and anchoring yourself in the aliveness of the moment. These three aspects all lead to each other, because there is really only one way that shift happens in the brain.

These three aspects of directly BrainShifting, of doing something to shift your brain, may seem removed from your normal experience. Here's an easy example to show that they're not so unusual. If you were listening to a symphony, you wouldn't strain to hear individual notes, you'd open your awareness and allow in the experience of the entire piece being played. You'd welcome it to wash over you. And to be able to appreciate the quality of the piece, you'd also detach a bit to grasp the artistry of the composer or the conductor or the musicians. Finally, to really enjoy it, to feel the significance of hearing it at this very moment, to realize how lucky you are to be hearing a symphony, you'd anchor in the present experience of it. It's the experience that says (even without the words), "I'm alive in this moment and appreciating the fact that I get to be here." Are these really three separate maneuvers? Of course not, although they can be separated out for ease of applying the skills to all your life experiences.

Whether you work on one or all of the skills at the same time is just a matter of what is easiest and most productive for you at the time in that situation. For example, a common and very useful way to BrainShift is when you find yourself in Tunnel Vision, after just recognizing the Tunnel Vision by itself is not enough to release its hold on your attention, is to use the "and" technique. That is, be aware of what is grabbing your attention, what you are preoccupied with or fixated on, *plus notice* some "thing" outside the Tunnel Vision you didn't notice before. Or notice some "thing" inside your Tunnel Vision but in a new way. (More to come on that.)

Practice Wholistic Life Wellness

In addition to happening on purpose, BrainShifting can happen on its own, when you're not trying to make it happen. We call that the indirect or outside-in approach. That's what the total wellness aspect of the SatoriWest Method does. It's represented by the six circles that surround the larger circle in the diagram. Think of it like six circles forcing air into the balloon-like inner circle, causing it to expand. Dozens of strategies and practices within the six spheres of wellness practically allow your brain to shift to its highest levels of development. More on this later as well.

Crisis as an Opportunity

This fourth avenue of practice, which is the fifth point of the SatoriWest approach to understand, is the heart of this book. We are all dealing with one or more crises at any one time in our lives, whether big or tiny. We are also managing the emotional, accumulated aftermath of a lifetime of crises. So this part has particular resonance if you are currently in the midst of a more serious crisis or hardship, such as a psychiatric condition.

The fifth point of the SatoriWest Method is that crises, though awful, show how they can have a silver lining. If allowed, they can transport your brain to the peak of its potential. Although even a modicum of Perspective, where you become a more rational and reasonable person, able to not take things as personally, could be all you need to have a more peaceful and content life. The highest degrees of Perspective of which your brain is capable, the levels where you feel the ecstasy of being alive, are wonderful to realize. They show you the full extent of your natural birthright of being born with a human brain. It's the peak of your own innate potential, it's the level of happiness and peace that on some level you realize you could be living. That's why it's been the "Holy Grail" of humanity for thousands of years. And although you may not seek them, crises have been a consistent means for people to realize these highest parts of themselves—aspects of themselves they either didn't know existed or that have been written about but are impossible to imagine.

As we'll explore, crises and hardships work in a few ways. First, severe Tunnel Vision is easier to see than less severe Tunnel Vision or even Perspective, maybe because it hurts so much. The tighter the Tunnel Vision, the more abnormal it is and the more apparent the aspects of its "anatomy" are. Seeing it is the premier way to release it, which is great if you have the centeredness to be able to see it.

The second way crises help us has to do with the fact that Tunnel Vision feeds on itself and can get unbearable. Yet as we said, because spirals of Tunnel Vision—from cultural to toxic to crisis—can become so earthshaking to our lives and our mistaken, ego-based habits of looking for relief and happiness, they can literally force us to surrender our egos. Then we can see them for what they are. That's the process of "bottoming out," so to speak—whether the floor of consequences is from drug and alcohol use or from our own toxic personalities.

Eventually the consequences of crisis levels of Tunnel Vision outweigh the rewards. It's as if we get shaken out of our stubborn patterns and habits of Tunnel Vision. The ego gets jolted out of its place of superiority in our minds. It can bring no relief, and we are forced to use other means to be happy. That's when extraordinary Perspective awaits us on the other side. Even though this is a process that happens on its own, we can be prepared for it just by knowing about it.

The third main way crises and hardships help us also happens on its own, and nothing can adequately prepare us for it. It's when emotional or physical pain becomes so severe that our brains literally, physiologically, shift themselves. We'll address this more in Part V, as it's not really a daily practice that we can use.

Let's drill more into the "how to" aspects of BrainShifting in the following chapters.

. . . .

Extremely impressed! My past eight years have evolved to chronic crisis events. The more I put into this program, the more I [received] back! Thank you so very much!

—Kimberly

12

Core Skills of BrainShifting: Notice Tunnel Vision and Split Attention

We mentioned that there are four avenues you can take on your SatoriWest journey from Tunnel Vision to Perspective: 1) noticing Tunnel Vision; 2) practicing the skills of BrainShifting daily and on the fly; 3) accelerating key areas of wellness from within the six spheres of wellness, so BrainShifting happens on its own; and 4) using crises and hardships as springboards to Perspective.

These four avenues to Perspective are not actually different; they're just different angles on the same process. In this chapter, we'll delve into the first two avenues of these SatoriWest strategies. Later we will explore the other paths.

SatoriWest Journey, Avenue One: Noticing Tunnel Vision

We described Tunnel Vision and its eight facets in Chapters 3 and 4. Tunnel Vision can be immediately rewarding and comforting in its familiarity, and so rob us of our awareness of it and our desire to do anything about it. To help us discern it in ourselves we labeled three degrees of Tunnel Vision—cultural, toxic, and crisis. Each of them comes with different challenges for recognizing and unwinding it.

The task in this chapter is to learn how to become a vigilant Tunnel Vision detective. To do that, we first need to review a few points.

Tips for Being a Tunnel Vision Detective

Being motivated to do it is the most important part of being an effective Tunnel Vision detective. Seeing your human condition in the waves of challenges and crises that you have faced so far in your life, and that you know you will face, should be impetus enough to make you want to search out the causes of your suffering and reverse them. Of course, the sadness, anxiety, and anger you faced in your life's trials could also be big motivators. You might also be inspired to search your mind for Tunnel Vision by the promise of great Perspective.

What's important is that you understand that the process of detecting Tunnel Vision doesn't have to feel tedious or burdensome. Think of it as occasionally checking in with yourself or being aware of it when you feel stressed and unhappy, and then relaxing a bit so your energy gets restored. That's what people use cigarettes for. BrainShifting is healthier, more effective in the long run, and won't kill you.

Whatever your motivation, bolster it by recognizing that expanding beyond Tunnel Vision is *the most important* task you can undertake in your life. Looking for happiness in any other way or in places outside yourself is a fool's errand. That kind of happiness is really pleasure that will be either fleeting or sabotaged by the Tunnel Vision it causes.

What is it that you do moment by moment to search for Tunnel Vision? In your work as a detective, you must look for clues about what around or within you may trigger Tunnel Vision, what is being expressed as the eight facets of Tunnel Vision, and what has occurred that might be an episode of Tunnel Vision.

To start, it may be helpful to identify whether the Tunnel Vision you're experiencing is cultural, toxic, or crisis. If you can get that far, you're well into unwinding the Tunnel Vision.

Knowing you are in cultural Tunnel Vision helps you recognize that its pulls on your attention and the reward for keeping it going are often promoted by society. When quick fulfillment and pleasure from others, food, sex, or the thought of an ideal time really get ahold of us, it can be stressful and even painful.

You can notice toxic Tunnel Vision when you find yourself believing your own opinion without being interested in evidence to the contrary. Or you defend your honor beyond all reason. Or your personality is entrenched to the point that it causes you discomfort, if not grief and suffering. Of course, crisis Tunnel Vision comes with such extreme effects on your mind that you can't miss it. If you've become a danger to yourself or others, or your health and safety are seriously impacted, it's likely from Tunnel Vision. These descriptions will help you become a better Tunnel Vision detective.

Whether you do it when you feel stressed or unhappy or decide to take scheduled breaks throughout the day to detect Tunnel Vision and BrainShift, it is also important to realize that Tunnel Vision doesn't travel alone most of the time. Tunnel Vision and Perspective work together at the same time—unless you are at the extremes of each. For example, you may be transfixed by and fantasizing about someone who is beautiful yet have enough Perspective to know it may be hurtful to the person, and ultimately yourself, to stare. Know that, see both, and you are strengthening the wisdom circuits in your brain.

Also guard against getting frustrated because you believe that whatever you do to BrainShift should be enough to give you relief from whatever stress or unhappiness you feel. Remember, reaching for a specific outcome that you imagine will happen is a form of Tunnel Vision. Perspective comes from being with the moment the way it is, with a widened and detached awareness, and anchored in the feeling of presence. Nothing needs to change, even frustration with the process. Change does come, but it's up to your brain, not all of which you consciously control.

Shifting your brain toward greater and greater degrees of Perspective is most often a gradual process. You notice it in small and big ways. If you happen to catch yourself being pigheaded about something, and know you are wrong, acknowledging it may seem small, but it is an important insight. Not trying to protect your ego by defending yourself against your mistake or denying it in public is another incremental step in the right direction. Delaying eating for emotional reasons, even if for a few seconds while you feel more about the moment, is an incremental shift of your brain. In essence, becoming a Tunnel Vision detective means becoming a self-therapist.

The nitty-gritty work of being a Tunnel Vision detective comes from noticing what is triggering your Tunnel Vision or, if you're looking back at it, what the reward for it was. Let's again look at the eight facets of Tunnel Vision to help you better notice them. Then we'll delve into some tips.

- *Attention:* Your attention is taken from you or freely surrendered.
- *Control:* Your ability to control your impulses is lessened.
- *Awareness:* Your ability to see things that are not directly related to your focus of attention is diminished.
- *Suggestibility:* You become easier to convince of the rightness of a thought, image, or idea.
- *Imagination:* You are pulled into your imagination, conflating it with reality.
- *Ego:* Your ego is inflated.
- *Thinking:* Your belief system gets warped toward irrationality, unreasonableness, and fantasy.
- *Time:* You experience time as if you are living in the past or the future.

Noticing Tunnel Vision When Attention Is Compelled or Freely Given Up

Your attention is grabbed because something extraordinary has captured it. For instance, a loud, unexpected noise in the house would automatically capture your attention. In and of itself, the fact that anything grabs your attention for a second is not going to create a serious episode of Tunnel Vision, although the better you get at noticing subtle manifestations of Tunnel Vision, the more powerful your detective skills become.

You'll be witnessing the pulls on your attention after the fact—unless you are choosing to freely hand over your exclusive attention. Ideally, it won't be too long after it happens, because you'll want to feel the energy of the attraction. You'll want to feel its pull so your brain can shift out of it or around it (widening and detaching, which we'll practice with later on). Let's break this down by things that grab your attention and things you freely give your attention to. Is there a story there that you are captivated to understand?

Noticing Tunnel Vision at Times When Your Attention Is Grabbed from You

It is not often that an unusual noise, sight, or bodily sensation grabs your attention. Maybe it's a bee buzzing by. You could simply notice how that happened a second after it grabbed your attention. You would notice how your attention became exclusive, meaning the bee focused your awareness and cut you off from anything else but the stimulus—in this case, its buzzing, the thought of being stung, and the fear around that.

If you are noticing getting pulled into the sensation of hunger that arises on its own or from the smell of food, this first part of your detective work entails feeling the amount and quality of drive you experience. How hungry is it making you? Where do you feel the hunger? How much of a "tractor beam" power does it have over your mind?

Noticing Tunnel Vision When Your Attention Is Freely Given Over

Examples of noticing Tunnel Vision when your attention is freely given over are fairly common. Advertising executives use this strategy when, for example, showing sexy young people in bathing suits on a beach for a soda commercial. This might cause you to give over more of your attention than usual. There are commercials that show a dinosaur walking a city street, a man sitting in the intersection of a busy city street with cars barely missing him, and other unusual circumstances, such as a car sitting on the bottom of a gigantic aquarium. Notice how commercials cause you to pay closer attention and focus in on these images to the exclusion of other things.

Other examples include rubbernecking as you drive by a car accident, seeing an attractive person in real life or on television, looking for attractive people in a crowd, and walking by a bakery and seeing cakes in the window. Notice how you give up your attention. The more you simply notice these incidents in the context of the moment—for instance, with awareness of where you are, what is happening around the incident, what is happening around you—the less your attention will be co-opted from you.

More common examples include your attention being captured by a list of goals that you must accomplish or by just desiring something. Perhaps you are preoccupied with taking a lunchtime break, trying to make a good impression on someone or everyone, or trying to avoid looking incompetent in front of someone whose respect you want to earn. That all comes from or causes Tunnel Vision, which is stressful and not as effective as being in Perspective.

Whatever it is that you are opting to focus exclusive attention on, notice the emotional drive to do that. If you are freely giving up your attention by watching two children tussle with each other, notice whether the story is attracting you because you are concerned for their safety or because you are just curious. See the power of whatever the draw is.

There is a special case of things that you freely give your attention to. You focus on them not because they are of interest for their own sake but because you don't want to be doing nothing. People don't want to experience the moment the way it is because they don't want to feel whatever negative emotions are lurking below the surface and could come up when they're doing nothing. That's when you freely give your attention over to fingering through your cell phone, playing games that aren't that interesting to you, or checking email that you don't need to check.

We know we carry hurt and emotional pain from our past and significant stress and emotional issues from the present. The last thing people with a lot of these feelings want to do is feel them, even though experiencing them fully, with Perspective, is the point of the SatoriWest Method. It's captured in the saying "The best way out is through."

Notice when you use your attention to scan the environment for something to do, something to freely give your attention to. Keeping busy is an effective way to temporarily avoid feelings. Notice if you are obsessively, even desperately, going from one focus to the next: watching TV, surfing the internet, talking on the phone, texting, exercising, cleaning, planning, eating for emotional reasons, or creating drama in your life. Of course, these activities in and of themselves are not the problem, although they will put us in Tunnel Vision.

Noticing Tunnel Vision in Your Loss of Control

As soon as you notice how your attention is grabbed or given over, you might notice how it robs you of some level of self-control. See if you can feel how much self-control you are compelled to give up.

We've previously given examples of this. The more you stare down or imagine a delicious dessert that you know you should not eat, the greater the likelihood that you are going to eat it. This also applies to people with a substance-use disorder who see or imagine a substance they know they should not use again but somehow manage to consistently and repeatedly use it. Feel the power of the urge over your impulses.

You might also notice this with triggers. For example, if someone is critical of you, it may trigger a defensive reaction, even if you know it is not a good idea to react defensively or in anger. Feel the desire to curse them out or even strike them, see its power, feel its force.

Noticing Tunnel Vision as Being Less Aware

How do you notice not being aware? This is a retrospective aspect of your detective work. It's no lighthearted issue, but if you are lost in thought walking down a street and then bump into a pole, that would be a sure sign. If your spouse rightly confronted you for how difficult you've been, and you've been that way for a while, that would be a learning opportunity to detect your Tunnel Vision.

Much of this is seeing how much your Tunnel Vision blocked out other things that you really wanted to pay attention to or should have paid attention to. Noticing how important these other things were to you is a measure of how much Tunnel Vision you were in.

Noticing Tunnel Vision in Being More Suggestible

We previously spoke about how a hypnotist can induce you to believe and feel like you are freezing in a warm room, at least in part by getting you to exclusively focus your attention. Of course, there are many ways to induce your attention. Television commercials are meant to grab your attention. Why? To get you to buy things. Notice this effect on you. It can be subtle or unconscious. However, like many of the facets of Tunnel Vision, it may be easier to see in the rearview mirror than around or within you at the moment.

Notice if objects that grab your attention, such as the image of a political leader, get you to believe their rhetoric without questioning it. They may be right. It's just that the Tunnel Vision they induce can steal your ability to reason for yourself. Or if someone is speaking disrespectfully to you, the judgment that they are "a jerk," or disturbed, or should be assaulted, may have greater resonance, be more believed, the more you focus on them. If that happens, see if you can notice any workings of Tunnel Vision.

However, the biggest problem with suggestibility is not so much about believing what you see and hear as it is about believing your own thoughts and opinions. Being convinced of your own rightness has a lot to do with ego. It is also what gives reality to distorted thinking. In essence, believing your own thoughts and opinions with absolute certainty comes from being so focused on your own ideas that they take a life of their own. They become self-validating. Be careful of this most insidious aspect of Tunnel Vision: it can be hard to see. Sure, you can call out with some degree of certainty, "This is the way it is," "He is that," "Life is this," while having enough distance from your own mind to know that the process is fallible. It's like adding the caveat to each of the declarations, "as far as I know right now." Question yourself with openness. Be like a scientist investigating your own mind, which is all the process of recognizing Tunnel Vision is anyway.

Noticing Tunnel Vision in Being Pulled into Your Imagination

Is being totally immersed in your imagination any different from being less aware of what is going on? No. Again, these facets of Tunnel Vision are artificially separate. They overlap and, in some instances, are the same thing. Therefore, believing your own thoughts would, by itself, cause you to be more in your imagination. In other words, if you are that certain of your beliefs and all the mental imagery that comes with them, you are, for all intents and purposes, existing in your mind more than in the changing new reality that each moment brings.

Author's note: I think of this facet of Tunnel Vision when I see my patients with psychosis on a psychiatric unit believe that nurses are poisoning their food or that everyone is colluding against them. They draw inferences where there are none. It's not so different from how we jump to conclusions at times.

Notice when you are lost in thought and mental imagery. For instance, think about being very anxious about something that might happen. An image of what might happen, if it grabs your attention, will cause you to live more in your imagination than in the reality of the moment. See how it grabbed your attention. See how it fed on itself, causing you to believe your own inner reality. Notice when you are pulled into your head or mind as much as you are experiencing the reality of the moment. This is not to say that your imagination is not part of the moment. It is. It's just that being pulled into it, or lost in it, to whatever extent, removes you from the reality of the moment. The next time you have strong feelings about something, notice how immersed in your imagination you are or were. Merely noticing how absorbed you are is a way to not be so wrapped up in your mind.

Noticing Tunnel Vision Driven by Ego

Everything we experience is experienced through the gravitational force of the ego. In this sense, the mind can be thought of as the same as ego. This is why I prefer to use the term "awareness" instead of "mindfulness." Being full of mind is Tunnel Vision. Being aware of mind (and anything else) is Perspective. Noticing our ego is a powerful way to notice our Tunnel Vision—and a powerful way to begin to find great Perspective.

Below are some ways that you can notice your ego in action and more fully recognize your Tunnel Vision when negative emotions are not enough or are not even present.

- Notice Tunnel Vision driven by ego when your relationship with events, objects, and people feels possessive. For example, imagine looking at an exceptionally beautiful sunset. If, instead of fully absorbing the visual and emotional experience of the moment, you find yourself wishing it would never end, or wanting to take a photo of it instead of directly experiencing it, you may be in Tunnel Vision.

You can easily see the possessiveness of your ego causing Tunnel Vision when it comes to personal relationships. If you've noticed yourself trying to control someone with whom you are in a relationship to feel more secure, you are caught up in Tunnel Vision. Sometimes this comes with jealousy, neediness, or fear of abandonment.

- Notice Tunnel Vision driven by ego when you are so competitive or obsessed with comparisons that you overlook what is of greater importance. For instance, notice when you are driven hard to attain something you don't necessarily need, such as a promotion, more possessions, or a better car. See how it serves mainly or only to make you feel better about yourself. That is a sign of ego effect from Tunnel Vision. If you are overlooking important relationships, such as with your children, significant other, family, or important friends, you are definitely stuck in Tunnel Vision.

- Notice Tunnel Vision driven by ego when you are so concerned with propriety, or with the opinion of others, that you can't relax and enjoy yourself. That's when you can't act naturally or express your feelings authentically. Do you obsessively shush family members from speaking louder than other people at fancy restaurants or hotels? Are you relaxed and yourself when in public or are you putting on airs, acting differently from how you normally would? You may also notice this when you feel stilted, stifled, and unexpressive.

Of course, the Perspective version of this does not include acting in ways that are inconsiderate, such as laughing loudly and making excessive noise when coming in late to a hotel. However, there are also limits to being considerate. It is ego based if you inhibit yourself so much to be considerate that you become stressed out.

- Notice Tunnel Vision driven by ego when you feel inferior to others. For example, imagine yourself in a social gathering with highly accomplished or wealthy people. Honestly, even those people can feel inadequate in social situations.

- Notice Tunnel Vision driven by ego when you feel superior to others. Even if you are, at heart, a humble or caring person, you can fall prey to this kind of Tunnel Vision. We all hold prejudices and preconceptions about people. Notice how those prejudices come up when you focus on someone who triggers them. For example, if someone looks very different from you—perhaps because of race, gender, sexual orientation, or religious or social beliefs—you will easily form prejudices. If you notice that you hold these beliefs without being interested in challenging them, you are stuck in Tunnel Vision.

  Remember, your mission is not to punish yourself or even inhibit yourself from thinking prejudiced thoughts. Your goal is to notice them and peg them to Tunnel Vision.

- Notice Tunnel Vision driven by ego when reacting to hurt feelings. In a situation where, for instance, you feel embarrassed or hurt by someone you think berated you in public on purpose, your immediate reaction might be to soothe your inflamed ego and hurt feelings with more ego. You might think, I hate them. They're idiots. You might even chastise yourself for being embarrassed.

  Noticing ego when our feelings are hurt is hard to do. When we are really hurting, our impulse is to revert to old habits of ego, like blaming others or ourselves—whatever will get rid of the painful feelings and replace them with feelings we can express—even if those strategies cause us to feel worse in the long run. At least in the immediate present we get relief. It's similar to the reason why people use intoxicants to rid themselves of negative feelings.

Noticing Tunnel Vision in Distorted Thinking

As you now know, an inflated ego of whatever type distorts your thinking. That largely happens because our thinking gets egocentric, which stands to reason. If you experience the world and yourself through the lens of a highly personalized reality, your thinking is going to get warped right along with it. And when your thinking is distorted, you will believe what you think. That's the next step.

The practice here is to notice when your thinking does not seem to be reasonable or rational *even to you*. This is admittedly hard to do, although it's not impossible. Once you believe your own thoughts, it is a challenge to step outside them and notice it as Tunnel Vision, with objectivity. Nevertheless, if you are able to question or have cause to question your thinking, ask yourself if the belief seems reasonable or rational.

For instance, when you think something *always* or *never* is one way or another, do you mean it literally, exactly as you thought it? If not, it is not reasonable or rational, and it is *likely* causing you suffering. When you think something *must be, has to be, should be, ought to be*, ask yourself, *Who says it has to be that way?* Is it more accurate to think that something *would be best if* or *would be nice if* it were one way or another?

When you make assumptions with little evidence and can catch yourself doing so, ask yourself if there could be any other explanation. When you experience yourself having racial, ethnic, religious, political, or gender prejudices, ask yourself if you are infallible in that belief. Ask yourself if it is at all possible that you are mistaken, but make sure not to judge yourself negatively for having the belief. We all have beliefs. It's programming. Just recognize it with honesty and compassion for how your mind has been programmed and appreciate yourself for questioning that subjective reality.

When you hear yourself being certain you know what the future holds—no less catastrophizing about it—ask if it is rational or reasonable to be that convinced. Keep in mind that there is a world of difference between being certain that you know what the future will bring and thinking something *might or might not* happen.

The last thought distortion you need to notice is rationalization. This means finding excuses or convenient reasons for doing what you want to do, even though it is not a desirable thing. This happens when your Tunnel Vision is so strong that it controls you so that you need to justify it with a reason. For instance, if you want to eat cake while on a diet or relapse on drugs when you know it is a bad idea, your mind may unconsciously find ways to justify your actions. This can look like thinking, *It doesn't really matter*, or *One more time won't hurt*, or *No one cares*, or *I have a right*, or *I deserve it*. These and other distorted thoughts and beliefs are not subtle, insignificant differences in word usage. Noticing when you think like that can make the difference between a life of honesty with yourself and one where you lie to yourself and others.

Noticing Tunnel Vision with Negative Emotions

Given all the above ways to notice Tunnel Vision, there may be one tool in your detective bag that rises above all else: negative emotions. You won't need your magnifying glass for this one. Remember, Tunnel Vision doesn't always come from or immediately cause negative feelings. It can feel great at first. But when it does lead to difficult feelings, you'll want to use them to check in with yourself.

Remember when we discussed the hurt feelings that come from a bruised ego? It was a strong way to notice your ego and its Tunnel Vision. Here we're doing the same thing, only in a more general, similarly effective way. It becomes a reminder to notice your Tunnel Vision when any negative feeling comes up. Don't be choosy. Notice any and all negative emotions you may have whenever they come up. Of course, we all drag along negative feelings through life. That's part of the human condition. That's fine. Notice even feelings that you have harbored for decades. There's a reason why you are noticing them. However, you'll also notice stronger-than-usual negative feelings when they come up.

Negative feelings usually come in some form of one or more of these basic groups: anxiety, from mild worry to dread and panic; anger, from irritation to hostility and rage; sadness, from mild sorrow to grief and hopeless despondency; and boredom, from mild impatience to more intense restlessness and feelings of meaninglessness. These emotions may come in combination or separately.

Notice the feelings and see how they are involved in grabbing your attention, lessening your control, pulling you more into your imagination, changing how readily you believe, inflaming your ego, and distorting your beliefs. The strategy here is to notice the Tunnel Vision associated with the feeling.

It bears repeating: the crucial way this strategy brings Perspective from noticing these negative feelings is to *not* try to make these feelings go away. You don't try to avoid them or any other aspect of your Tunnel Vision. You gain Perspective by recognizing your Tunnel Vision and the feelings that come with it *just as they are*.

This can be very challenging. Tunnel Vision can be extremely stressful. Think of being fearful of losing someone you love or even being in the midst of a panic attack. Yet the key to happiness in the long run is to accept the inevitability and reality of each moment as it exists. Then you can use the other aspects of BrainShifting to make that noticing even more potent. When you get good at this strategy, you'll notice more and more subtle negative feelings that are lurking in your heart and mind most of the time.

Noticing Tunnel Vision: Conclusion

Noticing Tunnel Vision is the most important aspect of the SatoriWest Method. It's the most important skill you can acquire in life. Until you are clued in to the infinite number of ways it can show up, and the ways it can fool you, you will not be able to unwind them when it takes over your mind. Remember, Tunnel Vision is the *only* reason why you suffer. If you don't address it, you will never enjoy a day of true peace and happiness, let alone experience the profound fulfillment that your brain is capable of achieving.

But be warned. As a Tunnel Vision detective, you'll find the trail is fraught with tricks and illusions. When you realize you are in Tunnel Vision, it usually feels good. It feels like a relief—usually. Don't make the mistake of chasing after the pleasure of getting some Perspective. That could turn into a form of Tunnel Vision. If you notice your mind in Tunnel Vision and it feels good, don't hang on to the feeling. Be ready for the next episode of Tunnel Vision. Eventually, if you keep noticing them, the Tunnel Vision episodes will get less frequent and severe. Then you'll be left with a subtle but delicious feeling of peace and easy contentment with the moments in each day.

Being a Tunnel Vision detective comes with other challenges as well, depending on whether you are noticing it in a cultural, toxic, or crisis context. We've already addressed this in this book, although I'll repeat it to help the concepts soak in.

The biggest challenge of noticing cultural Tunnel Vision in the course of your daily life is that it is so invisible. You go to work every day highly focused on expectations of getting recognized for what you do. You're busy making plans without really noticing the subtle and sublime going on around you. Toxic Tunnel Vision might be so entrenched in your sense of who you are that you won't want to see it—for instance, if you're an overly defensive person. Or, if your toxic Tunnel Vision has led to clinical depression, believing your irrational version of the future provides a perverse kind of comfort, like being in the water when you can't swim and hanging on to a sinking rowboat. Or you are so hooked into some addictive trigger, like eating or watching too much television, that you don't want to take the second it requires to see it for what it is.

Crisis Tunnel Vision is hard to notice, because whatever has grabbed your attention has grabbed it tight. The saving grace, as we've been saying, is that once you are willing to look, the eight facets of Tunnel Vision are much more apparent in crisis Tunnel Vision.

In these cases, being a detective presents unusual challenges, because you are both detector and subject. It's not impossible, though. And it does get easier with time. It can also be hugely helpful to have someone to talk to about your use of the SatoriWest Method.

SatoriWest Journey, Avenue Two: Split Attention BrainShifting

The paradox at the center of this book is that the more severe the Tunnel Vision, the easier it is to notice. Think of that in reverse. It is sure easy to notice someone else's Tunnel Vision when they're coming unhinged from it, perhaps being hysterical, irrational, lost in their own mind.

So if you've started to notice Tunnel Vision in its subtler forms, good job. It's not easy. It takes time. It also takes practice. Yet what if noticing your Tunnel Vision is not enough to release you from it? It's possible, for instance, that your mind has such a strong grip on your attention that you *can* witness yourself but are mostly witnessing your mind heading down the rabbit hole of a serious spiral of Tunnel Vision.

Yes, recognizing any Tunnel Vision will relieve the intensity of the suffering it has caused and may release it into some degree of Perspective. However, some Tunnel Vision experiences call on you to intentionally BrainShift further than recognizing them. Awareness of some episodes of Tunnel Vision may not be strong enough to sustain objectivity long enough to relieve their intensity. The force of the Tunnel Vision can then pull you back into it, which will cause you to start suffering from it again.

This next strategy will be your first intentional encounter with the basic direct skill of BrainShifting: splitting attention. Splitting attention is simply this: after noticing your Tunnel Vision or any facet of it, add an "and" awareness of something else unrelated to the Tunnel Vision.

Here's a lighthearted example, although for some it could be more serious. Say you come out of a public restroom dragging a piece of toilet paper on your shoe, and you see someone notice it and giggle. Of course, you immediately remove the toilet paper. However, most of us might feel embarrassed, and some of us might hold on to that embarrassment long after the person who noticed it walks away. There might be ego dilation, or feeling self-conscious or inferior. Or there might be distorted thinking, such as, *That person who giggled is a jerk*, or *No one should do that to someone else*, or *If I could hurt them back, I would*, or *These bathrooms are never cleaned up enough*.

If recognizing the Tunnel Vision of that moment is not enough for you to wind out of it and perhaps stop ruminating on it, then to split attention you would *also* notice anything you are not currently aware of outside your Tunnel Vision. This could be anything—your toenails, sounds outside, wood patterns in furniture, or the feeling of moving your legs while walking. With attention splitting, you would hold on to the awareness of all the features of Tunnel Vision, feeling them completely—the ego dilation, the distorted thoughts, and the rough associated feelings—*along* with the object you are splitting your attention with. All at the same time.

Make sure to hold the full force of the Tunnel Vision experience and the other unrelated awareness in consciousness at the same time for several seconds to minutes. Without wishing for the moment to be any different, you will notice a change. As Perspective dawns, there will likely be positive changes to your mood. Your body will feel different, calmer, with a slight increase in energy, as opposed to feeling drained from anger or shame. You may notice that you feel more compassion for your own ego that got embarrassed. You may notice yourself giggling at the absurdity of the situation, giving you more insight into the person who giggled first. In any case, you will likely be better able to move into the next moment free of the last one.

Here's another, more extreme example. Say you were having a panic attack. It feels terrifying, like suffocating. In Tunnel Vision, your attention is grabbed by these feelings and the sensation of asphyxiating. As Tunnel Vision takes hold, you will likely have obsessive thoughts that you're not going to survive. As you get pulled into your imagination, you envision dying. You become desperate to make that feeling go away. It's tantamount to screaming to yourself, *Don't let me die!* Of course, that feeds on itself, worsening the anxiety more than it might have otherwise.

If, once you notice the Tunnel Vision in the experience, it is not going to work to give you a modicum of Perspective—enough to realize you aren't going to die—then split your attention. Extend your awareness to include the following:

- something(s) outside the Tunnel Vision you hadn't noticed before. This can be anything, like the temperature of the room on your face, cracks in the wall, the color of light in the room, the feeling of your toenails, bird sounds coming from outside. So while you are noticing that "I" am having thoughts of "dying," with breathless suffocation, and severe anxiety, leave all that in place, feel it, and then include any of the above. Or

- seeing whatever is inside the Tunnel Vision in a new way. This can include the quality of your emotions, such as the heaviness in your chest, stiffness in your throat, tightness in your abdomen, or sweaty palms.

Or if you get really good at this, expand your awareness to include

- just knowing you are alive and aware. To experience what knowing you are alive fully means, let's consider the Thought Exercises that were previously presented, which brought your attention to the present moment. It showed each moment as unique and apart from any other moment. Ideally you came to the experience of what it is like to immediately appear into being or to be transported somewhere else. It's akin to the practice that tries to foster an existential sense of aliveness by having people contemplate what this moment would be like if this were the last second they were going to be alive.

These are two of the nuts and bolts of moving from being in Tunnel Vision to having Perspective. Remember, experience the causes and conditions of your Tunnel Vision just the way they are. Having Perspective in each moment *doesn't require you to change anything*. Then BrainShifting concludes by opening up and detaching your awareness so that you can more fully experience from the vantage point of a brain that takes in everything—including the sense of being you.

Author's note: This understanding can elude even the most advanced meditator, so I apologize for repeating this so many times.

Our powerful Tunnel Vision impulses will force us to want to make whatever hurt or negative feeling we have go away, immediately. Yet we don't BrainShift to change the moment. We want to experience the moment exactly the way it is. We don't BrainShift to be someone different from who we are each moment. We are not chasing some fantasy of being someone with great Perspective, like Jesus, Buddha, or an idealized guru. We aren't trying to become someone who we believe has attained perfect happiness. We don't BrainShift to be somewhere better or do something better. We BrainShift to get more in touch with being alive right now no matter what is happening, while detaching and expanding our awareness of exactly what is.

I will continue to repeat this in this book, because I, too, have to remind myself of it over and over again. It trips up people all the time. No one wants to feel and be aware of anything bad. Our instinct is to run to avoid feeling those things. But in pushing away bad feelings and thoughts, we often wind up giving them more power. In trying to control bad impulses, without fully feeling them and surrounding them with Perspective, we wind up losing executive control over them. If bad habits can be redirected early through awareness alone, we could save ourselves frustration later on, and BrainShifting will be that much more satisfying.

Here are a few examples to show you how to work with the purposeful BrainShifting skills of noticing Tunnel Vision and splitting attention to something else.

Example 1

Let's delve a bit deeper into the experience of panic attacks, which many people reading this book have had. Exploring one example in more depth may be useful.

Author's note: I had a panic attack that came on unexpectedly during a shower. It came at a time of great stress in my life. Granted, 40 years of meditation and being a psychiatrist helped me to, first, know it was a panic attack and, second, find some distance from the sensations of it. Nevertheless, it was frightening at first. Yet the journey of witnessing it and the Tunnel Vision triggered by it became a memorable and fascinating experience.

I surrendered to it and experienced the sensation of breathlessness with interest, and the Perspective came to me in the form of, So this is what a panic attack actually feels like. It became fascinating. It seemed to abate faster than I believe it would have otherwise. Time seemed to stop. In the moment after the experience wound down, I felt more alive. I would never wish to have that experience again, but knowing that I could manage it if I need to is confidence building.

As most panic attacks seem to come out of the blue, the aspect of surprise can overwhelm your BrainShifting ability—that is, unless your brain has been altered because of the daily practice of BrainShifting. The sensation of suffocating, like something heavy is sitting on your chest, occurs because your heart rate speeds up and your lungs cannot get enough oxygen into the blood; it feels like you are going to die or might be having a heart attack.

Panic attacks can be a powerful pull into Tunnel Vision. They are quintessential survival wiring that tells your brain to lock its attention onto a source of extreme anxiety. The stronger the stimulus that grabs your attention, the more it distorts your mind. As a result, you believe your own thoughts, and predictions of dying become more realistic. The more you are pulled into your imagination, the more everything else is blocked out, leading you to become lost in the nightmarish fantasy of the worst-case scenario of dying.

The more your mind struggles to control the situation—which it cannot do—the worse it makes the situation. For example, the more irrational your thinking gets, such as catastrophizing about dying, being certain you know the future, the "shoulds" that fight the reality of the moment. It is a central point of this book that Tunnel Vision can ruin ordinary moments and make bad moments worse.

The first step toward getting Perspective in the presence of your panic attack is obviously to notice the facets of the Tunnel Vision it induces, some of which we spelled out above. Let's assume then that noticing is not enough to keep you from being pulled into your Tunnel Vision and unable to objectively witness. That's when widening awareness by splitting attention comes in. It can help further detach your attention from the stimuli of the panic and help you expand awareness beyond the panic and its Tunnel Vision.

After you see the Tunnel Vision episode you're in, the insight of Perspective may come to you—namely, knowing you are having a panic attack. You'll likely begin to see that the world is okay; it's just that your brain is having an episode of extreme anxiety. Maybe it'll occur to you that people don't die from panic attacks.

Then, if needed, you can add to that initial Perspective by noticing something outside the Tunnel Vision, such as cracks in the wall, or inside the Tunnel Vision, like the sensation of breathing in your nostrils, that you hadn't been noticing. So while you are noticing your pounding heart and thoughts of death, become aware of something different.

To repeat this essential point, you are not trying to distract yourself from the panic attack by noticing something different. That will be your impulse. Splitting attention is an "and," not an "or" situation. Other examples of noticing things outside the Tunnel Vision might be to note what your fingernails feel like, seeing patterns in the wood of your chair you hadn't seen before, or hearing the sounds you hadn't heard before the panic attack. Inside your Tunnel Vision, you might feel the sensation of breathlessness in a way you hadn't noticed before, as a rapid breath that you don't consciously control. You can also notice the creative way your mind catastrophizes.

That is the next step in putting your Tunnel Vision in Perspective—by noticing around or alongside it, widening awareness into a new, more alive, way of being in the moment.

Example 2

Author's note: This is an actual experience I had not too long ago. I was a chief medical officer, heading to the hospital where I worked.

I was leading an important meeting that morning and headed out early enough to make it on time in normal traffic.

Driving on the freeway in my typical state of cultural Tunnel Vision, I was focused on the meeting and how it would affect the participants. I was also focused on the long list of things I had to do at work, and then after work, in my personal life. That's when I saw an unexpected traffic jam ahead.

My attention was grabbed by the long row of traffic lights a half mile ahead. I began to get anxious, thinking about how I might escape it. I was focused on how long the delay would be, which was making me frustrated and angry. I began fantasizing about people sitting around waiting for me or even starting the meeting without me, wondering what they might say or think.

I was presenting something important at this meeting and knew it would have been best to leave home earlier. Distortion of reality started to really set in. I started to think, This is just my luck (ego dilation); There's so much traffic in this city, why do I even live here? (magnifying the negative, minimizing the positive). I was getting myself even angrier. It wasn't a fully conscious thought, but was an impression that, All these cars are on the road just to block me (ego dilation).

Then I thought, I'm such an idiot—I should have anticipated this and left earlier (ego dilation, absolutisms of should); When I walk in late, they'll all think I'm flaky and scattered (ego, future certainty); My boss will think I'm not reliable. Maybe I could get fired for this (not true, catastrophizing).

My Tunnel Vision entered slightly into a crisis phase as I got really frustrated and angry, and more and more anxious. I pounded the wheel a couple of times and started driving more aggressively, weaving in and out of traffic.

Something about the sheer drop in my mood, coupled with this irrational thinking, triggered a recognition in me. Likely because I'd practiced and taught the SatoriWest Method for so long, it caused me to pause for a second. And in that moment the realization came to me, Wow, I'm in Tunnel Vision! How obvious is this?

That started me BrainShifting even further. My awareness fell open and expanded. I noticed my hands on the wheel and my foot on the gas pedal. I slowly detached and experienced the sensations of driving, the road, and my own reactions with neutrality. I didn't try to change anything about my reaction. The anxiety and the aftermath of my irrational beliefs were still there.

As you might guess, I started to feel a lowering of stress in a matter of seconds. By this time traffic had started to slow down significantly. With new eyes, I noticed the other cars and drivers around me. As the traffic came to a crawl, the realization dawned, We are all stuck in traffic together. I started to feel compassion for the other drivers. I realized, They must be as distressed as me. They have places to go, too, maybe meetings they have to be at. The thought came to me, It's not just my bad luck, it's all of our bad luck. I'm not sure love is the right name for the feeling, but something like it surged to the surface. I felt connected to my fellow commuters. It was an ineffable feeling of belonging, as if my mind were taking a bird's-eye view of the traffic, with me as a small piece of this amazing whole.

My thinking definitely started to shift. There was a softening of my anger toward myself: I could have [instead of should have] left earlier. Interesting life lesson—I'll factor that in in the future. Turning to the image of the meeting, and the senior management team sitting there waiting for me, I thought, If people judge me for walking in late, that's not the end of the world. And, actually, they like me, so they're not going to stress too much over this. Plus, They may get worried about me.

Then I started to feel so grateful I had a job, and a car, and important meetings to lead. By the time I was completely stopped in traffic, I noticed the freeway in ways I hadn't before—the trees alongside it, the patchwork of covered potholes—and cloud patterns in the sky. I looked at my beautiful car and all its modern gadgets and realized how much I loved that car. I was calm. Happy, even. It was a chance to relax and see the Tunnel Vision I put myself under when I was racing to work. By the time the traffic started to move again,

I was actually disappointed that I couldn't enjoy the experience of taking a little longer time-out from life.

Example 3

Suppose you happen across two men fighting on the sidewalk, really punching each other. Your attention is drawn into the fight and the thought of needing to save the one who is being badly beaten. On seeing this, your anxiety increases.

As your attention is locked on the two men, your mind assumes one is being attacked by the other (Tunnel Vision distortion: assumptions based on biases in your imagination). You are lost in thought, imagining what you should do to intervene. You imagine running up to them and screaming at them to stop or even pulling them apart. You might be preoccupied with calculating the risks of doing that. The more anxious you are, the less capable you are of deciding what to do, and the more anxious you get. You're approaching crisis levels of Tunnel Vision.

Then, somehow, in the midst of that, you use the "and" technique. You widen your awareness to notice more about the scenario: the sounds and images of the neighborhood, other people looking out their apartment windows, a gun lying on the sidewalk. You feel the anxiety in your body and realize that you're smaller than the dominant attacker.

You relax a bit from that wider noticing. Then the idea enters your mind that the seeming attacker was fending off an attack by someone with a gun, which is why the bystanders are just looking on. A plan seems to emerge by itself. You run up to the people looking from their window and yell, "Call 911. Tell them there's a gun here!" You then take out your phone and start taking a video.

This may not be the best solution. It is one solution, but it is driven by intuition born of allowing unconscious processing of different ideas and feelings to emerge, instead of solely relying on anxiety based on a single thought. The point here is to illustrate Perspective.

Reminder: Perspective does not begin with a thought; it begins with a change in awareness.

In this chapter we began to give you a concrete sense of how to purposefully invoke the skills of BrainShifting. In Chapter 13 we'll build on this by showing you other types of BrainShifting skills.

For now, it is important to remember this subtle fact: in times of significant Tunnel Vision, you don't impose Perspective on your brain. Instead, Perspective results from a change in how you control attention and use awareness. For instance, if you use the "and" technique of widening your awareness, eventually your attention begins to focus inward on the energy of your aliveness.

What this means is greater and greater Perspective does not really come from changing your thinking. Sure, it can, to an extent. You can practice wellness, like the practice of existential wellness that has you trying to see beauty in small things. Yet the true nature of Perspective is not a thought: it's a way of perceiving reality. It doesn't even need thinking or labeling. If you widen your awareness in a difficult situation, you likely won't even need to try to think what the best Perspective is. The thoughts emanating from Perspective will come on their own. Creative ideas will arise. New options will present themselves.

The SatoriWest Method is all about the bidirectional aspect of BrainShifting. We learn and practice awareness-changing skills to directly BrainShift, and we use wellness strategies to allow Perspective to unfold on its own. Like all wellness strategies, you *can* create the conditions that create Perspective, but to a *limited* extent. For example, someone who has a philosophical Perspective, such as "Live and let live," can use that philosophy when annoyed to keep their Perspective, chill out, and not overreact. Or in a challenging situation you can stop and think what your parent or mentor would do in the same situation. It's just that most of your Perspective will need to come from your direct practice with BrainShifting skills.

That's because if we are really distressed by something, we won't easily be able to think our way out of it. If we are pulled into Tunnel Vision by craving food or a drug, we probably won't be able to have enough Perspective by thinking Perspective-based thoughts alone, such as, *I should think about how this will affect my kids* or *I shouldn't do this—it isn't right.*

We need some degree of widened awareness to *really* see our own predicament clearly. It is in releasing the hold of attention that we gain self-control. It's by detaching from our ego that we best allow for a spontaneous gesture to emerge. To be truly creative, to get a brilliant new idea that we can't consciously anticipate, we need to change our brain first. It's hard to be "open minded" if we don't have the open-minded awareness that goes along with it.

....

I was having suicidal and homicidal ideations. With the SatoriWest Method I was able to see how I was acting in immature ways. I realized I don't have to be controlled by [my emotions]. I can feel those feelings and not act in ways that are toxic [levels of Tunnel Vision]. Somehow something broke through to that core. I'm riding the waves of those emotions instead of trying to fight them all the time. I think this is a new beginning for me.

—Greg

13

A Model for BrainShifting: What Shifts?

Let's take a brief break from the how-to aspects of learning to BrainShift to get a better sense of what the BrainShifting skills are doing in your brain—at least a hypothesized model. It may help you better relate to your inner experience when we present the skills of BrainShifting you haven't learned about yet in Chapter 14.

The SatoriWest Model of the Brain as It Shifts Toward Perspective

If each of us lived 200 or 300 years, our brains would naturally evolve by themselves. They would BrainShift to their highest level on their own. Since we live only 80 to 100 years, we need to learn how to make that shift happen faster.

But what does it mean for your brain to shift? We spoke about the two sides of your brain being trained on each other so that self-awareness could be intensified. But how does that happen? Here's our model, which starts with the so-called dominant hemisphere—which for most of us is the left side, so for convenience, we'll just refer to the dominant side as "left" and the nondominant side as "right."

The Two Brains: Dominant and Nondominant

Because we are an intelligent species, we experience reality and have structured society in a way that relies heavily on language. Language frames our every waking second. And as we've seen, words and concepts pull the brain into Tunnel Vision. Tunnel Vision then distorts how we experience reality.

Verbal language comes from the dominant cerebral hemisphere, the left side. By the way, the tricky thing about our brain is that each of the two cerebral cortices of each hemisphere control the opposite side of our body, and each receives sensory information from the opposite side. For example, the left hemisphere is dominant, so you become right-handed, right-legged, and right-eyed. Or, if you have a massive stroke on the right side of your brain, you may not be able to feel or move the left side of your body.

In other words, because the left side of your brain is the side that speaks and uses language to understand the world, that becomes the dominant way that you experience the world. Technically, 65 percent of the population has verbal language in the left hemisphere, which is why they are right-handed. For ease of discussion, I will use the majority configuration—"left" hemisphere is dominant and controls language and right-handedness—in explaining this aspect of the SatoriWest Method.

Your left brain dissects its experience into quanta: this is this, that is that, this versus that, and you and me. Language is what creates the experience of being you, the ego, "I," or sense of self. Because the left side of your brain has language, and language is such a powerful way to express and perceive things, the left side took over your entire brain, which again is why most people *are* right-handed.

This has been a survival advantage for us. When we see or feel something we want or don't want, our brain uses language to identify it. That enhances our brain's attentional mechanism to focus even more on it, which is how Tunnel Vision really gets locked in. Also, because language is intimately tied to the sense of self, having a strong sense of "me," or "I am me," becomes another way that language divides up the world. It's software on the left side of the brain that says (or thinks), *I am me, and everything else is separate from me.* It can then think, *I want that, and I don't want that.* It divides the world into what you want and what you don't want, and all the rest gets overlooked. This way of seeing things is helpful in that we do get what we want and what we *think* we want, and we do avoid what scares or repels us and what we think might scare or repel us. The problem is that each moment becomes a way for "me" to achieve something. And that fosters Tunnel Vision and makes it the dominant way we go through life. Hence, it creates the human condition.

The right cerebral cortex or hemisphere doesn't experience things in the same way as the left. It is aware of the moment "wholistically." It doesn't have a center "me" versus everything else. There is no separate this versus that. Perhaps you can see Tunnel Vision and facets of Perspective in the description of the left and right sides of the brain?

The experience of the right side of our brain is always operating; it's part of our day-to-day experience. It's just that it is in the background of our experience. It emerges normally when we use it to experience the entirety of the moment, like listening to a symphony. We relax and pay attention to the entirety of the piece rather than to one note or collection of separate notes at a time. A music critic might listen for the various sections of the orchestra and how they are doing, but with a pure, nondiscriminatory ear, the rest of us are open to the piece as a whole.

This way of experiencing, this sense of the entirety of the moment, has many advantages. It gives us a truer sense of what the moment is—a whole experience, a gestalt, a symphony of life. A symphony that includes us, our own mind and body. This way of experiencing tells us how the elements of our experience— everything we see, hear, think, touch, and feel—combine like the unique moments of a symphony to give a fresh and novel take on what is happening each moment. That's what Perspective— being able to discern context—requires. This way of perceiving is valuable information for intuitively understanding what is going on, for being able to anticipate where things are heading, which is a benefit for our physical safety. It has many uses. It's a big part of what having Perspective means.

When we're growing up, we need to develop the left side of our brain. It helps us be able to identify things, name them, separate them out, and study them. This includes our sense of being us. Our ego has to develop during childhood to help us relate better to the world. Use of language and ego are *basic* mechanisms for survival and for accomplishing tasks. It tells us that there is a predictable way that things work, so we can be efficient in how we move through life. Think of that way of experiencing as training wheels for orienting to later life.

In adulthood, exclusively experiencing reality that way becomes less necessary and less useful. In other words, we don't need ego or even explicit language as much as we did when we were kids. We don't need to categorize everything and habitually react in similar ways. As adults, we need to experience and understand each moment and everything and everyone in it as unique. That's so we can understand what is going on better, but also so we can feel less stale and more excited about the novelty of each moment. We can still isolate and analyze things, but when that is done in the *context* of other factors, with a more wholistic awareness, the analysis is more accurate.

BrainShifting allows the right side of our brain more and more airtime. We teach our brain how to access that aspect of its experience with more clarity. That's how we head down the road of changing our experience of life and of each moment: without Tunnel Vision, without focused and exclusive attention, but as a whole.

Higher and Lower Brain Areas

Besides the left-right interplay, there's another interplay in the brain. It's between higher and lower areas. Each hemisphere, right and left, has separate areas that allow each side to become aware of the world inside and outside us. Along with a separate awareness, each side can then act and react independently. There are literally two separate brains inside our head, as weird as that may be to contemplate. Each sees the world in a different way and then responds differently—although the left side usually wins out.

When we think of how the two sides of the brain are different, we can think of all the areas that make them different as the "lower brain." Can you see how the lower areas of the two brains, but especially the left side, are involved in Tunnel Vision, in reacting to the world? When the right half of the brain is more activated, we have more and more Perspective and less and less Tunnel Vision. Yet that is only part of the picture of what Perspective is.

How do we complete the picture of what Perspective is? It requires the higher brain to be more activated. The higher brain, remember, is the awareness of each brain working together, seeing or realizing each other. Together, this combined area, the higher area, makes us "self"-aware or aware of being aware. Self-awareness can be more easily thought of as awareness of being here now or awareness of being alive.

Just like the awareness of each side of the brain brings the ability to respond to things differently, self-awareness comes with the ability to act and think as well. It's an even higher way to act and think that is a macro-management style involving executive decision making, where we can make decisions and assess actions that incorporate information from both sides of the brain. It relies on intuition that combines sequential logic with wholistic perceptions. It is also a less reactive, but more spontaneous, easy, and authentic way of acting and expressing one's self.

BrainShifting Brings It All Together

The SatoriWest model hypothesizes that when we're in Tunnel Vision, we overuse language and a sense of "me" to chop up our experience so that we can react based on what we learned in the past. That draws heavily on the left brain, with its reliance on language, with wiring that makes it action oriented and geared to action with immediate consequences. As a result, we go through life overusing our left brain, extensively leaning on the sense of "me" to relate to the world. We believe that is the only way we can be. Yet this is not so. We can live perfectly well unselfconsciously. We can live life without leaning heavily on habits to experience the moment and react to it, whether we know we are doing that or not.

We may not realize it all the time, but we react unconsciously more than we know. We are driven to be rewarded by things, by idealized goals reinforced by our culture or family that satisfy our ego more than fulfill actual needs. Less than fully conscious choice is involved when we are influenced this way and being driven so powerfully toward future rewards. It is similar to laboratory mice being rewarded when they press a lever to get food even when they aren't hungry.

In other words, we are not as in control of our lives as we think. That is the condition of Tunnel Vision, generated by overreliance on our lower, left brains. It can be analogized to accomplishing a lot by climbing very high on a ladder without focusing on making sure the ladder is heading where it needs to go. What we miss is the wholistic and fresh experience of each moment (right brain) and the amazement of being alive (higher brain), subtle but powerful things that are often much more rewarding than anything we can achieve.

Going through life leaning heavily on our lower, left brain is not always bad in the short run. You get stuff done. Yet it can feel suffocating and depressing in the long run to be so stuck in being the same "me" you've always been. It's a more primitive way of being human. We don't need the training wheels: they may even be getting in the way. There are more sophisticated and effective ways to not only survive but thrive. We can be more intuitively and spontaneously effective while more fully enjoying and meeting the uniqueness of each moment.

With Perspective, as we said, we use the right side of our brain to experience the world more as a whole without relying exhaustively on a "me" to figure everything out and know what to do. We also use our higher brain more intensely to anchor us in reality, in the ineffable now. Our higher brain is what ultimately gives life its greatest sense of meaning, suffusing it with gratitude for what we are and what we already have. In that state of Perspective we can relax more and let life unfold. We don't take things that happen personally. We don't even need to decide in words what is best to do, because the right side of our brain gives us the intuition to sense what is best.

This is where the notion of spiritual levels of experience comes in. Known throughout history, and given many different explanations, these higher ways of experiencing are now commonly called "transpersonal" states (meaning beyond the personal) and studied in the field of psychology called transpersonal psychology. However, as far as the SatoriWest Method is concerned, they happen as the result of our brains somehow shifting how they function. It's where the right side of the brain becomes increasingly activated relative to the left, giving the person a greater experience of oneness and much-needed relief from an overactive, controlling, and often suffocating ego. In addition, there is greater use of the higher brain (which are the two brains realizing each other) to feel a heightened sense of aliveness and of micromanagement. This becomes a new center of experience and control, switching from ego-based experience and control.

Using more of your right brain and your higher brain is what makes life rewarding just for living it. There's no need to do or accomplish anything, because being alive is reward in itself. That's how to really feel more fully alive without needing to jump from an airplane (unless you want to). That's how the moment feels complete. It's the shift to Perspective. It's been called an ecstatic state because, as Buddha described in the *Dhammapada*, "joy follows you like a shadow that never leaves you." It's a state of deep tranquility.

Eventually very ecstatic states settle down into a new normal that offers a balanced Perspective involving left and right hemisphere processing as well as a more general activation of the cells in your higher brain.

However, this book is not about achieving fully transpersonal ways of experiencing. It is about learning what the path is and then taking the journey to whatever point you want. We don't need fully transpersonal or spiritual states to feel better. Any degree of BrainShifting can help you see life with more Perspective. Any amount of BrainShifting can allow you to feel at least a bit more content with each moment, with less ego-based fear—basically to develop all the facets of Perspective you learned about.

Any degree of self-awareness (a sense of aliveness, not what we think of as being self-conscious) is enlivening, empowering, and self-validating. The more our brain consciously takes in the moment in its entirety—the more we perceive interrelatedness, context, and uniqueness—the less we use the thick lens of ego to personalize it. The more authenticity and spontaneity flow, the more liberated we feel. As the saying goes, be more of a "human being" than a "human doing."

In essence, it comes down to the fact that by BrainShifting we are allowing our brain to mature to its max, where we are living the "extra" ordinary life that on some level we know we are capable of. Simplistically, this happens as the brain shifts more from left to right and from lower to higher. This lowers the veil that Tunnel Vision puts over reality. The shift releases us from past traumas, which are not forgotten, just remembered with distance, while the present becomes more salient. This shift opens the moment with greater intensity to the reality of our aliveness, which by its very nature gives us humbling gratitude, happiness, and meaning.

Mindfulness: A BrainShifting Tool

Before we present a few more BrainShifting skills in the next chapter, many of which can be said to overlap with (and in some circles are synonymous with) the practice of mindfulness, it may be important to note that the SatoriWest Method as a model doesn't actually use the term "mindfulness." That's because we refer to the term "mind" in describing thoughts, feelings, mental imagery, and a sense of self, so it might be confusing when we say a focus on the human mind causes Tunnel Vision, or when we talk about witnessing our thoughts, feelings, and ego as aspects of the mind. In other words, being "mind-full" would mean we are more focused on thoughts, feelings, and sense of self than we are on awareness of our aliveness.

Instead, the SatoriWest Method uses the terms "awareness," "self-awareness," and even "awarefulness." Yet "mindfulness" is a very popular term. It means being intentionally aware of something. The idea of mindfulness as a skill was extracted from Eastern religious traditions by Buddhist Westerners who wanted to share its essence as a healing skill. It was thus removed from its spiritual and religious context and taught as a simple, secular technique.

This made it much simpler and easier to understand and teach. And easier to study. To date there are tens of thousands of articles about it, and journals dedicated exclusively to mindfulness research. As such, the data showing the effectiveness of mindfulness is extensive—phenomenal, really. Mindfulness lowers anxiety, stress, depression, anger, PTSD, and mood-related symptoms. It treats addictions and insomnia and improves self-esteem, memory, and focus. It decreases perception of pain, lowers inflammation in the body, improves the immune system and the body's ability to fight infections, improves digestion, and lowers blood pressure and heart rate. It boosts creativity and enhances new learning, visuospatial ability, decision making, and self-awareness. Many, if not most, mental health professionals are using mindfulness practices in treatment. It is used therapeutically in prisons, the military, primary schools, universities, health clubs, and hospitals.

Of course, not all the studies showed the same benefits, and all research comes with warnings about drawing strict conclusions. Nevertheless, the research indicates that being more mindful is extremely beneficial across the board in helping people on many levels. Since BrainShifting incorporates mindfulness, it accrues the benefits that are attributed to it, plus the other facets of Perspective you learned about.

Unfortunately, something was lost when mindfulness was taken out of its Buddhist context. Its main advantage was overlooked: its use as a vehicle to attain the highest level of human development, to specifically raise Perspective—and in the case of Buddhism, to raise it to the point of an Awakening, which is just a very high degree of Perspective.

As we said, mindfulness—which the SatoriWest Method calls awareness—is just the first aspect of BrainShifting. What this means is that the more mindful we are, the more intentionally aware the brain is of *anything* and the more aware it is of *everything*. Eventually this leads to the cascading events of BrainShifting you just learned about.

What we'll talk about in Chapter 14 is how to use the skills of BrainShifting to strengthen the circuits that cause our brains to shift to the Perspective side more permanently. In other words, we'll learn how to better experience our right hemisphere and higher brain.

. . . .

The [BrainShifting] practice that I added to my daily routine is invaluable—claiming and centering. I truly experienced a crisis and how Tunnel Vision made me feel like life wasn't worth living. The SatoriWest Method helped me learn how to recognize Tunnel Vision thinking and ways to shift into seeing a broader Perspective and glimpses of life flowing.

While learning the SatoriWest Method, I loved the bits of neuroscience that I learned on how our brains work and the benefits of meditation.

—Dee Dee

14

More BrainShifting Skills

We'll now explore other BrainShifting skills, mainly awareness widening, but also some aspects of detachment and the experience of aliveness. It is important to know, though, that BrainShifting is a single maneuver that we divided up for ease of learning. Therefore, any one piece of the BrainShifting pie will eventually spread to include all the other pieces, and then the whole pie. So don't fret about not learning any or all of the parts right away. With patience, it *will* happen.

We start with the common mindfulness practice called the Body Scan. It is very relaxing, which is likely why it has so much data supporting it as a stress-reduction strategy. We will end with our own emphasis on its BrainShifting application: awareness of the whole body.

Preparing for This Chapter's Exercises

To prepare for this and any of these exercises, do the following:

- Find a comfortable location to sit. Don't lie down. In fact, sit up as much as possible, with your lower back slightly arched inward (because to activate those neural circuits we spoke about before, we want to send more energy to the brain during these exercises, and that happens with the spine straightened). Get comfortable.

- Keep your eyes open, even slightly, but not necessarily focused.

If it is easier to hear the instructions, go to SatoriWest.com and subscribe to get the BrainShifting exercise recordings for free.

BrainShifting Part I: Awareness Widening

BrainShifting starts with activating awareness of many different things. We actually started to do this with the "and" exercise we addressed in previous chapters. That's where we were aware of what was co-opting our attention plus something unrelated. This next exercise in the awareness-widening aspect of BrainShifting starts with body awareness. It is a common mindfulness exercise taught in many places. Our emphasis is in how it leads to wider awareness.

> ### The Body Scan Exercise
>
> In the Body Scan exercise we are going to bring our attention to different parts of our bodies. Like "beaming" up on the starship *Enterprise* from the show *Star Trek*, we will beam our attention up our bodies. Along the way, we will try to notice body sensations we may have never noticed before—even though they were always there.
>
> The ellipsis (...) is the cue to take a second or two and feel that sensation. Now, let's get started.
>
> Begin by moving your attention way down—to the big toe of your right foot ... Swirl your attention all around the skin of your right big toe ... What does the skin on your toe feel like? ... Now, settle your attention on the sides and web of your right big toe ... Now, move your attention to the bottom. What does the skin on the bottom of your big toe feel like? ... Does it tingle? Can it feel the softness of a sock, the pressure of the floor pressing on it or a shoe pressing into it? ... Now, move

your attention to the front of your right big toe ... Now, to the top ... See if you can feel your toenail ...

Now, move your attention to the big toe of your left foot ... Swirl your attention all around and settle it in on the sides ... front ... bottom. Do you feel the softness of a sock or the pressure of the floor or shoe? ... Now, feel the top and see if you can notice your toenail ...

Now, spread your attention to all of your toes on both feet ... Swirl your awareness around all your toes, aware of the sides and webs, bottoms, fronts, and tops ... See if you can feel all your toenails ...

Now, move your attention along the bottom of both feet, noticing what the skin there feels like, along the balls of your feet ... the arches ... the heels ... and now over the sides ... to the top of your feet ... and over to your ankles. What does the skin on your ankles feel like? ... Can you notice your anklebones? ...

As you move your attention up your legs to your shins and calves, notice the skin over them as well as the shinbones and calf muscles ... Now, move up to your knees. Feel the skin on the back of your knees and the front ... See if you can notice your kneecap ...

Now move up to your thighs. What does the skin on your thighs feel like? ... See if you can notice the skin there like it was the bottom of tight shorts ... Can you feel the pressure of a chair on your thighs pushing on your thigh muscles? ... Does it feel even or does it feel stronger on one leg than the other? ... Is the pressure on your thighs comfortable or uncomfortable? ...

Move up to your pelvis and buttocks. What does the skin of your genitals and buttocks feel like? ... Is it pleasant or stimulating? ... Notice it like you were noticing the bottom of a bathing suit ... If you are sitting, can you feel the pressure of the chair on the gluteal muscles of your buttocks? ...

Now, we'll move up to your lower abdomen and lower back. See if you can notice the wide band of skin around your lower abdomen and back as if it were a three- or four-inch-wide belt ... If you are sitting, can you feel the muscles below your skin that are tensing to help you sit? You may not have noticed that before. See if you can now ... Now let your attention glide up to the skin over your middle abdomen and middle back—like the bottom part of a tight shirt ... Can you feel any clothing that is touching your skin there? ... Is it soft? Can you feel the muscles of your abdomen and back that are tensing to help you sit? ... Now, move your attention up to the skin that surrounds your chest and upper back ... Notice it like the top of a shirt ... Can you feel your nipples? Can you feel any muscles in your back that feel tense? ...

Stop here for a moment to notice the breath. Notice your breath as cool, dry air automatically is sucked up past your nostrils, cooling your throat, inflating your lungs, and expanding your rib cage ... Then, when it runs its course, the in-breath slows, and at some barely perceptible moment, the process changes course ... The warm, moist air starts to pass over your nostrils and throat; your lungs deflate and your rib cage narrows ... Now, notice your breath at any point in that journey from your nostrils to your lungs ... Let's sit with your breathing for a few seconds, noticing it at the spot you chose. What you are going to look for are the points at the top and bottom of your breath—at the moments when your breathing progressively slows to the point that it starts to reverse course and either leaves or enters in. Notice the top and bottom of your breath at this point or throughout its journey for about 30 seconds ...

Now, keep moving your attention over to the skin and bones of your shoulders ... and down your arms, past your deltoids, triceps, and biceps. What does the skin over your deltoids, triceps, and biceps feel like? ... As your attention moves down past your elbows, front and back ... forearms ... wrists ... palms and back of your hands ... what does the skin on your hands feel like? ... Can you feel the temperature of the room on your hands? ... Are your hands still or shaky? ... Now, move your attention down to your fingers to the tips ... See if you can feel your fingernails ...

Now, move your attention up to the skin around your neck, and feel it like it's a wide necklace ... Now, let your attention dive into your throat ... Is it dry or wet? ... Now, pay attention to your tongue ... jaw ... teeth ... and to the muscles of your face ... Can you notice emotions in your face that have been etched in them for years? Now, let your attention glide out to the skin of your face ... your ears ... and up to your scalp ... to the top of your head ...

Now for the most important part of this exercise: it takes a bit of concentration and relaxation. Try to be aware of your entire body, all at once, from the top of your head, down your face, neck, chest and arms, trunk, legs, down to your toes ... One, single, continuous skin ... your body sitting there blinking, swallowing, and breathing ...

The Body Scan is a common mindfulness exercise, recommended in many mindfulness programs. Although the exercise does not always include the last part, it is essential in the SatoriWest Method context: widening attention to include your whole body. This is incorporated into the other BrainShifting exercises you will learn.

You should practice the Body Scan exercise every day to start—maybe more than once a day if you can. Later we'll make some recommendations about how to combine them for a daily BrainShifting practice.

Let's proceed to the next exercise in the progression of BrainShifting exercises: the Brain Sweep, Phase 1.

> ### Brain Sweep, Phase 1 Exercise
>
> For this exercise, your eyes can be open to keep you awake and attentive. However, you'll need to read each paragraph of this exercise right before practicing it. Recordings are available at SatoriWest.com.
>
> Let's get started.
>
> Focus your attention on the sounds around you. You can close your eyes during this part if it helps. Notice sounds you have not been paying attention to, that you have never noticed before, in addition to the ones you may easily be aware of. Take about two minutes.
>
> Now, slowly open your eyes and look around you. Try to notice things you have not noticed before. There will be many things that you may have seen but that didn't quite register, such as the way items are arranged, or imperfections in the color of things, or even objects you hadn't noticed before at all. Spend a minute or two looking around you as if you were seeing this area for the first time.

Now, remembering the Body Scan exercise, feel your entire body—from the top of your head all the way down to the tip of your toes. Feel the vibrations in the sensors of your skin as one big organ. This takes a bit of concentration. Hold it all in your awareness at the same time. Take a minute or two to do this.

Now, we're going to dive deeper within, to your core, where there are three aspects of your inner body we will focus on.

First, feel your emotions. There are always some positive and negative feelings churning around inside you. Notice your feelings manifesting in your body in some way, such as in the muscles of your face, tightness in your throat, sensations in your gut. Second, notice any drives in you, such as hunger, thirst, sexual urges. Third, notice your level of arousal, such as whether you're tired, restless, alert. Take a minute or two to notice all the emotions, drives, and levels of arousal inside you.

Now, pay attention inside your head. Notice thoughts—either ones flowing through on their own or ones you are thinking on purpose. Hear that constant inner narrator telling you what to do, commenting on what is happening, helping you make decisions. With that, notice any mental images either as memories or imagination that come into your head. Take a minute or two to notice the activity going on in your head.

Now, back to your body, notice what your body is *doing*—either on purpose or on its own. Your body is doing something every moment—certainly it is blinking and breathing. It is either still on purpose or adjusting itself. You might even be running or walking during this

> exercise. Feel the sensations either of movement or of intentionally staying still. All movements, automatic or intentional. Take a minute or two and become aware of all the movements of your body—such as shifting posture, stretching your neck—and little movements, like blinking, swallowing, and breathing.

The remaining exercise in this awareness-widening set of BrainShifting skills builds on the previous Brain Sweep by doing it in a different way. In it we'll repeat the Brain Sweep exercise while noticing the entirety of each channel of experience. For example, in the Body Scan exercise, we moved from detailed parts of your body to your entire body all at once. We're going to do the same thing here. We'll move from all the details of each part of the Brain Sweep to experience each aspect as a totality, as a whole or gestalt.

> **Brain Sweep, Phase 2 Exercise**
>
> Notice the sounds around you. Instead of listening to individual sounds, listen as if it were a symphony. When you listen to a symphony, you hear the entirety of the orchestra and all the music instead of focusing on individual instruments and notes. Here, notice the sounds around you as a whole, like it is a "symphony" of sounds. You might experience it like an imaginary "composer" wants you to hear the entire piece all at once, where each part presents itself on purpose. Include everything in your environment—refrigerator noises, birds chirping outside, people talking in the next room—try to hear it all as if it were a single soundtrack. Take a minute or two to do that ...

Now, look at the area around you. Try to see things you hadn't noticed before, but witness them as if this were a single virtual reality scene, a unified landscape. Like you would look at a vista or a painting. See it as a composition. Imagine that the entirety of what you're seeing was designed on purpose, with everything placed for an artistic reason. You wouldn't necessarily look at single elements of a beautiful painting, but you would "stand back" and see it as a whole. Take a minute or two to do the same with your vision ...

Now, feel the entirety of your body again, as you did in the last two exercises. Take a minute or two to do it again. This is a very important aspect of the Brain Sweep.

Now, feel the mixture of emotions, drives, and states that your body is experiencing, all blended together, all at the same time. It does take a second to do that. After all, feeling tired and feeling anxious are very different. Take a minute or two to do this ...

Now, notice the general activity in your head: thoughts, ideas, beliefs, and aspects of your imagination. There are mostly words, but there are also visual images, sometimes music. Include even songs going through your head. Notice your inner narrator. It may be chattering away, commenting on and processing whatever is going on ...

Now, we'll experience the sense of animation of your body. Include any movement your body may be making. This includes breathing, blinking, and swallowing, and subtle movements, like tremors or slight adjustments. It also includes the act of being

> relatively still. That is a form of movement that takes effort. Even when you're sitting in a chair without moving, you have muscles tensing in your abdomen and back, your neck, and legs that allow you to sit up. Take a minute or two to feel the sensation of movement, of animation in your body ...

The main reason to do these Brain Sweep exercises is to strengthen the circuits in your brain that allow you to be more aware. As you strengthen those circuits, everything in each moment gets more vivid. You feel things more intensely. You notice more. You feel more awake.

Here is a poem that can help you make switching easier. "Ears" refers to the symphony of sounds in a soundscape and "eyes" the landscape.

Ears, eyes, skin
And deeper within
Up into your head,
Body moving on its own, guided from deeper within.

The goal of future Brain Sweep exercises is to be able to shift from one channel of experience to the next without getting too bogged down in any particular channel. This will lead to a greater ability to be aware of everything together in one unified and heightened experience— *to the point that you'll find it easy to do.*

As we said, all aspects of BrainShifting, even if practiced as a single exercise, eventually lead to all the other aspects. My suggestion is to practice the Body Scan until you are comfortable being aware of your entire body all at once. Then move on to each of the Brain Sweep exercises, 1 and 2, as you feel comfortable.

BrainShifting Part II: Detachment

Again, detachment is a common mindfulness exercise with a BrainShifting twist. For this exercise you'll need to set a timer. Begin with three minutes and increase the amount of time each day by five minutes, until you are at 20 or 30 minutes.

> ### Breathing Flow Exercise
>
> Begin by noticing your nostrils. Feel the cold, dry air as it gets sucked up into your nose past your nostrils. Then, at some delicate, subtle point, the cycle reverses itself. Notice that point—where cold, dry air turns into warm or even hot air. This moist air leaves and is felt in your nostrils. Then, at another point, the airflow reverses again. Notice both the top and bottom of the cycle and the change in sensations in your nostrils.
>
> The important point of this exercise for a BrainShifting twist is this: notice how you *do not* need to control your breath at all. Notice how the air is sucked up into your nose or chest on its own. No help from you is required. Then, on its own, at some subtle point, the air releases past your nostrils until it slows and readies to begin the cycle over again. Surrender to your breath and witness it.

Like the Body Scan, this exercise will relax you, but you also need to remain constantly alert. It will likely relax you to the point that your breath will begin to slow down. Not a problem. Your breath may even slow down to a point that it stops for a brief period. This also is not a problem—unless that makes you anxious. Be assured, your brain has this, it will not fail you, and you will not be affected at all. On the contrary, naturally slowed or stopped breathing is a sign of deep relaxation, which is good for you. The thing to remember is to not get scared and try to control your breath. Just wait, surrender, and witness your remarkable brain and how it breathes. That's the detachment aspect of the practice. You'll need to be vigilant about noticing how you *don't control* your breath. Again, that's the main feature of the practice.

Later on, as you improve, the skill will generalize to other aspects of your experience. You will witness how your brain does other things by itself. That will give you spontaneity—so-called "flow." Remember, spontaneity is the action side of having Perspective.

Putting Them All Together

There is another element of the Brain Sweep that we left out because it can be tricky to feel at first: the sense of being you. If you are a beginner, then wait until your awareness is strong enough to include that. You can include it if you are experienced at meditation or when you become more experienced at BrainShifting.

The objective with these three exercises is to put them all together. To sit and experience the totality of sounds, sights, bodily sensations outside and in, the activity in your head, and the activity of your body—all happening on their own, without the need for control. It is a sensation of surrender. Like skiing or surfing or riding a bicycle down a gentle hill, there is a global awareness of what is happening and a riding of the experience without micromanaging it.

In the next section, we'll give you some advice on how to put these together. However, please start wherever you feel comfortable. If it's doing a Body Scan alone, then stick with that. If you like either of the Brain Sweeps, do those. If you find the Breathing Flow liberating and easy, then by all means do that. When you are ready, you can combine them all. Pace it to what helps you and feels right. The only suggestion is to pick one practice and stick with it for some days before exploring another one.

A Daily Practice Suggestion

Here is a step-by-step way to develop a daily practice.

- Find a place that you devote to practicing BrainShifting, somewhere you already meditate or somewhere private that is conducive to concentration.

- Sit on something comfortable, but where your knees are lower than your hips and your lower back is arched inward a bit—so that you are sitting up straight. A kneeling chair or meditation cushion is great, but a regular chair with a pillow to support your lower back works fine if you tuck your legs underneath so your knees are lower than your hips.

- Find a regular time to practice BrainShifting. Morning is best for most people because they are more alert before they start their day, and their mind is not busy remembering the day's activities. In the evening people tend to be tired and more internally distracted. However, find whatever time works best for you. Choose a regular time that fits into your other activities, like before showering or getting dressed.

- Find a timer, either via a phone app or an alarm clock. Choose one that uses bells or chimes because they aren't jarring and can create an atmosphere of importance.

- Start with two minutes each day. Increase your time at each session until you are doing each skill for 10 to 15 minutes at a time.

- When the timer starts, do a brief Brain Sweep using the poem presented in this chapter, spending perhaps 10 seconds in each area, such as hearing. (The purpose is to get your brain grounded in the moment. If you want to spend more time with this part of the practice, that's encouraged.)

- Spend the remaining time doing the Breathing Flow exercise. If you find that your attention wanes, you can count your inhalations or exhalations up to 10, over and over until the timer runs out.

- If your attention is led astray into fantasy, that's okay—it's common. The circuits that control attention in your brain will get stronger. One of the ways you can strengthen them is by constantly bringing your attention back to the task of noticing how you don't control your breath. (It is like doing repetitions with weights at a gym instead of just holding them still. That's how you build muscle. It's another way to activate nerve cells that control attention.)

Now that you have skills to practice, let's complete the picture of the SatoriWest Method by diving into the world of wellness.

....

The SatoriWest Method's view of Tunnel Vision and expanding Perspective and the focus on meditation and balancing areas in our lives made a huge difference to me and my outlook.

I'm never going to forget my experiences here. I felt like my problems, no one could understand them because they were so unique to me. Then, I would be talking [to my peers] about how my life is so terrible and we would realize I was in Tunnel Vision. [The SatoriWest Method] really can explain why I was so unhappy. When I focused so tightly on my addiction and heroin use, that I'm never going to be happy again, that's all you can see. If you can just widen your Perspective a bit and not get too focused on the terrible, you can pull through. And if I can pull through, anyone can. It's not just a run-of-the-mill program. It really has changed my life.

—Stephen

15
The Wellnesses and BrainShifting

We're now going to approach BrainShifting from a different direction: focusing on indirect BrainShifting through wellness. That's the way to get your brain to shift on its own. In the way it is defined in the SatoriWest Method, wellness is solely for the purpose of BrainShifting, even though this approach will assuredly improve areas within the six spheres of wellness for their own sake: physical, mental, social, cultural, moral, and existential.

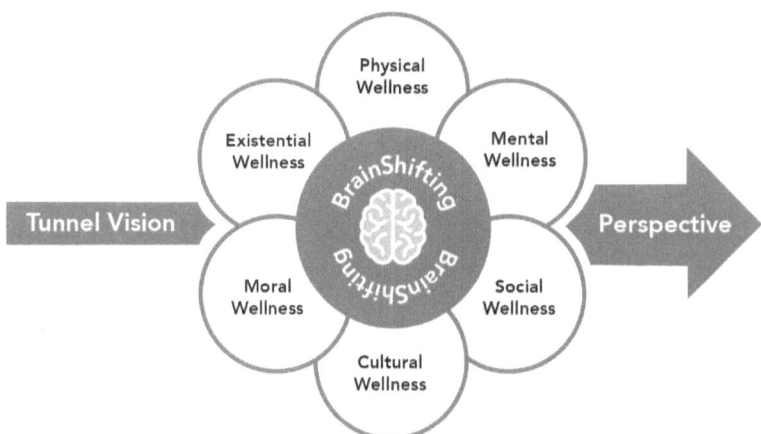

Figure 2. *The SatoriWest Method*

Indirect BrainShifting Through Wellness

Let's illustrate the SatoriWest Method's for integrating wellness, starting with mental wellness.

Many kinds of psychotherapy are about trying to make negative feelings go away as quickly as possible. In cognitive behavioral therapy, for instance, you are instructed to notice distortions in your thinking and then challenge them with a rational counterargument. In the SatoriWest Method, this is incorporated into the sphere of mental wellness.

In the SatoriWest Method, we're doing the same thing: recognizing Tunnel Vision's distorted thinking. From there, the SatoriWest approach splits. The direct BrainShifting approach is to just notice the thoughts along with any or all of the other seven facets of Tunnel Vision that are detectable. If the belief and the feeling that come with it persist, BrainShift further using the "and" technique or a Brain Sweep that opens awareness to everything, including the belief.

Then, with time dedicated to mental wellness, either with a therapist or on your own, perhaps with a self-help book, you can challenge distorted thoughts and replace them with so-called rational or Perspective-based thoughts. The point is that cognitive behavioral therapy is a mental wellness strategy that indirectly fosters BrainShifting. It is meant to enhance the direct opening of your awareness using the awareness skills of BrainShifting.

Again, the mental wellness or *indirect* approach to creating Perspective supports the *direct* BrainShifting practice, and vice versa. In the direct practice, the rational thought would just appear to you as Perspective emerges.

So which is best? Do you notice the distorted thought and the Tunnel Vision that caused it, and eventually, with Perspective, hope the thought will be replaced with a more rational, Perspective-based one? Or do you notice the irrational thought and try to challenge it right away?

There's no right answer. It really depends. They both start with noticing. If the awareness-widening and detaching aspects of the BrainShifting skill don't give you the Perspective you need to see the situation more clearly and rationally, then maybe it's time to think through the rational counterresponse. If you're in a therapist's office and they do cognitive behavioral therapy, then do that first. Your daily BrainShifting practice will cause you to think more rationally from a position of Perspective. Both directions lead to each other.

Eventually, if you practice BrainShifting every day as a form of meditation, for a set period of time, and you make a consistent practice of noticing your Tunnel Vision when it arises, you are not going to have to spend a lot of energy challenging your irrational thoughts: they just won't arise in the first place.

The cognitive behavioral therapy strategy of teaching you how to counter irrational thoughts distorted by Tunnel Vision is one single area in the mental wellness sphere. There are other mental wellness strategies, too, like examining your self-esteem or other aspects of your personality.

There are dozens of wellness areas in the SatoriWest Method organized into the six spheres of wellness: physical, mental, social, organizational, cultural, moral, and existential. For example, the sphere of physical wellness has exercise, nutrition, stretching, and medical care, among others, as its areas. And within each area are dozens of strategies; for example, within the area of nutrition there are dietary recommendations, hydration, and fasting strategies. All the spheres, areas, and strategies naturally and automatically help your brain BrainShift into Perspective. That's the beauty of the SatoriWest Method. It reveals the direct ways to BrainShift and links them with the indirect wellness aspects of BrainShifting. That's what gives the Method its power to change your life. Both directions are usually needed if you are going to liberate yourself from the powerful clutches of Tunnel Vision.

There is another aspect of these wellness strategies that you need to know about before you embark on your complete SatoriWest Method journey. That is, they're not really separate. They all need each other. Picking one and sticking with it alone will not work as well as having a wholistic plan. Let's explore this important point.

The Interconnectedness of Wellnesses

The smaller spheres of wellness overlap for a reason. It's important to explain those interconnections before showing how the wellness spheres cause BrainShifting.

Physical Wellness

Everyone wants to be healthy and well. I'm sure you want to be physically strong, able to walk or run long distances, lift heavier objects, quickly fight off infections, and prevent serious illnesses. We want to live as long as we can and be as fully functional as possible until the day we die.

Most people know that to be physically healthy they need to do the right things: eat and hydrate correctly and in the right amounts, exercise, stretch, relax, sleep well, be in natural settings, take needed supplements, and help themselves when they get mild illnesses, from taking supplements and medications to advocating for themselves with the medical profession.

But there's something else we need to know. We can do everything experts recommend—run and lift weights till we drop, eat the right food every day, take the perfect supplements—and still not be as physically well as we could be without *mental wellness*.

Mental Wellness

We all want to be mentally well, to be generally happy and calm, to feel good about ourselves, to have self-respect, to know and like ourselves and our personality, to think and react to situations effectively. We all want to know how to avoid being stressed so that we take things in stride and avoid getting anxious. We want to be appropriately optimistic so we don't get discouraged and stop trying to make a difference. We want to know what triggers and motivates us so that we have better self-control. We want to learn how to be true to ourselves, and authentic and spontaneous in expressing our feelings and thoughts.

Well, there's something you need to know about mental wellness. To have a high degree of it we can do all the right things. We can explore our personalities, go to psychotherapy and read self-help books, practice self-reward, essentially do everything experts recommend or do it with experts, but it will still be hard, if not impossible, to have a high degree of mental wellness if we don't have *social wellness*.

Social Wellness

We all want social wellness. It means understanding that because we evolved over millions of years as a tribal species, we are more comfortable and feel safer living in communities. Communities give us logistical support, emotional guidance, and companionship. Social wellness means knowing how to make that happen.

More than that, we feel energized and happier when we have romantic love in our lives. We feel more natural as part of a couple, with a close family nearby, who all identify as a tribe with a common identity. Families can give us meaning and an understanding of who we are and where we came from. Social wellness means being able to create good family ties. Loving family, great friends, even companion animals can give these things to us.

Social wellness means knowing how to communicate our feelings, beliefs, and needs. It means being able to set limits in a kind, honest, empathetic, and clear way. It requires us to be able to establish interdependent connections so we can be dependent and independent at the same time. It can involve having the wisdom and balance it takes to raise happy, well-adjusted children. In general, it means we're good at create empowering, loving, and supportive relationships and communities.

If we want a high degree of social wellness, there's something we should realize: we can try to find love, fantastic relationships, and a great community, but it will still be hard, if not impossible, to maintain if we don't have enough *cultural wellness*.

Cultural Wellness

Cultural wellness means being competent at living in this complex, modern world of ours, in society. It means living up to our ability as a member of an extremely intelligent species that is capable of highly complex and creative work. Having cultural wellness means we can accomplish complicated tasks, make difficult decisions, and prepare for the future. It means we are well equipped for all eventualities and emergencies. It also means we can schedule our time in a way that allows us to accomplish what we want and need to do: take care of our house, car, and belongings; find great recreation and enjoyment opportunities to recharge ourselves; and manage the logistics of raising children and caring for each other. It also means knowing how to spend, invest, and save money and how to live in the world, use technology, and negotiate fashion and other trends. In general, cultural wellness means being good at navigating the complexities and competing priorities of modern life and creating order.

Of course, it is one thing to be good at organizing: it's another to be successful. If we want to be culturally successful, we should realize it is hard to have true or lasting cultural wellness if we don't have *moral wellness*.

Moral Wellness

Moral wellness means being wise in how we act and even think. It means understanding what is most important to us, not just what gives us immediate pleasure. Moral wellness means living according to the values—such as love, honor, and family—that are most important to us. It means following ethical principles or guidelines in our actions and decisions, such as treating others as we want to be treated, as if we were walking "a mile in their moccasins." Moral principles inspire us to make ourselves, others, and the world better. They serve us when our impulses might lead us to make other choices. Being morally well means living with integrity, being honest, being kind, not being wasteful, and doing what is in your best or others' best interests.

Morality in the SatoriWest context is also about being wise and balanced in all the areas of wellness, because all the areas and spheres of wellness can bring you to a higher plane of existence, *to greater Perspective*, not just behaviors and attitudes that are traditionally considered moral. In other words, being morally well is not only about doing what is right as far as harming others; it means knowing whether to spend time with family or give yourself some alone time, and whether to eat healthful food or give yourself a treat. It means knowing whether it is best to get more sleep or keep up with an exercise routine in any particular moment. Whether it is best to spend money on exercise equipment or save money for the future. Whether it is best to risk hurting someone's feelings by being honest or by being silent. These are all decisions that are about making our lives and the lives of others better, decisions that can bring our brain to a higher plane of Perspective.

Being morally well means having wisdom and balance that changes with the uniqueness of each moment. This requires Perspective, so moral wellness and Perspective go hand in hand.

Moral wellness helps us be culturally successful. That's because the more people lack integrity, the greater their chances are of not being successful—at least in the long run. Imagine running a business or working at a job or raising kids without a moral compass to guide you to do what is right. Running a business with only short-term benefits in mind, without regard for its customers' welfare or even society's interest, would damage its reputation. Amassing a fortune by skirting the rules will likely get you into trouble. Working with others but putting your own interests first all the time would cause your coworkers to dislike you or not want to work with you. Raising kids without balancing everyone's best interests might cause them to resent you or vice versa, or end in them being maladjusted.

For some, the highest coordinating principle of moral wellness is discerning and working toward a life purpose, a mission that aims to use our talents and passions to make the world a better place. It can inform all our wellness choices. Plus, without moral wellness, people aren't very happy at the end of the day, which speaks to the connection between moral wellness, mental wellness, social wellness, and all the other wellness areas.

If we truly want moral wellness, there's something we should know: it's hard, if not impossible, to have or sustain moral wellness if we don't have some amount of *existential wellness*.

Existential Wellness

Existential wellness means realizing the true worth of our existence. It means being amazed and awed at the incomprehensibly unlikely odds that we got to be born and are alive in this very moment, at how precious a gift that is. To be in wonder about the fact that anything came into being. Think about it: the universe didn't have to come into existence. There might as well have just been nothing. Even if you believe in a god who created you and the universe, who says that god had to exist in the first place?

Existential wellness often comes with the expression of deep gratitude for the source of our existence, whatever we perceive that to be. The term existential includes notions that have been called "spiritual," if supernatural, metaphysical, or religious beliefs help you put your existence in Perspective. However, religious and spiritual beliefs (for example, the ideas of a god, spirits, angels, reincarnation) are not necessary when it comes to appreciating the magnificence of one's existence, or of all existence.

When we have existential wellness, we see beauty and artistry in the sublime and seemingly mundane. We are humbled and awed by our experience of seeing, hearing, smelling, tasting, touching, thinking, and feeling—anything. Existential wellness means practicing being grateful every day, sometimes in a ritualistic way—at mealtimes or before bed or when with family. It means having practices that cause us to appreciate our existence. We get existentially well through the study of and belief and faith in religion. We also arrive at it through the study of science and philosophy and in communing with nature.

If we want true experiential wellness, there's something we should realize. First, moral wellness allows your brain to focus in on its existence. It encourages it. As we'll explore, your brain has to shift for you to experience existential wellness.

Perspective and Wellness

Each of the six spheres of wellness need the other five to fully work. You can't have total wellness without integrating physical, mental, social, cultural, moral, and existential aspects of your brain.

For example, if you're in bad health (physical wellness), your brain won't be able to sustain the energy to take care of life's business (cultural wellness). If you are miserable and stressed (mental wellness), you won't be able to care about anyone else's feelings (social wellness). If you are lonely or despised by others (social wellness), you could wind up becoming greedy and selfish (moral wellness). If you are disorganized in your life (cultural wellness), you won't be able to take care of your hygiene and medical health (physical wellness). If you are in violation of universal laws of morality so that you seek immediate pleasure above all else (moral wellness), you will overlook the beauty and magnificence of the world around you (existential wellness).

In fact, if any one of the six spheres is way out of balance, it will throw the others off balance, and your life will be the worse for it. In the diagram of the SatoriWest Method, the wellness spheres are connected to their neighbor but not to all the other spheres. That is not fully accurate, although depicting that would make the image complicated to look at.

So what's left after all the areas of wellness are working in concert toward our total wellness?

The Link Between Wellness and BrainShifting

This is where we pull together the two aspects of the SatoriWest Method, the direct skills of BrainShifting and the indirect wellness practices that shift our brains, with one other element. Yes, if you practice wellness, it will lead your brain to Perspective. That's indirect BrainShifting. And yes, if you practice the direct skills of BrainShifting, that will also cause Perspective to emerge.

We should point out another obvious fact: wellness is not just good for your brain. If you practice physical wellness, your body will be healthier. If you practice mental wellness, you'll be happier and more rational. If you practice social wellness, your relationships will improve. The same for cultural wellness—your life will be more organized, and you'll be more successful in what you do. To be clear, traditional wellness strategies are a means to accomplish the improvements needed in those areas.

With SatoriWest, a cleaner home and a happier marital life are not the main ends. The main reason for practicing wellness is so your brain can shift. The purpose of shifting your brain is to realize the magnitude of your existence, in the context of the entirety of each unique moment. That's the main reason for practicing wellness. Keeping your bed made lifts and calms the energy in your brain. Going on vacation, being loved by a spouse, energizes your higher brain and supports a shift toward seeing the nondominant hemisphere.

Now let's see this in the opposite direction. As your brain shifts, as you use your higher brain and shift to a more balanced experience with both hemispheres so that you have more Perspective, your health and wellness will magically (not really) improve. Your thinking will be more effective, you'll have more satisfying relationships, and you'll have more success. In other words, the more we learn to shift our brain through daily practice, the better off we are in the various areas of our life. And the more wellness we practice in each sphere, the more it changes our brain so it gets natural Perspective. Here are a few examples of this two-way relationship.

How a Shifted Brain Creates Wellness

These are the ways in which a shifted brain creates wellness.

Physical Wellness

This isn't addressed in the chapters on BrainShifting, but BrainShifting comes with a physical lift in energy into your head as well as significant relaxation. Sometimes stimulants have a similar effect of energizing your mental functions while relaxing your body. Opening up to the moment with heightened, wide, and detached awareness is good for your body. It's a natural antidote to stress. This allows your body to function better, with improved digestion, immunity, cognition, and circulation.

Mental Wellness

A brain that can BrainShift won't drown in its own Tunnel Vision, in overcontrolling its mind, ego, and imagination. This leads to stress, anxiety, prolonged grief, and hostility.

A brain with Perspective can more easily overcome even biological depression and anxiety, first and foremost, because it can recognize the illness as an illness and not objective reality. A widened and detached style of paying attention allows you to experience thoughts and feelings with objectivity so you don't take your feelings, your beliefs, and even your "self" as absolute truth instead of as information. If nothing else, Perspective lets you see each moment as unique, as fresh and new, so you don't get bored. Each moment can be interesting, if not fascinating.

Social Wellness

A shifted brain can fall madly in love with someone, but not so madly that it loses boundaries and sabotages the experience. It can only enhance it.

A brain in Perspective will have deep and meaningful relationships in part because it sees the gift each person really is. If your brain is in Tunnel Vision, you will quickly take things personally. You will take people for granted or experience them as objects to meet your needs. A BrainShifted brain in Perspective lets you deeply appreciate the people in your life exactly as they are. Perspective allows for empathy. A brain in Tunnel Vision cannot empathize; it cannot be truly authentic and expressive with others.

Cultural Wellness

Your brain needs Perspective to be truly competent in this world. Perspective is practical. It allows you to make better decisions. A shifted brain in Perspective can integrate diverse pieces of information, like deciding whether to save, invest, or spend a gift of cash. In Tunnel Vision most people might spend that money without a second thought. Perspective makes you functionally smarter because you need it to weigh opposing factors, for instance knowing how much insurance to buy for the potential risk you face.

Moral Wellness

It is virtually impossible to be moral if your brain is in Tunnel Vision, particularly the role of ego in aspects of immorality. A brain in Tunnel Vision that is geared exclusively toward escaping and avoiding feelings of pain or what it dislikes will do anything to accomplish that end, including what could be considered immoral. A brain in Perspective will have wisdom, forgiveness, compassion, and understanding.

Existential Wellness

You cannot feel the wonder and magnitude of your existence, feel gratitude beyond words and devotion to the source of your existence, appreciating everything you have in your life, if your brain doesn't widen and detach its awareness and penetrate its aliveness.

Key Wellness Strategies that Cause Your Brain to Shift

Can you really, practically, practice every strategy recommended in the SatoriWest Method at around the same time? What does it even mean to practice something: you can always reach higher and higher levels of wellness? Can you even work on every single strategy, since there are so many?

My previous book, *Awaken Your Brain: Coming Alive to Vibrant Well-being and a New Reality*, is a detailed guide to wholistic wellness with over 80 strategies from within the six spheres of wellness. Its level of detail is beyond the scope of this book. The aim of this chapter is to show that wellness practiced specifically with the goal of BrainShifting—opening up the brain toward Perspective—is a qualitatively different kind of wellness practice. Remember, wellness practices are the indirect routes to Perspective.

So the answer to the question of whether you can realistically do everything and do it to perfection is, obviously, no. Knowing which areas and strategies to work on within each sphere, and knowing when to stop working on them for a while because the place you've reached with them is good enough, takes Perspective.

However, there are a few guidelines that may help. First, identify the key areas of wellness within each sphere that are out of balance, that are not going so well. Then create a plan to work on them around the same time. Here are a few key wellness strategies to think about, research, and add to your total wellness regimen.

Physical Wellness

Physical wellness strategies include the following:

- If you need medication, take it. If you need to see a doctor, do so, and follow their advice. However, be an informed consumer of medical services, educated to the extent you can be, and able to practice self-health when necessary.
- Eat and drink nutrient-dense foods and beverages (as opposed to foods and beverages with empty calories) that are from natural sources (unprocessed) and organic.
- Drink at least eight cups of pure water a day.
- If it is medically allowed, consider a water or raw juice fast for 24–36 hours once a month and maybe for a few days once a year.
- Get at least a moderate amount of aerobic exercise several times a week. Please consult your healthcare professional before undertaking any physical wellness program.
- Engage in a breathing/stretching practice such as yoga a few times a week.
- Put yourself in a natural outdoors or wilderness setting for at least an hour once a week.

Mental Wellness

Key mental wellness strategies include the following:

- Seek out professional assistance or objective guidance from someone you trust whenever you encounter a stressor that seems to last.

- Talk about yourself openly and regularly, but in appropriate circumstances.
- Practice cognitive behavioral self-therapy when you feel overly sad, anxious, angry, stressed, or guilty. Recording or noting your negative feelings, the thoughts that create them, how those thoughts might be irrational (warped from Tunnel Vision), and the countering rational thought (Perspective) is a mental wellness / cognitive self-therapy strategy.
- Practice stimulus-control awareness, noting the stimuli that trigger unhealthy behavior, such as eating when the television is turned on or vice versa, or driving aggressively.
- Practice contingency self-management, where you reward yourself for healthy behavior and do not reward yourself for unhealthy behavior.

Social Wellness

Key social wellness strategies include the following:

- Practice empathetic listening regularly while listening to friends and family about their issues, thoughts, and concerns.
- Be assertive as soon as you realize you need to be.
- Make time with family and friends a priority.
- Create family meetings with prearranged ways to make decisions about important issues, such as finances, wills, healthcare, and vacations.
- Give yourself the opportunity to fall in love. That can start with instant physical chemistry or grow over years with someone with whom you are greatly compatible.

Cultural Wellness

Key cultural wellness strategies include the following:

- Find out what natural disasters are prevalent in your area and prepare for them.
- Buy the right kind and amount of insurance and adjust it regularly for changing needs.
- Raise your financial IQ, invest wisely, save appropriately, then spend joyfully.
- Create a LifePlan® (find a downloadable document at SatoriWest.com) that organizes all the areas within the six spheres of wellness and attaches them to a daily schedule.

Moral Wellness

Key moral wellness strategies include the following:

- Create a list of 30 or more values (for example, love, family, success, admiration, global warming, mental health) and prioritize them within highest, medium, and lowest in groups of 10 or more.
- For every wellness strategy you devise, create a list of principles that can help guide you during challenging times. For example, your goal may be to save 10 percent of your salary for the future. Your guiding principles might be "A penny saved is a penny earned," and "If you can't pay cash, you can't afford it."
- Generate a list of 10–15 precepts or vows that you promise yourself to follow to the best of your ability. Structure each precept so that it is preceded by the reason for it. Here are some examples:
    - To keep my mind and body healthy, I vow to not abuse intoxicants.

– To keep my relationship strong, I vow to be honest with my spouse about all things, all the time.

Existential Wellness

Key existential wellness strategies include the following:

- Stop periodically and appreciate the moment and how you and everything in it got there.
- If you are religious, practice your religion if you are a better person for it.
- If you are spiritual, do your spiritual practice if you are a healthier person for it.
- Regularly create art, appreciate conventional art, or see art and beauty everywhere.
- Regularly practice gratitude, for example, with family before meals, as you begin meetings, or every night before bed.
- Take daily and extended contemplative time in a conducive setting to think about your life, where you've been, what you have enjoyed, what has gone wrong, and where you want to go. Spend part of this time practicing BrainShifting.

Balance and Perspective

Perspective is wonderful. Seeing life with wisdom, humor, compassion, creativity, and all the rest makes it much better. Having wellness is wonderful, too. Being able to live in ways that are effective and healthy also makes life better. Yet there's an ingredient that both of these things independently require. It's a skill and a talent that we've only touched on throughout this book yet is worthy of praise and exploration. It's balance.

Balance is the ingredient that binds together Perspective and wellness. It's the ingredient that helps you effectively practice the skill of BrainShifting, to know when to try hard and when to relax and realize. It's the ingredient that will help you better work each specific wellness strategy and know how to work several or all of your wellness strategies together. It's the ingredient that helps you know when it is time to employ the direct avenue to Perspective and when to use the indirect avenues.

Balance is an integral aspect of what it means to have Perspective. It's as fundamental to Perspective as it is to walking and standing.

Balance was mentioned earlier in this chapter in the context of moral wellness. It's knowing when to be honest and when to hold back honesty in service to someone's feelings. Wisdom and balance go hand in hand; so do balance and creativity. When making art, you need balance to know how much and how little to put where. Balance is also knowing when enough is enough, when not enough is not enough, when to switch wellness strategies, and when and how to combine strategies.

There are many balances when it comes to wellness alone. There are balances *within each specific area*: we need to know when to eat to keep our strength and nutrition up and when to stop eating, and whether to spend time at the gym doing aerobic exercise or strength training.

There are also balances within each *sphere* of wellness. For example, in the sphere of physical wellness, it's choosing how to balance our limited time between nature, exercising, and sleep.

There are balances *between each of the spheres* and their respective areas. For example, it's knowing how much of our limited time to devote to home organization, physical exercise, family outings, and religious activities, to name a few.

There is also a balance between wellness and BrainShifting. We must, in my opinion, spend a bit of time each day practicing the skills of BrainShifting while making sure that all the areas within the six spheres of wellness are also looked after.

The key to the wellness aspect of the SatoriWest journey is to have the spheres of wellness and BrainShifting in balance. This takes planning and wisdom, time management, and moment-to-moment awareness. In other words, it takes Perspective. Perspective gives you balance. Balance helps you get Perspective.

To help you accomplish all these balances, you can download the LifePlan® document (find it at SatoriWest.com). It not only helps you find balance in wellness but provides another indirect way to get Perspective using tools such as an Identity Statement, Historical Timeline, and Mission Statement in addition to wellness goals and steps.

. . . .

[The SatoriWest Method] was insightful, interesting, helpful, thought-provoking, useful, and challenging. This was the program I needed and have been seeking for almost three years, since my diagnosis. I feel hopeful and giddy about the possibilities for healing and perspective. Thank you so much for giving me more tools, and especially for giving me hope that my healing will be durable and long-lasting.

—Anonymous

Part V
Blessed by Distress

16

Suffering and the History of Crisis and Opportunities

The poet Henry David Thoreau said, "Most men lead lives of quiet desperation." The rest of that line (often cited but misattributed to Thoreau) is "and go to the grave with the song still in them."

What song does this refer to? Perspective, of course. What does quiet desperation point to? The suffering in the human condition caused by Tunnel Vision.

Blessed by Distress

So far on our journey through the SatoriWest Method we've talked about Tunnel Vision in its cultural, toxic, and crisis manifestations as the cause of suffering. We then addressed the solution: a subtle shift in what your brain pays attention to, called BrainShifting, which can open up a world of Perspective— Perspective encapsulating everything a person could want out of life, which is freely derived from within. We then touched on the main subject repeatedly throughout the book: the paradox that crises and suffering can be beneficial to discovering this inner source of ultimate happiness.

Crises come in many different forms. Some are self-induced, some are thrust upon us by life, and some are a combination of both. So what does it really mean to be "blessed by distress"? How can pain, hardship, and emotional distress be opportunities for life-altering Perspective? Before we explore how and why crises—or any "negative" feelings—can be a blessing in Chapter 17, let's reiterate something that is universally confusing: what it means to suffer.

To Suffer

It bears repeating: the feeling that life or an event is insufferable is *solely* the result of constricted Tunnel Vision. Again, what that means is that it is one thing to feel afraid, grief-stricken, or furious; it's quite another to suffer from those feelings.

In a sense, suffering means that negative emotions or even physical pain have penetrated to your core. They cause you to lose Perspective. For example, someone being tortured would not suffer as much, if at all, if they knew they were enduring it to save their family or a country, or as a religious calling.

This is admittedly a difficult concept to understand. We assume that suffering will inevitably follow physical pain, huge loss, and other traumatic events, so much so that the painful event and the suffering seem inexorably linked. Yet in our way of understanding it, anything that causes Tunnel Vision causes suffering. For instance, a traumatic event, like losing everything you own after a tornado, can inflate your ego so that you take this act of nature personally, feeling it defines your life or that it is bad luck directed at you. That makes the event even worse. It causes you to suffer from it, at least some if not a lot.

A traumatic event can make you more suggestible, so you utterly believe your assumptions about what is happening, with no room for doubt. In the instance of a loss caused by a tornado, any obstinate or unyielding beliefs that, for example, you can never be happy again, or that financial ruin is shameful—any belief fueled by ego—makes you suffer. Holding on to these beliefs, insisting that they are the truth, can cause you to feel anguish.

The very experience of Tunnel Vision itself is the experience of suffering. A difficult event that blocks your awareness, so all you can experience inside and around you is the trauma and the circumstances around the trauma, leaves you living in an experiential kind of hell. It's a kind of claustrophobia that is insufferable and doesn't allow you to see any positive options.

The inflation of your sense of self, by itself, comes with the experience of loneliness and alienation. Feeling separated from others and from the universe are forms of suffering. In essence, the warping of your mind makes you miserable.

Even changes to your brain that aren't from an external event cause Tunnel Vision, such as biological depression. These changes can warp your mind to the extent that you suffer *even when nothing bad is going on in your life.* People have had biological depression or extreme anxiety, and attempted suicide from its resulting Tunnel Vision, only to find that when medications brought them back to some degree of Perspective, they would *never* want to lose their lives. It is possible to be in a biological depression and not suffer from it. Any aspect of Perspective—humor, self-love, especially the certain knowledge that it is a medical illness—can relieve the suffering from it.

There is a popular saying that "stress is not what happens to you, it's how you react to it." This is another way of viewing suffering.

Don't misunderstand. Horrible things do, of course, happen. And they can cause you to feel mighty emotions, yet that is still not the same thing as suffering from them. When difficult things happen to someone with great Perspective, they feel—and want to feel—all the normal feelings you might feel; it's just that their sense of self doesn't get inflated, and their attention and thoughts aren't pulled into the event so that they cannot remember or experience anything positive.

Even physical pain doesn't hurt as much when you have Perspective. It is a known medical phenomenon that there is a difference between having pain and the perception of the same pain. That's how certain pain medications work—on the perception of pain, not on pain receptors. That's how mindfulness works in pain clinics. That's how Perspective works as well.

In this sense, there's a difference between a life crisis, where something objectively bad happens, and an emotional crisis. It is an emotional crisis because Tunnel Vision is at an extreme, when our sense of self, our beliefs, and our reality become so distorted that we can no longer cope.

Remember, the SatoriWest definition of a crisis is Tunnel Vision that is so extremely constricted that we risk serious health problems or become a danger to ourselves or others. In other words, two people can experience the same event and have similar feelings, but if one of them gets dragged into worsening Tunnel Vision, and the other keeps some degree of Perspective, the one with Perspective will not suffer as much, if at all.

Again, *suffering is not the same thing as experiencing grief, fear, hostility, or even physical pain.* People can experience difficult feelings and sensations in context, and they can frame them with gratitude for what they *do* have. They can face adversity with some amount of love or humor. They can juxtapose those difficult feelings with the love they feel for their family, who may be affected by what they are going through. They can also emote fully without holding back, which can feel liberating, like a release and a relief. There are many ways to use the various facets of Perspective to transform suffering. So the more Perspective you have, the less you are in emotional crisis.

Crisis as a Springboard

All of this is important to understanding how and why crises are opportunities. There are many reasons why adversity can be a chance for a breakthrough to a more fulfilling life. In Chapter 17 we'll explore four of them. For now, here's one way to think of the process. Imagine a rubber band sitting on the spectrum from Tunnel Vision to Perspective. Take one end of the rubber band, put it anywhere in the middle of the spectrum, and then pull the other end toward Tunnel Vision. The farther you pull it, the more potential energy is built up. When you let the Tunnel Vision side go, it flings the rubber band toward Perspective.

One way this happens is waking up to your life and to the fact that you are creating your own Tunnel Vision, even in the middle of a crisis—when most people would completely understand why you would be suffering.

Not Suffering

In the chapter on Perspective we explored Perspective as the opposite of Tunnel Vision. We looked at it as if it were the extreme opposite. We talked about being in love with life, happier, more at peace. We mentioned having an abundance of gratitude, deep fulfillment, a greater sense of irony and humor, wisdom and insight. It sounds ideal.

The first thing to understand about suffering is that *not* suffering is really the goal of life. Not suffering brings out the best in you, in your brain. Not suffering is liberation, a level of Perspective that comes with greater wisdom, creativity, humor, love, gratitude, and so on. This does not need to be as dramatic as the words Awakening or Nirvana imply.

If you suffered back pain your whole life, not having the pain or not suffering the pain would feel as amazing as having achieved something extraordinary. To suffer from depression for years and then suddenly not have depression or not suffer from it would feel like you had been emotionally suppressed but could now cry fully and completely, without shame or inhibition. That expressiveness would be purging and cathartic.

Siddhartha Gautama, the Buddha, pointed out that to not suffer *is* Enlightenment. Not to overstate this, but Tunnel Vision feels awful, all the time, even in its milder expression. That's why even a smidgeon of relief from severe Tunnel Vision can be so liberating that you want to "kiss the ground," so to speak, in gratitude. If you were drowning in the ocean and somehow managed to reach a shore, you wouldn't have to find the sandy beaches of Cancun to appreciate every rock and blade of grass. It might be the best place you've ever known, even if you'd led a life of extreme privilege.

One way that crises and adversity are opportunities is that relative to them, any degree of relief, any amount of Perspective, can feel life altering. Many people believe that you must know suffering to know great happiness. They think you have to know extreme Tunnel Vision to know extreme Perspective. That does *not* appear to be universally true—but it is often true. It would be a relief to be unshackled from a privileged but suffocating and meaningless life, even without trauma. It could cause you to feel in love with your existence, if only a tiny bit, if only for a moment.

Using Crisis and Hardship to Find Perspective

Do we absolutely need the springboard of severe crises and enormous hardships to find great Perspective, even great Perspective that is relative to the suffering? Again, it does not appear so. That's the good news. Yet no one is exempt from crisis. You may not live in a country torn by war and famine, but you will lose loved ones. You will get sick, even very sick at times. You will face the prospect of losing everything you have worked so hard to build or collect.

Suffering is a shortcut to Perspective, because any degree of relief from that suffering, with any degree of Perspective, makes that Perspective life changing. Of course, that dynamic goes hand in hand with slogging through the process of recognizing Tunnel Vision to get Perspective whenever you can find it. That's because no matter how good you are at recognizing your Tunnel Vision, no matter how effective you are at BrainShifting every day—whether with meditation or on the fly—no matter how successful you are at practicing wellness so that you feel naturally high, life has a way of hitting you with things from out of nowhere. Life can and will try to drag you into emotional crisis. You will experience crisis Tunnel Vision. That's when the SatoriWest Method will be your best friend. That is also when it will challenge your willingness to practice it the most.

Some of you have already lived a life of suffering or been dealt a bad hand in childhood or somewhere along the way through no fault of your own. For you, the SatoriWest Method probably makes sense already. You get it on a gut level that others who haven't suffered that much may not understand as well.

If you've suffered a lot, you probably don't need to be lured into learning and practicing the SatoriWest Method by the promise of fantastic levels of Perspective or even Awakening; even a little relief would be a blessing. You're probably more than ready to see your Tunnel Vision and how it hurts you.

Author's note: I've noticed this as a psychiatrist with my patients. Some of them have struggled every day of their lives, sometimes since early in childhood, with abuse, mental illness, or substance use. When I tell them about Tunnel Vision, they get it clearly and viscerally, immediately. They get it in ways that others don't. It never stops amazing me. When I present the same method to advanced Buddhist meditators, many of whom have not suffered as dramatically as my patients, they are often left trying to imagine what Tunnel Vision is, without having the same visceral, experiential understanding my patients had. People who have suffered less in life don't have the same drive to feel their Tunnel Vision for the source of pain that it is and then do what it takes to recover from it. I've seen this time and time again.

It reminds me of the proverbial Zen master having to hit his disciples on the head with a stick to get them to realize what he or she is talking about, so they can wake up to great Perspective.

The History of Crisis as Opportunity

Does this still seem like an odd concept—the idea of calamities and suffering as a launchpad to greater happiness and peace? Actually, it's not unusual. Throughout history many, many people have described it. It's such a widespread notion that the Chinese symbol for "crisis" is made of two characters: one for "danger," the other for "opportunity," as seen here.

"Crisis" = "Danger" + "Opportunity"

Consider people with substance-use or other compulsive disorders who really do get to the point that they "bottom out" from their addictions. That's when their Tunnel Vision has fed on itself so thoroughly that their lives have become smoldering wreckages of negative consequences. Their own physical health is often precariously bad, sometimes irreversibly so. Their finances and credit are sometimes in a deep hole, and they've usually burned many relationship bridges. Perhaps the worst part is that with a slim amount of Perspective, they can see what they've done to themselves and others. Yet out of that misery—because of that misery—many describe an opening to themselves and to their lives on a deeper level. It appears their misery and finally their desperation spurred them or switched something inside that caused a BrainShift, as we'll explore further in this chapter. Sometimes the BrainShift is radical and sometimes it's modest, but in either case, it's life opening.

In SatoriWest terms, it forces people out of their downward spiral of reactions, self-centered perceptions, and self-defeating thoughts and behaviors caused by Tunnel Vision. It throws them out of that spiral in a dramatic way. Crashing and burning in that way is like a "hard smack in the face." It gives victims of their own Tunnel Vision a new appreciation of life, more than regular hardships do for people who don't have a substance-use problem or compulsive behavior. From this "bottoming out" some have even had so-called spiritual Awakenings.

For example, Bill Wilson, the founder of Alcoholics Anonymous, described his spiritual Awakening in this well-known quote. Having been through many alcoholic benders with heart-wrenching consequences, he wound up once again in a hospital room after another binge and described this:

> My depression deepened unbearably and finally it seemed to me as though I were at the bottom of the pit. I still gagged badly on the notion of a Power greater than myself, but finally, just for the moment, the last vestige of my proud obstinacy was crushed. All at once I found myself crying out, "If there is a God, let Him show Himself, I am ready to do anything, anything!"
>
> Suddenly the room lit up with a great white light. I was caught up into an ecstasy which no words can describe. It seemed to me in the mind's eye that I was on a mountain and that a wind not of air but of spirit was blowing. And it was burst upon me that I was a free man. Slowly the ecstasy subsided. I lay on the bed, but now for a time I thought I was in another world, a new world of consciousness. All about me and through me there was a wonderful feeling of Presence and I thought to myself, "So this is the God of the preachers!" A great peace stole over me and I thought, "No matter how wrong things seem to be, they are all right. Things are all right with God and his world." (Ernest Kurtz, Not-God: A History of Alcoholics Anonymous [Center City, MN: Hazelden, 1991.])

Not many people experience an opening on the magnitude of Bill Wilson's. For most who reach "rock bottom" and change for the better, the opening happens in a more modest way. Maybe they realize for the first time that they've been behaving or experiencing life in self-defeating ways they couldn't see before their crisis. Maybe it helped them become humbler, less stuck in their ways, and more authentic, more at peace, less rigid and intolerant.

Wilson's words are an apt expression of extreme Perspective: the sense of freedom, the thought that even though things seem to be "wrong," there still can be amazement for one's existence. In other words, the notion that "things are all right with God and his world" depicts the wider experience of the moment, rather than being caught in Tunnel Vision.

It is important to say that bottoming out *can* be a disaster. Sometimes if you stretch the rubber band enough, it'll break. Some people bottom out and never really fully recover. Some die prematurely. Bottoming out does not guarantee an opening. Do not justify bottoming out or seeking any hardship *just* to wake yourself up. That's dangerous and unnecessary. As we said, life provides plenty of crises all by itself. There's no need to go looking for them. On the other hand, people throughout recorded history have lived through disasters and difficult predicaments and described how it opened their eyes to a world of appreciation and freedom they had never known before.

There are more lessons to be learned from the historic Buddha, Siddhartha Gautama. He was a prince sheltered from the world as a child and young adult who discovered to his horror and deep sadness that old age, sickness, pain, and death existed. This suffering drove him to seek Enlightenment. It was Siddhartha's *opportunity from adversity*. It motivated him to seek a different understanding of life. He sought something greater than the splendid, but obviously fleeting, pleasures he had as a privileged aristocrat. It compelled him to come out of his comfort zone and seek something more substantial and real.

The story of Buddha helps makes another point. As he began seeking Enlightenment, Siddhartha followed the ascetic practices of the day. These called for self-denial to the point of starvation, sometimes sleep deprivation, and self-inflicted pain. You could say that this practice engendered the mistaken belief that you must inflict suffering on yourself to know Awakening. Remember, that is sometimes true, but not always.

At some point, Siddhartha realized that the "mortification of the body" strategy, which was (and maybe still is) believed to be a requirement to release the mind to Nirvana, was not working. Instead of the two life extremes he experienced—indulged prince and self-inflicted sufferer, which are two ways to be in Tunnel Vision—he woke up from his suffering.

Author's note: What did Buddha do to Awaken himself? He had to have BrainShifted in one way or another. Sitting under the Bodhi tree, following his breath, he came to a realization. He recognized that he (his brain) was already Awakened, and that his suffering had been self-inflicted. All that was needed was to find an inner place of self-knowing, an aliveness beyond everyday experience from which he could let go of his attachments—his Tunnel Vision. He could then realize the miraculous reality of his and all existence, and his (brain's) ability to know it.

Many, many people describe opening experiences, which we'd call significant Perspective, that came from some adverse event. You probably know some of them. When asked, the people who opened up to greater Perspective would say they benefited in some significant, often life-changing ways. Here are some quotes from people who have posted their thoughts on the internet:

"Crisis ... shakes you into reflection and healing."
— Bryant McGill, Simple Reminders: Inspiration for Living Your Best Life

> *"Through each crisis in my life, with acceptance and hope, in a single defining moment, I finally gained the courage to do things differently."*
>
> — Sharon E. Rainey

Many modern-day, well-known spiritual teachers, such as Eckhart Tolle, Byron Katie, and Jeff Foster, speak firsthand about emergence from a so-called "dark night of the soul." The depths of their misery rebounded into a life infused with bliss, with great contentment for what is a wondrously alive reality. Their experiences are like Charles Dickens' story, "A Christmas Carol," where an otherwise unhappy, irritable, and unappreciative Ebenezer Scrooge is dragged into the harsh realities of his past, present, and future, only to come out a transformed, happier person.

Of course, the vast majority of us won't need such dramatic stories of great Awakenings from a "dark night of the soul" to find the Perspective that will change our lives for the better. Yet this history illustrates that there is a connection between *any* stress and *any* hardship and finding fulfillment.

Again, you don't need crises to find the highest sense of meaning and appreciation for life you are capable of. People can find great Perspective from intense meditative practice or religious contemplation. A few fall into it suddenly for no obvious reason. Most adults gradually find more Perspective in life as they mature. Emotional maturity happens naturally as people age in wisdom and Perspective—unless they are caught up in spiraling Tunnel Vision. Some people do age with a greater sense of peace and contentment than less emotionally mature adults who are stuck in serious habits of Tunnel Vision. Yet even the vast majority of people who mature naturally never do it enough to escape the traps of their cultural Tunnel Vision.

The SatoriWest Method is about using all strategies available to you. They will likely all be needed for the road to fulfillment. We should all be directly cultivating our brains with daily

BrainShifting meditation, recognizing Tunnel Vison where and however it shows itself, promoting Perspective and brain development by practicing wellness. And we should prepare for the inevitable crises and hardships that will befall us.

In case accounts of difficulties and traumas were not enough to demonstrate that you can find life-changing Perspective from them, there are plenty of examples right now in popular media. It's not *that* unusual. There are many published stories about people who describe their lives as shaken up for the better after surviving something bad. There are accounts of veterans who lost their limbs in a bomb blast during a war, people whose worldly possessions were lost in a flood, and even, I know it seems hard to fathom, some traumatized by sexual assault. They have described their experiences as "life changing" or "the best thing that ever happened to me."

Author's note: A college friend of mine lost the use of his legs after a motorcycle accident, yet he was one of the happiest and most loving people I had ever known. He was a magnet for all of our friends, who felt happy just being around him. Before the days of the Americans with Disabilities Act made access easier, we took turns carrying him up a flight of stairs to go a meeting. One day, carrying him up the stairs, I asked him why he was so at peace and happy. He told me the accident was the best thing that had ever happened to him. I was shocked. It was one of the strangest things I had ever heard; at the time, I didn't understand what he was talking about. I believe I know now that the accident forced him out of his narrow mindset and into greater Perspective.

Even life-disrupting events can be opportunities. During a major power outage and blackout in New York City in the 1970s, neighbors who never knew each other connected in deep and meaningful ways. People stopped habitually running, grasping, and seeking long enough to soak in the moment and connect with those around them. Without electricity they were able to more fully appreciate the small things they hadn't really appreciated before—photographs on the wall, furniture in their homes, the neighborhood. Some of these things were usually virtually invisible because they couldn't compete with the things that grabbed people's attention every moment of every day in Tunnel Vision. Similarly, the shock and horror of September 11, 2001, led many people to feel a sense of love and unity with strangers and an appreciation for life and what they had.

In Chapter 17, we'll show you how to use difficult times to your advantage.

....

Before I started [with SatoriWest], I was going to leave to live in the woods. I have since been able to find perspective through the SatoriWest Method. I appreciate all aspects of this program.

—Trevor

17

How to Use Crisis and Hardship as Opportunities

Right now, in millions of homes around the world, families are in cultural Tunnel Vision at the end of long workdays. Perhaps they have enough financially to be comfortable but they feel inadequate for not having even more. Instead of celebrating each other's company, they watch television. Each family member gets lost in his or her own room and world. Parents want their children to have the very best life has to offer, so they work extra hours and miss the chance to get to know and enjoy them. Families want to feel special in a world that rewards specialness. They dream of going on the best vacation and living in a more upscale neighborhood. Parents want children to be motivated to make their family proud in their career choices, so the children may make choices that ignore their psychological needs. Which leads to unhappy children, which is not what will ultimately make the parents happy. They are all in slowly heating water.

Yet the immediate payoff for those Tunnel Vision dreams feels less and less effective and motivating. They become sources of stress. We know something is wrong. Many of us can identify the problem. We know the culture is robbing them of the joy that comes from appreciating each miraculous moment of their lives. On some level, most of us know that those Tunnel Vision objectives, whether we achieve them or not, gradually numb us to feeling those pleasures. Many of us know that fame, fortune, and admiration will never be enough.

Tunnel Vision feeds on itself and doesn't allow for true satisfaction. Most intelligent people know that, even while they watch the consequences slowly mount. Teenagers start rebelling, wanting to follow their natural drives, not society's. Yet wise and smart parents still react with disappointment and anger. Otherwise loving and savvy couples live in increasing marital strife and suffer infidelity at best, and domestic violence at worst. Family members engage in some form of escapism, from overusing substances and overspending to codependency.

It's a waste of human potential for happiness, a squandering of the precious time we are given. And the vast majority of people realize this regrettable loss of the seismic gift each of us was given in being born human, at this time, with what we have.

The Emotional Impact of Crises

Enter crises on that gradual, downward course. Crises of any kind *always* happen in the context of some background of cultural or even toxic Tunnel Vision, and sometimes one crisis overlaps another. They're different versions of Tunnel Vision, like varying sizes and frequencies of waves in an ocean. People can't see anything gratifying to offset crises and their accompanying Tunnel Vision.

Whatever immediate payoff there was for cultural Tunnel Vision or even toxic Tunnel Vision abruptly ends. Being in a crisis or time of hardship with Tunnel Vision is punishing, and the distractions or pleasures we were using to cope with life just don't work anymore. Not to be glib about the misery that comes with emotional crises, but they can rescue us from ourselves.

Let's investigate what it is about crises and times of incredible hardship that are so useful.

The Four Factors

There are many ways in which hardships and crises can change your life for the better. Four principal ways are the Brain

Disruption Factor, the Ego Disruption Factor, the Visibility Factor, and the Motivation Factor. We point them out so you can strategically use them to develop yourself and evolve your brain; however, know that the Brain Disruption Factor is automatic and unconscious. Like everything else in the SatoriWest Method, we created these categories for ease of understanding.

For the first factor, remember that crises are not just events you experience: they also have a physical effect on your brain. They cause hormone secretion and deplete vitamins: in short, they rattle your brain. This is the Brain Disruption Factor.

The Brain Disruption Factor can cause a spontaneous release into Perspective. What appears to happen is that the Tunnel Vision from an intense crisis gets so constricted that its mechanisms in the brain cause it to spontaneously shift. The brain releases itself into Perspective. However, it isn't clear what is happening in the brain. Maybe the cerebral hemispheres get so out of balance, or the brain's chemistry gets so skewed, or the stress on the brain becomes so toxic, that the brain just lets go whether we consciously want it to or not. In this instance, we don't really "learn" anything as much as our brain experiences an involuntary disengagement from its own troubled mind.

It recalls the experience of Eckhart Tolle, who passed out, presumably from emotional exhaustion, after an evening of such severe nihilistic depression that he questioned his basic reality and the existence of his ego:

> I woke up ... with a feeling of absolute dread ... more intense than it had ever been ... The most loathsome thing of all, however, was my own existence. ...
> "I cannot live with myself any longer." This was the thought that kept repeating itself in my mind. Then suddenly I became aware of what a peculiar thought it was. "Am I one or two? If I cannot live with myself there must be two of me: the 'I' and the 'self' that I cannot live with." "Maybe," I thought, "only one of them is real."

He lost memory soon thereafter, and eventually awoke from sleep into a new world of profound Perspective, parts of which you may recognize from Chapters 8, 9, and 10 on Perspective.

> I got up and walked around the room, and yet I knew that I had never truly seen it before. Everything was fresh and pristine, as if it had just come into existence. I picked up things, a pencil, an empty bottle, marveling at the beauty and aliveness of it all." (Eckhart Tolle, *The Power of Now: A Guide to Spiritual Enlightenment* [Novato, CA: New World Library; Vancouver, BC: Namaste Publishing, 2004], 3–4.)

The second way that crises are opportunities is the Ego Disruption Factor. This is reminiscent of the movie *Moonstruck*, where the character Loretta slaps her lover in the face, saying "Snap out of it" while trying to get him to realize he is making a mistake about her. (There was no such luck.) In some ways, severely toxic or crisis Tunnel Vision can be a slap in the face, a wake-up call to appreciate your life, to stop causing your own suffering. Here the emotional pain of Tunnel Vision outweighs the rewards. It's as if our ego cries "uncle"—it gives up—and we surrender.

Our egos have to surrender, because our Tunnel Vision convinces us that Tunnel Vision itself, which relies on "you" controlling everything, is the way to happiness. "Just try harder. Acquire more and better of everything, and you'll feel better." Maybe this internalized message is so convincing because Tunnel Vision makes us more suggestible. Maybe Tunnel Vision is so powerful because our egos are so inflated by it, and our thoughts so distorted by it, that we justify our desire for more and better things as the right path to happiness. We think, *I've got this, I know what makes me feel better*, when in reality we don't. We believe all we need is a drink, or the perfect relationship yet to be attained, or enough money, and we will finally be happy and can stop seeking. Of course, only Perspective does that.

Stubbornness and egocentricity are usually the hallmarks of a brain trapped in its own loops of Tunnel Vision. That's why the ego benefits from being disrupted. If you add in the physical effects of addiction or compulsiveness, that degree of ego dilation becomes really toxic. Bottoming out from drug and alcohol use and our own toxic personality sometimes becomes the only way to "change our mind"—to really change our brain.

When that happens, our brain shifts on its own, like it did in the Brain Disruption Factor. And then Perspective comes to us. With the Ego Disruption Factor we know something or someone has shaken up our defiance, or our feeling of shame, but we don't know how. In other words, if we face a crisis that exposes our folly and ego, and that insight—that Perspective—works, it allows us to be more humble, more open, perhaps more willing to listen.

For example, if your car slid off the road in a snowstorm and one of your passengers was injured and no one stopped to help you, your usual pride or inhibitions might be replaced by desperation. A normally shy or arrogant person might find themselves flagging someone down, even waiving frantically or standing right in front of their car to stop them.

The third way crises help us is the Visibility Factor. It is related to the fact that Tunnel Vision *is,* as you now know, invisible when it is "ordinary." In other words, it is cultural Tunnel Vision, which is disguised as the normal way we are and the way things work in the world. Tunnel Vision is *more and more visible the worse it gets,* to the point that it can get so constricted (yet painfully visible) we wind up in crisis. That's crisis Tunnel Vision.

We spent several chapters delving into this aspect of the SatoriWest Method, as it is the centerpiece of the Method. For the SatoriWest Method the benefit of the Visibility Factor is that noticing Tunnel Vision means unwinding Tunnel Vision to some degree. The idea is to notice your Tunnel Vision in its milder forms so that you can find Perspective before life puts you in crisis.

Here's a possible glitch to the Visibility Factor we've been addressing throughout this book. When we're caught up in an extremely hard time, the Visibility Factor may not serve us, because we may not *want* to see how we are creating suffering for ourselves. We might be so upset that we fall into familiar habits, doing what we usually do to make pain go away, like consuming alcohol or pursuing people for sex. For instance, if you just went through the death of someone close to you, you may not want Perspective. You might think Perspective would short-circuit your grief. It doesn't. Perspective during grief allows you to go through normal grief. It actually helps you grieve by removing layers of other emotional elements, such as guilt for what you did or didn't do for the person, shame at crying, or believing your happiness is at an end. All things focused on your ego. None focused on your legitimate feelings of loss.

The benefit of the Visibility Factor is that the difficulty we all have in seeing our dysfunctional personalities is brought front and center during crises. For example, if you find out your spouse has been having an affair, your insecurities, your grandiosity, your fixation on your own pleasure, your inability to let go of past rivalries with your siblings—all of that is made abundantly clear when this real heartbreak and deep betrayal is your new reality.

Likewise, a light shines on the superficiality and banality of cultural Tunnel Vision in times of tragedy. Your concern with how you look in the mirror, the status symbols of your mode of transportation, and how wealthy you are compared with your siblings all dissolve, all become obvious Tunnel Vision, when a serious health scare strikes. The "mission impossible" of noticing relatively invisible Tunnel Vision is easier in contrast to a family tragedy.

In fact, all eight facets of Tunnel Vision stand out like a neon sign when you're in crisis. Look at the first facet of Tunnel Vision: attention. It would be impossible not to feel the pull of attention toward the sensation of suffocation during a panic attack. It would be a serious challenge to let go of obsessively imagining your teenage child in a car accident when they were late coming home. You'd be hard put to let go of your fixation on alcohol if you were an alcoholic sitting in a restaurant while everyone was drinking it.

Or let's look at the fifth aspect of Tunnel Vision: imagination. If you are heartbroken after a traumatic breakup, you should not be driving a car, because your attention will not be on the road, which increases the risk of an accident. But if you know the SatoriWest Method, witnessing that you are lost in your head should set off alarm bells that your Tunnel Vision is in crisis mode and potentially getting out of control. It's time to BrainShift.

With the sixth facet of Tunnel Vision, ego, you'll see your Tunnel Vision more clearly (if you've learned about the SatoriWest Method) when someone you're in love with leaves you. It could feel like a blow to your ego. You can feel your bruised ego in the feeling of rejection, in the hurt, in the thought *I'm not good enough*, or in your anger for taking it as a personal betrayal. You'll start examining your ego and how it may have played a role in the loss. You may see your arrogance or insecurity in a different light. The process can be therapeutic and cathartic and help you grow, although it's extremely painful.

Crises show us how distorted thoughts, the seventh facet of Tunnel Vision, get so warped, it defies logic. In the last example, you can't see how you are catastrophizing after a difficult breakup, but you'll quickly see it after someone points it out to you. Will your heart literally break? Will you really be *completely* alone the rest of your life? Will you really be looked at and pitied by *literally everyone* in the world?

Author's note: A word of caution. These examples of catastrophizing may seem childish, even absurd, perhaps even laughable. That means you have Perspective. Yet I would just caution you to be careful if you're judging them as something you could never think or believe. When adversity strikes, we are always vulnerable to a "fall from grace" into serious Tunnel Vision. You might catch yourself catastrophizing someday and ideally will remember how you felt about it.

The eighth facet of Tunnel Vision, time, shows us that we act as if we are living in the past. Using the same example as above, the breakup may hurt so much because it is reminiscent of past loss. You'll then need to ask yourself, Does it feel the same as when your first crush in middle school rejected you? If so, is it *really* happening again? Or is this time different? The answer to the last question is always yes, although Tunnel Vision does create eerie patterns. You are not the same person you were a few months ago, let alone years ago. Again, even a quick foray into BrainShifting can relieve you of the reality-connection to that past event.

Cultural Tunnel Vision can seem so normal when the situation is slight and so grossly distorted in crises. Again, crises and emotional hardship are paradoxically easier to see and detach from *if we know what we are looking for.*

What else do suffering, hardship, and crises do for us? They motivate us to change. We'll call this the Motivation Factor.

Crises and hardships can provoke us to come out of the comfort zone Tunnel Vision lulls us into. For example, learning we have cancer can energize us to make changes to our wellness practices we never found time for before because we were caught up in Tunnel Vision pursuits. Traumatized by an assault, we might devote ourselves more fully to our religion in a way that we hadn't before—maybe coming to a greater level of appreciation for life, assuming our religion is a source of goodness, love, and other features of true Perspective. After suffering flood damage to our house and belongings, we might see what material things we want to salvage more than others, might realize what we really care about. Enduring a contentious divorce, we might be honest with ourselves in ways we hadn't before.

These times of crises and tragedies can not only motivate us to make changes that foster Perspective, but cause Perspective themselves. They shake us out of Tunnel Vision. They loosen the traps that kept us captive by immediate rewards or ego gratification. In a sense, they can motivate us to look at life differently—if we choose to do that.

If your child were gravely ill, you might care less about what people think about your titles or status. You would not give a whit about whether your child is an A student or an F student when they are lying in a hospital bed. If you were in a hospital with other parents of gravely sick children, you might give up your judgments about their class, race, or differences. If you've just survived a natural disaster, your petty differences with your neighbors might dissolve into greater empathy and compassion.

If your child becomes gravely ill, you might be motivated to meditate more regularly to cope with the fear and pain. With such strong emotions, you might feel the *need* to do something. That's when BrainShifting may come to mind. Strong emotions motivate us to look inward. They can not only spur us to BrainShift but make BrainShifting more powerful.

If you can remember to BrainShift during times of high emotionality, it will be more effective. You can acutely feel the relief that comes from widening and detaching awareness. You can clearly experience the liberation that comes from watching your breath without controlling it. If you weren't upset, you'd have to muster up that much energy—sometimes by bringing up whatever negative emotions are lying deeper down—to experience BrainShifting in the same way.

Crises can make us desperate to change. That level of motivation can translate into a spontaneous BrainShift. We can let go of habitual ways of seeing and thinking and experience life with new eyes. The feelings of being in crisis can stimulate your mind—your brain—to wake up to the intensity of the moment, to feel the energy of the moment. That brings its uniqueness and preciousness into focus. After living through a serious disaster, perhaps coming close to death, people say they treasure each moment in ways they hadn't before. They BrainShifted. They surrendered to the moment the way it was instead of insisting it be one way or another.

The most drastic way crises help motivate us to look for or discover great Perspective is when we "bottom out." It's a harsh and dangerous path, to be avoided at all cost. Yet it happens because people become victims of their Tunnel Vision, spiraling down until the consequences become so unbearable or dangerous that it becomes a final motivation.

For instance, some people become so attached to drugs or alcohol through the Tunnel Vision mechanisms of surrendered attention, and experience such rapidly devolving Tunnel Vision, that their egos become hyper-inflamed. They convince themselves that the next glass of alcohol will finally solve their problems. They believe their own rationalizations instead of what everyone is trying to tell them. Except for moments of a bit more Perspective, when they come up for air, they might say they understand how much they are controlled by their desires, their minds, which is Tunnel Vision; they might have the conviction that they can stop Tunnel Vision by force if necessary. After repeatedly falling prey to their addiction, they bottom out—or come close to it. Consequences outweigh any conceivable benefits. The Tunnel Vision strategy is vividly revealed, whether it is called that or not.

Sometimes when people bottom out, a Brain Disruption Factor can open into an unparalleled level of Perspective— which is what happened to Bill W. during his alcoholic episode described above. Sometimes, needed motivation emerges. These people allow their brain to powerfully shift, and a new world of Perspective appears.

Bottoming out also happens when formidable toxic Tunnel Vision heads into crisis levels. Some people can feel such self-hatred that they cut on their wrists to avoid feeling emotional pain, but this just strengthens the self-hatred. It gets to the point where this vicious cycle gets unbearable and they give up trying to solve their problems by creating deeper problems—that is, with more Tunnel Vision. They stop trying. This surrendering is an aspect of BrainShifting. Strategic surrender opens our minds to Perspective. Sometimes bottoming out in this way lets them hear what others are saying in ways they couldn't or wouldn't before.

Author's note: A patient of mine was involuntarily hospitalized because of extreme behavior; he had gotten into arguments that caused him to angrily overreact in an ever-escalating series of retaliations. He eventually burned every bridge in his life and felt suicidal.

When I explained his Tunnel Vision to him, and then demonstrated it by putting my hands together in a circle and looking through them, he countered with a description of his experience with Tunnel Vision. He squeezed part of his thumb and index finger into a tiny circle so tight that light barely got through. It was his recognition that his Tunnel Vision, already at crisis levels, had gotten so extreme that light could barely get through.

The SatoriWest Method changed him. We reinforced his change with some simple BrainShifting exercises. Light bulbs seemed to come on for him, and over the course of a few days he seemed transformed. His participation in group therapy was reported to be substantially more insightful, and his maturity level increased dramatically. Even he, other staff, and his spouse were amazed at the change.

I had another patient who was committed to a psychiatric hospital with such severe borderline personality disorder that, furious with everyone and herself, she fought and attacked staff. She had to be restrained for her safety and the staff's.

I met her when she was in restraints and explained her Tunnel Vision. You could see the insight light up her mind. She calmed and took control of herself. The entire interaction lasted not more than 20 minutes. She aged psychologically before my eyes.

I asked the staff to release her restraints after only 10 minutes of sitting with her. When we were finished talking, I had her released from the seclusion room. Staff were fearful but did as I asked. She was a different person. I noticed a nurse with dropped jaws.

When I asked the patient later, I learned that the biggest takeaway she heard from me in that seclusion room was that her behavior and emotions had a science-based explanation. It focused on her brain and not on her. It lessened her shame and started a reverse cycle of Perspective that did not need a lot of further explanation from me. I discharged her from the hospital two days later; she was a very different person.

These are only two dramatic examples from many of my own patients. However, the therapists in the mental health partial hospital program that exclusively used the SatoriWest Method saw similar results. Were these striking effects in part the result of the Motivation Factor? Undoubtedly, yes.

Crisis Tunnel Vision can get to the point that the rewards that help us cope with crises no longer work. The immediate rewards of cultural Tunnel Vision—such as screaming at someone to feel instant relief or drinking alcohol to make frustration with life disappear—don't work anymore.

Eventually the consequences of crisis levels of Tunnel Vision outweigh the rewards. It's as if people need to get shaken out of their devotion to patterns and habits of Tunnel Vision, because people caught in a rapidly deteriorating cycle of Tunnel Vision are nothing if not stubborn. Drug addicts and alcoholics who know they are addicts can convince themselves that the next use or drink will not be a problem. They do this by exploiting the elements of their own Tunnel Vision, such as denial, rationalizing their behavior, or relying on their ego to tell them they are right. The same holds for compulsive eaters, shoppers, gamblers, and sex addicts.

People with these issues rapidly head to crisis levels of Tunnel Vision. They need the motivation of extreme consequences, or a dangerous situation, to be willing to change. Bottoming out from substance use can rescue us from death. Bottoming out from emotional dysregulation can save us from a life of misery. The ego of our Tunnel Vision can find no footing in the midst of this degree of pain. We are practically forced to discover the extraordinary Perspective awaiting on the other side.

When Crises Wouldn't Work

Of course, the opposite is true: crises and hardships can shut us down. They can cause us to rely on old Tunnel Vision strategies even more, like engaging in even more compulsive behavior or becoming even more stubborn and inflexible. And it's odd, but there can be a perverse reward for being in some level of crisis. Some people are most comfortable in hardship. Some families are attracted to dysfunction and stress and unknowingly cause it for themselves. There may be many reasons for this, although the payoff of Tunnel Vision is the underlying cause. For some, it's so familiar, it is all they know.

Others almost want a crisis to shake up their lives, almost daring life to help them. Maybe they instinctively hope drama and crises will force them out of their destructive habits of Tunnel Vision. That may be the case with some people who take increasing risks in sports, gambling, or infidelity. There may be a reality in the pathological state of Munchausen syndrome, where people feign medical conditions to get the attention of the healthcare system.

Seeking what is superficially rewarding, like familiarity, may be why people repeatedly get into abusive relationships. It's possible there are perverse rewards to fostering dramatic life situations and painful emotions, similar to why we love horror movies or apocalyptic films. Whatever the rewards may be, we know on some level when we're in deep crisis that those superficial rewards are dwarfed during times of extreme problems.

The Use of Psychiatric Illness

So far we've referred to crises and hardships as things that happen to us from the world—a terrible life event, a loss, a disaster, or something outside us, even a medical crisis. Yet disaster can often come from inside our brain in the form of a psychiatric illness. Of course, events do trigger psychiatric illness and substance-use disorders. Either way, these illnesses can be as devastating as a traumatic event.

Now that you are more familiar with the SatoriWest Method, I hope you can see how central Perspective is to the treatment of depression, anxiety, other mental health issues, and substance-use disorders. This applies even to compulsive behaviors like gambling or shopping addiction. (This category of mental health—which includes substance-use and other compulsive disorders—is called "behavioral health.") Major depression and bipolar disorder can put people who deal with them in crisis every time the disorder manifests. And every time they do show up, another opportunity for Perspective also appears.

Dealing with the misery of a behavioral illness can shake people loose from the traps of cultural Tunnel Vision. If it is well handled, they might come out of an episode better appreciating what they have in life and experience mental peace and hopefulness. People struggling with behavioral health issues can wind up happier than the general population because of their struggles. They can come to relish the important things in life more than they would a fancy house, perfect vacation, or other cultural trappings.

Although Perspective may not cure mental illnesses, it can make the negative feelings that come with those illnesses more than tolerable. Even a bit of Perspective can add a layer of positive emotions. For example, if you deeply appreciate what you were given in life, it's hard to be lost in the negativity and guilt that often accompanies a biological depression.

The notion of suffering presented throughout this book applies equally to psychiatric issues. Great Perspective may mean you don't suffer any longer. That doesn't mean you *don't* feel anxiety or sadness, or that you don't have to deal with fatigue, insomnia, memory concerns, or sexual dysfunction. Yes, symptoms may be lessened or eliminated with Perspective or with the whole SatoriWest Method itself. Not suffering means the same thing: you're not brought down by those symptoms; you don't lose heart, optimism, humor, context, insight, or compassion. You cannot suffer what you don't attach to via Tunnel Vision.

Author's note: I'm always amazed to see my patients who take psychiatric medications naturally get Perspective just from the medication. When I teach them about the SatoriWest Method before they take the medication, the idea of Tunnel Vision and Perspective makes sense to them. Yet after the medication starts to work, pointing out the Perspective they've developed because of it adds exponentially to their understanding of the grip Tunnel Vision had on them and how vital it is to have Perspective. In other words, the SatoriWest Method helps them learn from the medication. They can put the process their brain went through to get Perspective under the proverbial microscope, learning from the effects of the medication on their brain how to find Perspective even when they don't take it.

One final word about the benefit of behavioral health issues. The Perspective they generate has a special quality that can be particularly powerful. For example, any BrainShifting helps lessen ego. Someone with bipolar disorder can watch their ego go from the depths of a depression, with so much self-loathing that it physically hurts, to the heights of grandiose absurdity in a manic state. Any amount of Perspective that you can glean about your ego from witnessing how bipolar disorder causes the brain to change it would be an epic amount of Perspective. For an Enlightened master with an advanced level of Perspective, ego will appear unreal or in the background of their experience. Yet you could be an Enlightened master or meditate for 50 years and not comprehend the nature of your ego as well as someone who has experienced bipolar disorder—or really any psychiatric condition—and recovered enough to have some insight into it.

If one day you are committed to a psychiatric hospital against your will because you had paranoid delusions that caused you to be a danger to others, and a week later, on medications, could see that none of that was true—and you could acknowledge that as a trip through the nightmares of Tunnel Vision—you could teach the SatoriWest Method. Or at least the words in this book would jump off the pages.

Seeing how any psychiatric disorder, from obsessive compulsive disorder to panic disorder, depression, or schizophrenia, can alter your brain tells you that your brain is in charge of you, not the other way around. If you can see that fact, unambiguously, with that degree of detachment—it's a BrainShifting skill—you will experience significant liberation from Tunnel Vision.

When you experience the symptoms of your psychiatric disorder as a brain disorder, that is BrainShifting supreme. You have to shift from the very hold on your mind and body that drugs like cocaine or alcohol have over your brain. That is no easy feat. Psychiatric illnesses are something you wouldn't wish on anyone, not even your worst enemy, yet they are like that rubber band that stretches so far, it can fling you into the heights of Perspective.

When you can see the raw power of your brain causing your addiction, so that willpower (mind or ego) alone cannot defeat it, there is a "spiritual"-like quality to that Perspective like nothing else.

The upshot of this is that the benefits of high Perspective from objectively witnessing a behavioral health issue are immense; the fullest extent of these benefits is not to be underestimated. They can be a springboard to a level of insight, maturity, compassion, and appreciation for life that anyone would envy. You just need to find and nurture the amount of Perspective that gives your brain the power to evolve. I wouldn't wish a behavioral health issue on anyone, but it can be a gift if approached the right way. That kind of deep shift is what spiritual Awakening is about.

Author's note: The SatoriWest Method destigmatizes behavioral health issues. There are many reasons for this, one of which is that the Method defines behavioral dysfunction as Tunnel Vision, not by a diagnosis. It's that simple. You could have schizophrenia, bipolar disorder, or a brain tumor, but if you have more Perspective than Tunnel Vision, you are in reality. According to the SatoriWest Method, if you have more Perspective than Tunnel Vision, you are mentally healthier than someone who does not have a psychiatric or substance-use brain disorder.

This applies to a corporate executive as much as it does to the person on disability with a diagnosis of mental illness. If over time you have more Tunnel Vision than Perspective, you are mentally unwell. Again, this has nothing to do with having symptoms. It has everything to do with control over your mind and brain. The person with Perspective would make a much better employee than someone in Tunnel Vision.

This chapter has been almost exclusively about how crises can help you, or how you can use them. In Chapter 18 we'll spend a little more time on how others can help you get needed Perspective on your crises.

. . . .

> *I was extremely distraught, despondent, and my husband was in the process of trying to find a way of getting me out of where I was. I was in the hospital and then started the outpatient program. I just wasn't doing well. I was in such bad shape because of the extent of my bad experience with the bipolar [disorder].*
>
> *I began crying. My husband would hold me and just try to get me out of these episodes of crying and being fearful, and worried, and fear and just regret from the past situations that I had. And I just didn't see any way that I could get free from this. I was entangled in it, and that's when my husband started researching the programs that I could be involved in.*

Thankfully, I was able to start going to this program.

You know, when I first started it I had all the enthusiasm in the world to, even though I was in fear, and worry, and anxiety. I thought, This is good, I'm gonna apply myself, I'm gonna learn what was taught to me. *I saw videos that explained the SatoriWest Method and it calculated. And I just thought,* Oh, you know, I'm going to absorb all I can about it and all the different aspects of it. *And the premise of going from Tunnel Vision into Perspective was just fascinating to me. I just glommed onto it. And I thought,* If this is the procedure I can do it. *You know, it showed me that there is a definite program that could see me through and help me get on the path to health again.*

[After the program]

It was mainly sharing with my husband that I wanted to make sure that I didn't go back down into the bipolar, it didn't have a lifelong hold on me. I was starting to worry that it's gonna come back. And I started, you know, really going down that tunnel and then I was able to just step back, like I learned, to just step back from it and then BrainShift. I learned about BrainShifting; that was just life changing for me. And then to BrainShift into right perspective and step back and say, No, I don't have to have that fear. I've got the tools that I've learned through the SatoriWest Method, *and I was able to have a hold on it, getting the Perspective, and not letting myself go back down into any negative situation. I was able to get on top of it.*

—Debbie

18
Crises and Going It Alone

Some crises come at you fast, out of nowhere, like finding out you have a serious illness. Or being surprised someone you're in love with has left you. Or getting assaulted, or into a car accident or natural disaster.

Some crises are slow burning. Like slowly mounting financial troubles. Or a gradually escalating chemical dependency problem that you can't admit to yourself. You might even live a rolling crisis by bringing the pain and memories of an abusive childhood into the rest of your life.

These things are powerful. They hurt more than you would ever expect, sometimes more than you express to others. Even knowing the SatoriWest Method, you couldn't be blamed for wanting to immediately make the hurt and pain go away. Anyone would be challenged to want to do otherwise, even if they were skilled at BrainShifting, even if they were living life with natural Perspective. Because once you're in a crisis, it can wash over you like a roaring wave and you can feel like you're drowning. Your instinct is to kick and thrash and try to escape. Again, you're only human. That impulse, as we said, is a hardwired survival instinct.

Then there's our human condition. It will cause enduring suffering, lasting as we ride the waves of one crisis after another. As Sheldon Kopp said so well, "[I]t is very hard to be an on-your-own, take-care-of-yourself-cause-there-is-no-one-to-do-it-for-you grown-up" (Sheldon Kopp, *If You Meet the Buddha on the Road, Kill Him!* [London: Sheldon Press, 1974] 165–167).

We must all ultimately face our reality alone; no one can do that for us. Although doctors can treat our brain, we have the responsibility to manage it ourselves, inside ourselves. Yet reaching out for support and guidance can help us do that more effectively, as long as it doesn't become another target of Tunnel Vision. Reading this book, cultivating your awareness and your brain, can prepare you to unwind suffering. It can take you far along the path toward recovery and resiliency, whether or not you are in crisis at the moment. It may be all you need.

Yet why face trauma alone? Why face life alone, if you can help it? We all have limits to what we can tolerate. We could turn a crisis into an opportunity *without* support if we needed to, but why would we want to? Not many people who have been through a crisis and found an amazing new Perspective would say that emotional support would not have helped them or did not help them.

It is important to reach out for help. Doing so is a form of social wellness. Plus, guidance can be essential to progress in BrainShifting, depending on what you are dealing with, especially if you reach your limit of tolerance for emotional and physical pain.

For guidance on how to BrainShift, understand that any form of mindfulness is a form of BrainShifting and many people can teach it. Many spiritual teachers are talking about the SatoriWest Method, whether they call it that or not. One benefit of the SatoriWest Method is that it brings many different therapies and models together, including all the areas of your life and wellness, under one umbrella, toward one end. That can make it a more powerful approach.

As far as the spiritual aspects of the SatoriWest Method, its roots can be understood through the lenses of Tunnel Vision and Perspective. The earliest humans created communal religious rituals to deal with life and death as they developed enough self-awareness to feel their mortality. That fear and angst caused versions of Tunnel Vision as they sought real and imagined ways to escape that Tunnel Vision–influenced reality. Of course, like every generation since then, they had to fight off real and imagined hardships at the same time—hardships made worse by Tunnel Vision.

Yet even with all these layers of Tunnel Vision causing early humans and their descendants to be incredibly cruel to each other and desperate to escape their own minds, a select few discovered ways to find Perspective, and their numbers increased. Some used one another. That is why religion is so focused on love, loving one's neighbor, and giving. These were avenues of powerful indirect BrainShifting. Ultimately, when contemplation or meditation or some variant of BrainShifting was discovered, people started to pass down those strategies.

Yet no one wants to face life and its very real challenges in isolation; that would be absurd. We need each other. Finding an empowering community to join you in your journey to actualize the SatoriWest Method is part of total wellness.

Professional Help

The direct BrainShifting skills and wellness practices of the SatoriWest Method can be challenging to master on your own, even without being in crisis. Keeping in mind that although this beginning book may be all you need to gain a healing amount of Perspective, it may be helpful to form support groups around the Method.

The SatoriWest Method was successfully used in a psychiatric hospital and partial hospital (outpatient) setting, because when it comes to serious mental health, substance-use, and other compulsive disorders, the SatoriWest Method may be best practiced with professional guidance. Crisis and hardship created by serious psychiatric illnesses and compulsive behaviors, although opportunities, can affect the very brain you are trying to evolve. In that case, your direct BrainShifting can be greatly enhanced by professionals trained to use the SatoriWest Method in association with biological treatments.

These biological approaches can include natural supplements as well as medications.

On the other hand, just reading this book may work for you if you have a mild condition. Regardless, social wellness will always include reaching out for help. The moral wellness aspect of indirect BrainShifting ought to always include being kind to yourself—basically fostering love—as a way to gain Perspective.

. . . .

At the end of January 2020, I was hired and trained to be the therapist in a partial hospitalization program (PHP)—a 15-day, daylong curriculum that treats mental illness and substance abuse. It was a program that exclusively used the SatoriWest Method.

What I saw was that moving out of Tunnel Vision isn't easy. Often it's all we know; there's a lot of comfort and familiarity in repeating patterns, even if they might cause harm. The idea of surrendering to the moment and experiencing something new can be anxiety-provoking, but the SatoriWest Method requires this action—it is a "do" method; participants must put it into action to reap the benefits. With application of the method an organic, authentic shifting happens. That sliver of anxiety diminishes, and the long-term gratification kicks in, resulting in feelings of empowerment and gratitude.

The method works. I've witnessed it in so many ways. It's amazing to watch someone express hopelessness at the beginning of their 15-day journey, only to end the program confident and full of hope. I've seen patients start to align with themselves instead of fighting against themselves. I've seen patients improve every symptom that they've come in with. Their physical postures change; when patients enter the program, they often have closed-off postures, and demonstrate hesitancy or disengagement from the group. By the end they're sitting up, with shoulders back, and are engaged in the group discussions and able to express themselves confidently.

As a therapist, being able to help empower individuals to therapeutically confront and become aware of themselves begins and ends with this method. Its effectiveness is the most inspiring part of it for me; to have patients go from years or sometimes entire lifetimes of struggle to experiencing states of happiness and hope, sometimes for the first time in their lives, in only 15 days is nothing short of incredible. There are not enough words to express the reward and gratification I feel from watching this method unfold in people's lives. *It's an honor to be a part of that journey.*

—Chrystal

Part VI
Conclusion

19

Completing the Circle

We've covered a lot of ground together on our journey through the SatoriWest approach. We progressed through the five points of the method one at a time: 1) accepting and validating to yourself the presence of your human condition; 2) understanding and recognizing Tunnel Vision in all its many manifestations and degrees; 3) understanding the immeasurable, life-affirming value of finding higher and higher degrees of Perspective; 4) making a life practice of BrainShifting—both its direct skills and indirect wellness strategies; and 5) readying yourself for inevitable crises, so that you can use them to your advantage to escape invisible Tunnel Vision and gain great Perspective.

However, now that we've completed them, we can see the bigger picture of how the five points work to shift your brain and open your mind. Much of what this book is about has to do with the human condition. That's why we started with the human condition, even though it's not the usual way for a self-help book to begin. We did this for many reasons, not the least of which was to gently pierce the denial that most people have around their human condition. No one wants to admit to others, let alone to themselves, that they are hurting inside. People might shame them for being weak—or worse, invalidate the suffering in their experience, or worse yet, not be moved at all, which is the height of paradox, since we all feel the same thing. Even if you are in crisis, it can be easier to share the fact that you are than to acknowledge long-standing feelings of inadequacy or self-doubt.

And so we started off by immersing ourselves in the human condition. Its first job was to help you get greater emotional

Perspective right away by reminding you, or informing you, that we are all in this together. Support, empathy, and reassurance from others who truly understand are indirect wellness ways for you to get Perspective. Truly realizing that we are all going through the same thing to different degrees is deep Perspective. When someone validates your feelings, it gives you permission to validate them for yourself. You can rest in the assurance that what you're going through is "normal," inasmuch as it affects every adult human—that is, before BrainShifting begins to transform it into something poignant and Awakening.

Remember, as the SatoriWest Method understands it, Perspective is not solely bliss that comes from falling in love in your experience. It is not solely an enhancement of your creativity, sense of humor, and insight into people and yourself. Perspective is also the ability to see the world as it is. It's the capacity to feel deeply and compassionately about what is going on with the people in your life and your fellow humans around the world, including the sociopolitical issues that face us all. Perspective is seeing how the human condition causes conflicts between people, immorality, crime, war, and behavioral disorders, including suicide. And even though you suffer it, you're trying to cope with it and ideally transform it by taking this journey.

Of course, seeing the human condition in yourself is of singular importance, both in its long-standing effect on your personality and in how it creates hardship and crisis. That aspect was meant to help you pause to reflect on your own psychological makeup as you prepared to take the SatoriWest journey. That kind of contemplation opens your heart for the trek into Perspective.

Another reason we started with the human condition is that it is ripe for learning. The human condition *is* cultural, toxic, and crisis Tunnel Vision all wrapped up in one. It's fabricated from waves of life problems and their accumulations of emotional distress—the suffering that's hidden—which serve as the backdrop for the tidal waves of life that can bring you to your knees, the suffering that's visible to you and everyone else. Really seeing it is motivational fuel. It's a level of clarity that could serve as a wake-up call, if you needed one, to give you the drive for the tricky work of continually looking inward. Because there is no getting around it: the SatoriWest Method is involved. It takes momentum to move down the road of the four avenues of BrainShifting. Remember, they are 1) recognize the eight facets of Tunnel Vision as often as possible, but especially when stressed or distressed; 2) employ the rudimentary skills of BrainShifting, such as the "and" technique, in difficult times, and practice other skills, such as Body Scan or Brain Sweep, daily; 3) use a LifePlan© or otherwise attend to key strategies of total wellness to encourage your brain to shift naturally; and 4) step up all the previous avenues in times of crisis and stress.

To that last end, as we said, Tunnel Vision is paradoxically much, much easier to witness when it is worse. By acknowledging the extent of your human condition, by bringing your suffering to the surface and making it palpable, the first part of the book was intended to help you see your Tunnel Vision as soon as it shows up in any noticeable form.

Besides validating your experience of it as a way to gain Perspective, offering you greater clarity to see your Tunnel Vision, and serving as a springboard for the detective work of looking for it, the most important reason to present the human condition early on was to help make this point: you must first accept it, as it is. You must see it as part of each moment exactly the way it is. Of course, the shift in your brain that allows you to do this is a shift in consciousness that can transform your life.

This notion of acceptance, of seeing the moment and yourself as they are, was reinforced repeatedly here. BrainShifting opens you up to radically appreciating the good, the bad, and the neutral as part of the amazing whole that makes up each moment.

All this talk of the human condition can give the impression that the SatoriWest Method is kind of depressing, or even that it takes a pessimistic view of life. Of course, this book is for those who may be struggling with an emotional hardship. Yet it is not meant to leave you more aware of the human condition so that you drown in it. It is meant to do the opposite—if not catapult you, then at least lift you up close to the height of what it really means to be human.

Seeing your human condition can help you realize your existence as the miraculous expression of a universe that evolved to finally see itself, via the "self"-awareness of two brains intimately tied to each other. (Remember, you have two separate brains in your head, each with its own awareness, that can be trained on each other and cause the miraculous emergence of self-awareness.) At the same time your awareness is directed inwardly on itself, your brain and its attention are redirected away from the particulars of survival and the pseudo-survival needs of your ego. Your brain is then poised to transform you.

Anchoring your brain more clearly in the experience of being alive means having a more effective way to embrace each moment in a radically different way. To experience events in your life with wisdom and emotional maturity, heart and humor, intuition and novelty. To move through life with creativity, authentically expressing your feelings and spontaneously responding to the unique calling of each second.

Of course, validation and inspiration, even education, were not where this journey left you. It took you into the weeds of your mind. It asked you to *do* something, not just passively receive. It asked you to do the work of looking for very specific elements of your Tunnel Vision and to do it under varying circumstances that challenged you in different ways. To look for the eight elements of Tunnel Vision when they are semi-invisible, in the cultural manifestation that controls your day-to-day life. It asked you to bring it to light in its much more visible but harder to swallow toxic phase. And it asked you to open up and see it when you might be least willing to do so—when it hurts the most but also when it becomes glaringly obvious: in times of crisis.

But the crossing of the SatoriWest passage into the life you want and are capable of having didn't end at that point, either. As if the work of recognizing your Tunnel Vision and actively shifting your brain were not enough, your journey required more of you still. It asked you to at least learn, if not take immediate action on, no less than all the trappings of your daily life. The six spheres of wellness, and all the areas within them, weave the rich tapestry of your daily experience, including what is going on inside you and around you. This interrelated network of complex requirements speaks again to what this book is all about: the organ sitting in your head. By paying attention to the reality of having a human brain, we laid the groundwork for this lifelong journey to continue downhill instead of uphill.

The SatoriWest Method is a cyclical journey, to be repeated over and over—the most important mission you can undertake to fulfill your highest destiny. To do this, this cycle was not yet over at this point. All four points of the SatoriWest Method were meant to steel you for the hardest part to come: how to handle the inevitable crises and traumas that life throws at you.

Sharing the history of how crises have worked their power to fulfill people's lives may have seemed either reasonable or mythical. Ideally you came to see the prospect as rational. Even though we proposed potential scenarios to use to your advantage, however, there is no adequate way to prepare you, because you are involuntarily on the world's biggest metaphorical roller coaster, with no way to get ready for its immense and unexpected drops, which plunge down with no foreseeable end. Except to say that they do end, but before they do, they can and do propel people to the summits of human existence.

If this book gave you at least a blueprint to make that happen, it has served its purpose.

Author's note: It's been an honor to present the journey to you, and to take it with you. This is sacred work. Your very existence and self-evolution are of immense importance to you and to the world.

My fervent wish is that you move from Tunnel Vision to Perspective at every turn and live the rest of your life deeply fulfilled and liberated.

If you would like more information on the SatoriWest Method and SatoriWest programs, find us at SatoriWest.com. Let us know how the book and the SatoriWest Method worked for you. We'd love to know. Our contact information is on the copyright page.

Warmly,
Jeff Skolnick

. . . .

The amazing thing is that when I was 18 years old, I was a giddy kid. I was out there in the world having a good time. For most of my life I have been downtrodden. I have been on medications, trying to get me to feel better. I'm ready to leave the program and I'm like a giddy kid again! So to people, a message. This is worth trying. It is worth having the experience.

—Clara

Appendix 1
Questions and Answers

Question
You emphasized that while practicing the direct skills of BrainShifting, nothing should be changed. You expand only your awareness of the moment. Don't the wellness strategies attempt to undo the symptoms of Tunnel Vision, for example, replacing irrational thoughts with rational thoughts and changing run-down bodies with health-promoting strategies?

Answer
It's correct that BrainShifting doesn't attempt to change anything about the moment, including your thoughts and feelings. The *direct* skills of BrainShifting are about encompassing with awareness the moment exactly the way it is—the good, the bad, and the ugly—and focusing in on the immediacy of being alive.

It is also correct that the indirect or wellness BrainShifting strategies do seem to attempt to undo the conditions of Tunnel Vision. However, the two strategies work hand in hand. If practiced together, Wellness BrainShifting, which compels and guides your brain toward Perspective, does not conflict with the direct skills of BrainShifting. They work together in synchrony. That's because, while opening to the moment exactly the way it is, you can engage in practices that make your brain more capable of doing that. You accept reality the way *it already is*, instead of denying it, trying to run from it, or fighting it before being fully aware of it, so that you can feel the miracle of your existence, which compels you forward to make the world a better place.

Question
So every time I want something or don't want something, it distorts my reality?

Answer
No. The more you focus on what you want or want to avoid to the exclusion of other things, the more you distort your reality. The stronger the drive toward or away from something that controls your attention, the more distortion of reality there is, and vice versa. Wanting a glass of water because you are thirsty and can't think of much else but water will distort your reality to the degree to which your attention was grabbed or taken over.

Question
Are you saying it is possible to have Tunnel Vision and Perspective at the same time, so that you can have Perspective into your Tunnel Vision? If so, how is that possible?

Answer
It's possible to have Perspective on how your attention is being drawn into something or on how you give over your attention to what you want or don't want.

Without going into too much detail, remember that you have not one but two separate brains in your head, each with the separate ability to be aware of the other, meaning the right brain can witness the left brain being in Tunnel Vision. Of course, with that recognition, Tunnel Vision is already unwinding.

Question
If crises and extreme drives, like hunger or sexual urges, as well as emotions, cause Tunnel Vision to be so severe, it can be more readily detected, would you advise me to put myself in dangerous situations to bring out a crisis-like experience?

Answer
Definitely not, although sometimes people do challenge themselves by engaging in behavior outside their comfort zones—for example, someone who's afraid of heights goes skydiving—and say it changed their Perspective on life.

My assertion is that life provides plenty of crises for you to make use of. You will get very sick at some point. Someone you love will die. You'll experience losses. Get ready for those; when they come, they will springboard your brain to a new, higher reality if you know how to BrainShift.

Question
Are there any barriers to learning the skills of BrainShifting?

Answer
Definitely. After all, BrainShifting needs a functional brain. You need a relatively intact and healthy brain to be able to shift your awareness. Of course, lack of wellness can propel you to purposefully BrainShift even more effectively. Yet all brains have limits. A brain lacking critical amounts of oxygen or glucose, for example, will not shift. Your mind, trapped in an excessive amount of ego, will not allow your brain to shift unless it is compelled to by external forces.

Question
Related to the human condition, are you saying that even when I think I'm happy and having fun, I have negative feelings in me, too?

Answer
Usually, yes. We carry deep moments of sadness, or anger, or fear through life, even though we have some or many lighter moments with laughter and lightheartedness.

Question

Is the object of having Perspective to have positive emotions and not negative ones?

Answer

This is an important question. If you still have the impression that a high degree of Perspective means having only positive emotions, that belief needs to be corrected. It's understandable that you might have that impression. Although it was reinforced many times that Perspective means accepting and embracing the moment just the way it is, the logical assumption is that the opposite of suffering is perfect bliss. It's even a widely believed myth that high levels of spiritual Awakening are like being in a drug-induced state of ecstasy all the time.

Consider this. If you didn't cry at a significant loss, if you didn't fear for the safety of your children when they were in harm's way, if you didn't feel anger at an injustice, you would not be fully human. The opposite of the human condition created by Tunnel Vision is a life of deep meaning, of passion and purpose, and yes, with the Perspective to appreciate what you have. That doesn't equate to a one-size-fits-all homogenous personality. It does equate to a personality that is fully expressive.

When your brain has Perspective, *feeling happy all the time doesn't determine your contentment with life*, as strange as it may be to hear that. You can cry with joy. You can be so angry with someone you love that it makes you love them even more. You can be so scared when taking a risk that you feel more alive than you have ever felt before.

So-called "negative" emotions are not your problem: Tunnel Vision is. Tunnel Vision turns "negative" emotions into suffering; it blocks the subtle and sublime things that exist around you. It accentuates your sense of self and warps your reality.

Question
I can really see how I am suffering from Tunnel Vision and feel dedicated to living a life of great Perspective. It's just that I'm in a really hard place right now and nothing seems to be going right. What advice do you have?

Answer
Life can be brutally unfair sometimes. Some of us get more than our share of bad cards in the game of life. If you are struggling, I'm truly sorry. Just know that there are people out there who care, so make sure you reach out to them. Someone who shows empathy and compassion to you is raising their own Perspective, and you can pay it forward.

Also know that suffering does help you appreciate what you have—which is always more than you realize—even if you are going through unthinkably hard times. I wish you well.

Question
Are you saying that I should accept my miserable thoughts, horrible feelings, warped reality, and shallow awareness?

Answer
Accept them in the sense of acknowledging their reality. Experience them with detachment, with self-empathy, with context. Remember James Baldwin's axiom, "Nothing can be changed until it is faced." Releasing the grip that these negative feelings, thoughts, beliefs, and situations have on our attention—the cause of Tunnel Vision and misery—is the meaning of liberation.

To see our Tunnel Vision the way it is means surrounding it with awareness, love, and compassion. In other words, trying to fight or resist Tunnel Vision only gives us more Tunnel Vision.

Question
How can I witness Tunnel Vision the way it is? Doesn't the act of witnessing it dissolve it?

Answer
Yes, it does. Yet you can still experience the conditions that created it without paying them exclusive attention. You can still feel the feelings that are being generated without reacting to them. You can still visualize painful memories in your head without trying to push them out while ignoring everything else going on. You can still be aware of your shame-producing, warped beliefs with distance and objectivity, which causes them to naturally lose power, without trying to run away from them.

Sure, the act of witnessing the conditions of Tunnel Vision is going to make the whole experience expand into Perspective. Yet you can still notice the conditions of your Tunnel Vision, *even the smallness of your world*, while it's happening. But you better hurry, because those conditions won't stay around for long.

Question
What if I have physical pain or body discomfort? Do I just witness that without changing it, too?

Answer
Remember that suffering from pain, suffering from anything, is not the same as feeling it. If you suddenly have a knife stuck in your abdomen, you are going to feel that pain. Yet focusing exclusively on that pain to the exclusion of everything else is, first of all, only going to make the pain feel worse. Plus, the pain will be worse if that narrow focus distorts your reality so that you are irrationally scared and begin future-tripping.

Pain management clinics use mindfulness strategies. They are a popular form of treatment. They show patients in chronic pain how to experience pain as changing patterns of energy, not as a "fixed thing" to try to push away with their minds in fear and rejection, which makes the pain worse. I believe it is a question of having Tunnel Vision or not that makes the difference in pain patients. Yogis of old, and maybe modern ones, too, have demonstrated sleeping on beds of nails to show that pain is less fixed than we believe. People practicing sadomasochistic sex define pain and pleasure differently than the mainstream.

Question
Is there a best way to practice the direct skills of BrainShifting?

Answer
Most experienced meditators, and I am one of them, would say to practice some aspect of formal BrainShifting (meditation) every day, without exception. Even just closing your eyes and listening to and feeling the symphony of sounds in your environment for two minutes every morning will prime your brain to BrainShift during a crisis. Advice for creating a daily practice of BrainShifting skills is in chapters 12 and 14.

Also, when you notice a moment of negative emotions and distorted reality during the day, *take advantage of it*. BrainShift. See how your attention is locked into the negativity. Notice all the aspects of the negative state of Tunnel Vision from an objective place. This will expand your Perspective right away.

Question
I've been meditating for a while, yet I still find myself getting frustrated. My mind seems to wander for long periods of time, and I can't settle it down. Is BrainShifting going to be any different?

Answer
With BrainShifting you do not need to change the contents or speed of your mind. It can race, it can be full of thoughts and mental images, you can be on a roller coaster and still BrainShift effectively. In fact, though I do sitting meditation each morning, I also get great benefit from BrainShifting while running, while watching a movie, and even while thinking and talking, though

the latter two instances can be very challenging for me. It's fruitful, so long as there is a conscious witnessing of it all.

When BrainShifting, does it matter if your brain is chattering away in thought? Not in the least, as long as you are anchored in the present. As long as you can witness the contents of your mind with some objectivity and distance. Does it matter if your mind wanders? Yes, but realizing what's happening and regaining your presence only strengthens the circuits of your higher brain that much more. If your imagination grabs your attention and pulls you into Tunnel Vision, and you are lost in fantasy, there is great use in realizing it and coming back to some degree of Perspective, some objective observation. Just as doing repetitions with weights at the gym strengthens your muscles, coming back time and time again to Perspective after wandering off in Tunnel Vision strengthens your brain in the sense that activating circuits causes a thickening of the cells in those areas.

Question
Does strengthening those nerve cells in your higher brain stop you from having a crisis?

Answer
Crisis is defined here as experiencing such extreme Tunnel Vision that you can become a danger to yourself or others or can't take care of your basic health and safety. Whatever you can do to mitigate that risk—the risk that we all face, regardless of how resistant we think we are—you would be well advised to do. BrainShifting that strengthens your higher brain may give you what you need to keep Perspective.

Appendix 2
Summary of the SatoriWest Method

Point 1: Recognize Your "Human Condition"

The journey that is the SatoriWest Method must start here. Appreciate that you are currently in the human condition—the impulse to deny it, distract yourself from it, or try to force it away is based in Tunnel Vision.

If you are struggling with a crisis at the moment, it is important to realize you are not alone in your suffering. Tunnel Vision causes us to feel alienated. Everyone has either just gotten over a crisis, whether large or small, is in one, or knows on some level they are due for another.

Point 2: Understand What Tunnel Vision Is

Tunnel Vision is a hardwired survival program in the brain that warps the human mind.

- Attention: grabbed or given over
- Control: decreased
- Awareness: blocked or reduced, denial
- Suggestibility: increased
- Imagination: conflating inner and outer reality
- Ego: inflated
    - Taking things personally
    - Self-righteous, believing you are right
    - Feeling self-conscious, like you are the center of attention
    - Feeling alienated, on the outside looking in
    - Feeling superior

- Feeling inferior
- Feeling competitive
- Obsessively comparing
- Self-blame

- **Thinking: Distorted**
  - All or nothing
  - Black or white
  - Absolutisms (for example, "shoulds")
  - Future certainty
  - Jumping to assumptions
  - Magnifying the negative / minimizing the positive
  - Catastrophizing
  - Rationalizing
  - Mind-reading

- **Time**
  - Negative transference
  - Flashbacking
  - Feels long during stress
  - Feels short overall

TUNNEL VISION					PERSPECTIVE
Crisis	Toxic	Cultural	Moderate	Great	Awakened

Point 3: Understand Perspective

Perspective is the opposite of Tunnel Vision. Just as there are degrees of Tunnel Vision, there are degrees of Perspective. The middle parts of the spectrum can have some degree of Tunnel Vision and some degree of Perspective at the same time. The details of Perspective are the converse of Tunnel Vision:

- Attention is inclusive, wider.
- Internal control is kept to the point of spontaneity and authenticity.

- Awareness is open, witnessing, processing multimodal input.
- Your imagination is experienced objectively.
- You are open-minded, able to perceive deceptions.
- You have humbleness and depersonalized experiencing.
- You think rationally.
  - All or nothing distortion versus seeing nuance and shades of gray
  - Distortion of absolutism "shoulds," versus asserting a preference, such as "would be nice if"
  - Future certainty distortion versus discerning the probability that something might occur
  - The distortion of "jumping to conclusions," versus making careful inferences, keeping an open mind
- You are immersed in the limitless, infinite moment.

Perspective affects personality with these qualities:
- Insight
- Wisdom
- Maturity
- Judgment
- Objectivity
- Empathy and compassion
- Love
- Spontaneity
- Authenticity
- A sense of humor and irony
- Creativity and seeing novelty
- Intuition
- Gratitude
- The experience of belonging
- A happier and peaceful disposition

Point 4: BrainShifting: The SatoriWest Method Journey to Perspective

There are four general ways to open your brain to the greatest Perspective it can have:

- Notice your Tunnel Vision as much as possible.
- Practice the skills of BrainShifting.
  - Daily BrainShift / meditate
  - BrainShift when you notice yourself trapped in Tunnel Vision
- Practice wellness BrainShifting.
  - Physical wellness
  - Mental wellness
  - Social wellness
  - Cultural wellness
  - Moral wellness
  - Existential wellness

Point 5: Use Pain and Suffering to Find Great Perspective

- Realize you're in crisis or toxic levels of Tunnel Vision and see their eight facets—they'll be clearer than ever.
- Realize your suffering *is* Tunnel Vision.
- Don't push away negative feelings and thoughts; feel their energy melding with the energy of a Body Scan or Brain Sweep.
- Step up wellness even if you don't want to.
  - *Physical*: Exercise; get outdoors, treat yourself to but don't binge on comfort food.
  - *Mental*: Note the ways in which your ego is suffering, such as feeling hurt, betrayed, alone, or humiliated, and expose it to awareness and love. If irrational thoughts persist after a Brain Sweep, challenge them with rational ones.

- *Social:* Do not isolate; talk about your experience and allow others to share your experience.
- *Cultural:* Keep order in your life—bathe, keep your home clean, take care of necessary business and tasks; reduce or let go of societal indulgences that distract you from your feelings, such as games, social media, even distressing news shows and media.
- *Moral:* Do something for someone else; keep to your precepts.
- *Existential:* Write a list of what you are grateful for (at least 10 items a day while in crisis or suffering); step up religious activity and/or engage with some subject that puts you in an existential mode, such as science, philosophy, spirituality.

Acknowledgments

I want to acknowledge the editing of an earlier version by Shoshana Alexander, and the developmental editing of this version by Rebecca Pillsbury. My sincere gratitude goes to Robyn Fritz, who edited and packaged my last book and provided the same inimitable abilities for this one. Laurel Robinson provided insights and proofreading, Sheryl Chieng created the evocative cover illustration, while Robert Lamphear's artistry created the cover and interior design. Lastly, many thanks to my sister, Joanne Sagona, who gave hours of invaluable and detailed editing feedback.

About the Author

Jeff Skolnick, MD, PhD, is a diplomate of the American Board of Psychiatry and Neurology, Clinical Assistant Professor of Psychiatry at the University of Washington, and Lifetime Fellow of the American Psychiatric Association. He has worked as a psychiatrist in a variety of settings, including a private psychotherapy practice, and as a chief medical officer in four different organizations. He has advanced training in neuropsychology and a doctorate in Natural Health Science.

Dr. Skolnick began a daily practice of Zen Buddhist meditation in 1980 while studying eastern philosophies and contemporary spiritual literature. He formulated the SatoriWest Method by combining 40 years of personal development in Zen with training and research on the brain, advanced education in wellness sciences, and years of clinical practice. His SatoriWest company has created successful curricula based on this method for psychiatric hospitals and outpatient programs as well as for SatoriWest LifeClubs, a longer-term membership program dedicated to healing, wellness, and advanced psychospiritual development.

www.ingramcontent.com/pod-product-compliance
Lightning Source LLC
LaVergne TN
LVHW091530060526
838200LV00036B/546